W9-ABI-130

Mapping Islamic Studies

Religion and Reason 38

Method and Theory
in the Study and Interpretation of Religion

Mouton de Gruyter

Mapping Islamic Studies

Genealogy, Continuity and Change

Edited by
Azim Nanji

Mouton de Gruyter
Berlin · New York 1997

Mouton de Gruyter (formerly Mouton, The Hague)
is a Division of Walter de Gruyter & Co., Berlin

Library of Congress Cataloging-in-Publication Data

Mapping Islamic Studies : genealogy, continuity, and change / edited by Azim Nanji.
p. cm. – (Religion and reason)
Includes bibliographical references.
ISBN 3-11-014187-6 (cloth ; alk. paper)
1. Islam – 20th century – Miscellanea. I. Nanji, Azim. II. Series.
BP163.M365 1997
297'.07–dc21 97-15820
CIP

Die Deutsche Bibliothek – Cataloging-in-Publication Data

Mapping Islamic studies : genealogy, continuity and change / ed. by Azim Nanji. – Berlin ; New York : Mouton de Gruyter, 1997
(Religion and reason ; 38)
ISBN 3-11-014187-6

♾ Printed on acid-free paper.

Printing: Ratzlow-Druck, Berlin. –
Binding: Lüderitz & Bauer, Berlin. Printed in Germany.

Preface

The volume was conceived after a Symposium held in London in 1983, under the auspices of the Institute of Ismaili Studies, to discuss emerging directions in Islamic Studies. There was also a concern to situate the debate about "Orientalism" in proper historical context and to evaluate its ramifications for scholarship that was being jointly undertaken by Muslim and Western scholars. The conversation continued informally, among those present and others, over several years and in different academic locations.

While we are grateful for the inclusion of Professor Mikoulski's contribution on Russia and the former Soviet Union, we are mindful, that other regions of European scholarship such as Italy, Scandinavia, the Iberian Peninsula and parts of Eastern Europe, as well as Japan, are not represented here. The growth of modern Islamic Studies in the Muslim world has been referred to and is expected to form a major part of a second volume.

I am grateful to the Institute for its encouragement to publish these papers and to Jacques Waardenburg for his support and suggestion that it be published as part of Mouton de Gruyter's series on *Religion and Reason*. The various contributors are to be thanked for their patience and agreement to allow additional ideas and papers presented elsewhere, to be included here. Finally, I wish to thank and acknowledge Susan Lewis for her assistance in the arduous task preparing a camera-ready copy for publication.

For the purposes of this volume, the system of transliteration of words from Muslim languages has been kept to a minimum and words or names which have a familiar English usage are retained in that form.

TABLE OF CONTENTS

CONTRIBUTORS

Mohammed Arkoun is Professor Emeritus and former Director of the Institute of Arab and Islamic Studies at the Sorbonne, and Editor of *Arabica*.

C. Edmund Bosworth is Professor Emeritus and former Head of the Department of Arabic and Islamic Studies at the University of Manchester, and Editor of the *Encyclopaedia of Islam*.

The late **Norman Daniel** was an historian of the Middle Ages and Intercultural Relations. He served for many years as a British Council representative in various countries and held the appointment of Cultural Attaché in Cairo.

Muhsin Mahdi is the James Richard Jewett Professor of Arabic at Harvard University and the author of numerous studies on Muslim Philosophy and Literature.

Dimitri Mikoulski is a member of the Russian Academy of Oriental Studies, specializing in the history and culture of Muslim Central Asia.

Azim Nanji is Professor and Chair of the Department of Religion at the University of Florida and the Editor of *The Muslim Almanac* (1996).

Sarah Roche-Mahdi specializes in the study of Medieval and Romantic European Literature and Thought. She is the author of *Silence: A Thirteenth Century French Romance* (1992).

Jacques Waardenburg holds the Chair of Science des religions at the University of Lausanne and serves on the Editorial Board of several series on the History of Religions.

Azim Nanji

Introduction

The study of Islam is both an ancient and a modern endeavor. The former has its roots among Muslims in a long-established and continuing tradition of scholarship and interpretation of their own faith. Among others, particularly medieval Christians, the study was motivated by polemical ends, aimed at establishing self-authenticity and pre-eminence, by attributing to Islam, often pejoratively, error or wilful misappropriation. The tendency has lingered on, though the medieval constructions and assaults on Islam have assumed different forms and emphasis. The academic study of modern Islam, on the other hand, grew primarily out of the Enlightenment tradition of European scholarship and interest in Asian and African cultures and peoples, and had assumed by the nineteenth and twentieth centuries some of the normative contours and institutional patterns that are associated with the general discipline of thought and expertise known as Oriental Studies or Orientalism.

The subject of most of the essays in this book, is an examination and a critical appreciation of this modern phase. They are intended as a contribution to the discussion of how the discipline of Islamic Studies, a branch of Oriental Studies, as it has come to be understood and practiced, evolved in its various historical contexts. They also seek to reflect upon the ironic effects, whereby "Orientalism" and "Islamic Studies", which emerged as European disciplines to study the "other" have themselves become texts and objects of study, as the "other".

Orientalism, Edward Said's critique of the discipline, its assumptions and practitioners, first published in 1978, elicited a steady stream of responses, some of which were denunciatory and hastened to defend the discipline and its authority; others, more self-reflective, began submitting the discipline to greater introspection and even rethinking in the light of developments in other disciplines. What is noteworthy, is that such a turn towards self-reflection, though stimulated in this case by someone outside the discipline, was by no means the first of its kind. Such a process has had its own history within Islamic Studies and Orientalism and was part of a general trend in academic culture after the Second World War.

In 1953, a conference of leading European Islamicists was organized by the late Gustav von Grunebaum, as part of a larger effort, to examine the relationship among Muslims, and between Islam and the various cultures and civilizations, to which it had spread over time. This marked probably the first organized and self-conscious endeavor in recent times to undertake a historical and critical self-understanding of the discipline in the light of developing methods and theories in the social sciences, particularly Redfield's notion of "great" and "little" traditions. It was noted at the time that the methods and assumptions used to study the history of Islam lagged a century behind those used for European history. A year later, at another conference, Claude Cahen reemphasized the point, quoting Bernard Lewis to the effect that the history of the Arabs had been written in Europe chiefly by historians who know no Arabic and Arabists who knew no history. Cahen argued that a new direction was necessary, one that would go beyond the hitherto philological orientation and study Muslim society as a total integrated organism. The sponsors and participants of such conferences, which took place against the back-drop of events and changes in the Muslim world, noted and emphasized the need to better understand Muslim civilization and history, and thereby the social and political problems of the Near East. They were conscious that the assumptions and methods of past generations of scholars, though meritorious in their own right, had become increasingly outmoded and detached from developments in other disciplines, as well as the changing realities in the relationship between Europe, America and the Muslim world. The next two decades of the sixties and seventies represent for Asia and Africa the era of decolonization, nationalism and revolution, whose impact was no longer local or regional, but was becoming increasingly global. These were turbulent times in the academic community as well. A newer, more assertive tone emerged to which many scholars from the now so-called "Third World", allied themselves. It argued for the dismantling and deconstruction of established metaphysical and epistemological systems and the "Eurocentric" institutional apparatus that accompanied them. This would not be the only straw in that wind of change, but among others it caused a questioning and revising of many of the assumptions of humanistic and social scientific inquiry into other cultures. This debate, whose contemporary games are played out within interdeterminate frameworks called post-modernism and post-structuralism, but also across disciplines in programs of "cultural studies", affected Islamic Studies only marginally. In part, this insulation explains both the defensiveness of the established community of Islamicists against criticisms, and the need felt by an emerging group of dissatisfied younger scholars, to escape from the narrower confines of philologically oriented scholarship to a more open-ended discourse, from which, in certain cases, they embraced uncritically the many new theories that had emerged. The community of scholars in Islamic Studies had indeed grown larger and more diverse and the subject matter too complex, to be contained any longer within one interpretive community. The debate about "Orientalism", reflected and heightened the ambivalence within the field. Its significance, in retrospect, seems to lie more in the way it highlighted this predicament through wider public discourse and by placing it within ongoing academic debates, than its particular claims and critique against European scholarship.

Said's claims and insights regarding the historical and ideological conditions necessary to produce a discipline such as Islamic Studies, intertwined issues of representation and construction of the discipline to reveal a Eurocentric pattern of domination and authority. At a time of cultural and political collision and preoccupation with assertions of identity and difference in some parts of the Muslim World, his linking of power and knowledge and his arguments against an hegemonic misrepresentation of Muslims by the West played into the hands of rhetoricians emboldened by its anti-imperialist and anti-Western stance. This narrow focus and the controversy the book aroused diverted attention from the scholarly task and opportunity to engage in a wider intellectual dialogue and exchange. The theorizing and extension of the boundaries of knowledge was by no means limited to Islamic Studies. Broadly speaking, the process reflected the larger debate (some might say disarray) among various communities of interpretation in the humanities and the social sciences on the questions of the role of intellectuals and scholarly settings in representing and misrepresenting various human groups and cultures and upon the stability of authors and texts as repositories of meaning. This *Introduction* to the essays that follow has two purposes. Firstly, to situate Islamic Studies against the background of questions and issues, as they are defined within the contemporary debate, in cultural studies and interpretation of texts; and secondly, to relate the discipline's future development to the history of Islamic Studies in different parts of the Western world. In this way, it is hoped that the essays will be seen as an attempt to engage practitioners of Islamic Studies in the mapping of the discipline by focussing on its various formations in European and American contexts, while also reflecting upon and responding to questions about intercultural discourse and scholarly and other representations of Islam and Muslims. The essays are thus products of a review and a conversation, motivated by a desire to frame responses that seek to go beyond the constraints and assumptions of a collective heritage, as well as the deconstructive and skeptical tendencies inherent in some contemporary critiques that imply severe shortcomings in any past or present modes of studying and writing about Islam.

The first part of the volume presents a historicized framework, locating the growth of Islamic Studies within its plural and geographically diverse European expressions. The core components of the study of Islam, have their roots in the archaeological and philological German tradition of critical scholarship of texts and cultures. As with the study of Christianity and Judaism and other religions, Islam was studied within three major frames: the critical edition, study and interpretation of primary texts; the study of doctrinal and theological developments and thirdly, the historical growth of Islam and institutions such as the Caliphate. There also developed in due course, as each European power established trade and colonies, a need to undertake studies of structures and peoples in their immediate settings, in particular the study of existing legal and social practices. While much of the collection of such information was an official task, it did involve individuals with scholarly interests, who subsequently helped encourage greater interest in the study of Muslim society, contemporary to them. However, the primary source of Islamic Studies remained textual (based on available and selected texts) and the mode of analysis remained philological (with Arabic, Persian and Turkish having priority). The history of European scholarship, as illustrated in the various essays here, was by no means monolithic. At times, it appears as competing and is certainly diverse. It also reflected the economic and religious involvement of these various countries and their own power relations within Europe.

However, the pattern of historical-linguistic scholarship on Islam, remained general for a long time and was often insulated from developments in other areas of humanistic scholarship, that affected academic trends in fields such as history and literature. The 1953 Conference referred to earlier marked somewhat of a departure particularly for the study of economic and social history and institutions. The focus of traditional Islamic Studies, the Middle and Near East, was shifted to include interactions between Muslims, Africans and other Asian peoples and current sociological and anthropological perspectives came to be employed in the analysis of the spread and development of Islam.

Two new global factors would affect the study of Islam in the 1960s: the institutionalization of the Cold War and the decolonization and creation of new nation states in much of Africa and Asia, including the Muslim region of these two continents. There was a corresponding development in the growth of higher education and research in Europe and the North America (accompanied by the migration of scholars and ideas from the former to the latter), and a transplanting of emerging intellectual trends in the theory and practice of scholarship. These factors highlighted attempts to study what were presumed to be the disorienting effects of colonial rule and the need to develop institutional strategies necessary to address the challenges as well as asymmetries created by independence.

A colloquium held in 1961, the *Colloque sur la Sociologie Musulmane*, affirmed the need to refine methods and develop new concerns informed by social science. Baber Johansen, in discussing the development of Islamic Studies in Germany, reflects on the loss of the dominant paradigm of historicism, since the 1960's. The changes in German society after the Second World War, and the subsequent breakdown of the colonial system, led to University reform and a restructuring of Oriental Studies. Scholarly authority shifted to the disciplines of social sciences, with their promise of better understanding of the transformation of economic, political and social life at home and abroad. The same patterns can be said to have affected Britain, France, Holland and other Western European countries, during the same period. The Russian example (and that of some other East European countries) presents a special case. Dimitri Mikoulsky's outline of developments suggests the strong constraints of ideologically grounded scholarship of a different kind - moulded as it was by assumptions that governed intellectual and cultural life in the former Soviet Union. In its engagement with some countries of the Muslims world an effort was also made to infiltrate intellectual life in these countries with a competing agenda meant to foster the Soviet Union's hegemonic aspirations.

It is also during this period, that the study of Islam expanded in Canada and the United States, in particular with the establishment of area studies centres, funded by government sources and foundations. It has been argued that such centers particularly in the United States, while advancing the study of regional languages and cultures, tended to have their intellectual rationale subverted by the matrix of Cold War concerns, strategies and ambiguities. This led to a fragmentary approach that very often, separated and pitted those who were in the Humanities against their counterparts in the Social Sciences, studying the same region. The various uses to which the conclusions of Thomas Kuhn's *Structure of Scientific Revolutions* (first published in 1962) suggested how even the most objective pursuits of scientific knowledge, operated within contingent and historicized contexts. The presumed failure of "bias-free" assumptions and methods, came to be evoked in those Social Science disciplines that studied other cultures and societies. This undermining of confidence in the inherited paradigms was also exacerbated by the availability of many works by those who lived or wrote from the perspective of the "Third World". In time, as these ideas took hold, the construction of knowledge became linked to issues of power and representation. Existing textual authority came to be questioned and many pretentious and arbitrary claims came to be made for and against established "canons". Said's work was a reflection and a development of this trend. The history of Islamic Studies reveals, there never was at any time in the past, a fixed paradigm, that operated universally; the boundaries were constantly being revised, not always by design, but invariably, because the dynamics of Muslim engagement with their history and heritage, was changing, as dramatically, as the relationship of Europe and America, with the Muslim world.

The essays by Sarah Roche-Mahdi and the late Norman Daniel remind us that the creation, reproduction and representation of Islam in the West, have a long and complex history. They deal with a catalogue of distortions and stereotypes, provoked by attitudes of denigration and also of myth-making, born of nationalistic fantasy, whose political consequences go far beyond the initial flights of romantic or distorted images.

The insights of these essays yield lessons about how new perspectives might be developed about old questions of conflict and the imagining of enemies. The late Norman Daniel, embodied such hopes, an aspiration to create an academic forum for expression of the trans-territorial landscape signified by "Islam and West" seen together in all their diversity, and not just as two contending civilizational clusters, inhabited by fixed and irreconcilable differences.

The confused world of shifting perspectives and changing methodologies, reflected in the proliferation of books and articles on the humanities and religion in general, need a frame of reference and some theoretical understanding of evolving scholarly practices. The essays by Professors Mahdi, Waardenburg and Arkoun under the theme "Retrospect and Prospect" offer a number of contexts within which to think anew the task of a future Islamic Studies. Their insights suggest some of the ways in which the study of Islam, as a diverse cluster of cultures and as a living faith in its present global context, might be studied. The abundance of current scholarship portrays the intellectual, spiritual and institutional pluralism of Islam, showing the development of a wide variety of Muslim societies within local and global contexts and illustrating the diversity that exists among individual Muslims, traditions, and periods of history.

They also suggest how we need to rethink ways in which we have geographically and intellectually mapped the Muslim world. Past legal constructs such as "Dar al-Islam" and "Dar al-Harb" have become irrelevant, which is not to say that they cannot be invoked for ideological reasons. The manner in which European scholarship in the past perceived the Muslim world, with a presumed center, the "Near or Middle East", led to the marginalization of large groups of Muslims who did not inhabit that geopolitical space and this marginalization affected the focus and practice of scholarship.

In addition to resisting the imposition of old boundaries, there is the caveat against present - mindedness and the undue focus on what has been termed "fundamentalist" expressions. While their relevance to contemporary politics and current affairs cannot be dismissed, it is individuous to make it the primary expression of Muslim identity in the modern world. There is among contemporary Muslims, as in all religious traditions, an inherent tension. One pattern expresses the growing differentiation in and separation of spheres and activity of life in which the inherited tradition occupies a place of differing degrees of personal and collective commitment. Another seeks to reintegrate all spheres within a totalizing conception of "Islam". Still others, seek broader intellectual, ethical and practical directions, without assuming a parochial or doctrinaire approach. The tools of intellectual modernity that are employed in all cases cannot be homogeneous. The task of scholarship is to further develop and refine mediating categories and tools of comprehension that allow us to negotiate the space between concept and practice, embeddedness and expression, past and present.

Perhaps the most encouraging trend in Islamic Studies in recent times is the cosmopolitan profile of the scholars and their methods in the field. The migration of European scholars to the Americas has been followed by the migration of scholars from the Muslim world to both Europe and America. As Muhsin Mahdi points out, one cannot easily separate contemporary scholarship in terms of "Western" and "Muslim". When combined with the rapid changes in communication made possible by advances in technology, such as the Internet, collaboration between scholars within a continent and across continents, has become much easier. This cross fertilization is reflected in the fact that Islamic Studies now radiates from within many departments and disciplines and finds expression in collaborative projects, institutes, journals and associations. This new constellation of interests and constituencies, has generated a profusion of scholarship and as the contributions suggest, augurs well for a transnational scholarly landscape.

The field of Islamic Studies will continue to be more diverse and encompassing in its scope, than in the past. There are many possibilities open for adding to its subject matter and methods, including the role of Islam as a cultural force of great diversity; the increasing public participation in society by women (whom contributions and role still await detailed study within Islamic Studies); the history of rural, agricultural and mountainous peoples of the Muslim world and new interactions among Muslims now living in the West. In this way, a vibrant humanistic scholarship can contribute to knowledge, linking a fifth of humanity that is Muslim, to others among whom Muslims live and with whom they share increasingly the task of building mutual understanding.

References

Akbar, Ahmed. *Postmodernism and Islam: Predicament and Promise*. London: Routledge, 1992.

Breckenridge, Carol A. And Peter van der Veer. *Orientalism and the Post-colonial Predicament*. Philadelphia: University of Pennsylvania Press, 1993.

Cahen, Claude. *Turcobyzantina et Oriens Christianus*. London: Variorum, 1974.

Clifford, James. "On Orientalism" in *The Predicament of Culture*. Cambridge, MA: Harvard University Press, 1988.

Geertz, Claude. *Local Knowledge: Further Essays in Interpretive Anthropology*. New York: Basic Books, 1983.

Hodgson, Marshall G. *Rethinking World History: Essays on Europe, Islam and World History*. Introduction by Edmund Burke III. Cambridge, New York: Cambridge University Press, 1993.

Hourani, Albert. *Islam in European Thought*. Cambridge: Cambridge University Press, 1991.

Huntington, Samuel P. "The Clash of Civilizations?" *Foreign Affairs* 72:3 (Summer 1993).

Johansen, Barber, "Politics and Scholarship: The Development of Islamic Studies in the Federal Republic of Germany" in *Middle East Studies: International Studies on the State of the Art*. Tareq Ismael, ed. New York: Praeger, 1990.

Kerr, Malcolm, ed. *Islamic Studies: A Tradition and Its Problems*. Malibu, CA: Undina Publications, 1980.

Lambropoulous, V. *The Rise of Eurocentrism: Anatomy of Interpretation*. Princeton: Princeton University Press, 1993.

Lewis, Bernard. *Islam and the West*. New York: Oxford University Press, 1993.

Lowe, Lisa. *Critical Terrains: French and British Orientalism*. Ithaca, NY: Cornell University Press, 1991.

Malek, Anwar Abdel. "Orientalism in Crisis," *Diogenes* 44 (Winter 1933).
Mernissi, Fatima. *Beyond the Veil*. Revised Edition. Bloomington, IN: Indiana University Press, 1987.
Mudimibe, Valentin. *The Invention of Africa*. Bloomington, IN: Indiana University Press, 1988.
Rahman, Fazlur. "Approaches to Islam in Religious Studies: Review Essay" in *Approaches to Islam in Religious Studies*. Richard C. Martin, ed. Tucson: The University of Arizona Press, 1985.
Said, Edward. "Orientalism Reconsidered" in *Literature, Politics and Theory*. Francis Baker et al, eds. London: Methuen, 1986.
Von Grunebaum, Gustav, ed. *Unity and Variety in Muslim Civilization*. Chicago: University of Chicago Press, 1955.

Permission is acknowledged to reprint excerpts from the following published material:

Muhsin Mahdi, "Orientalism and the Study of Islamic Philosophy," *Journal of Islamic Studies* 1 (1990); Muhammed Arkoun, "Rethinking Islam Today," Center for Contemporary Arab Studies, Georgetown University and Jacques Waardenburg, *Scholarly Approaches to Religion and Interreligious Perceptions and Islam*, Bern: Peter Lang, 1995.

Jacques Waardenburg

The Study of Islam in German Scholarship

> "The aim and purpose of our academic work is to break through the intellectual horizons of our society and to cast a glance into the world of the rising sun in order to improve our understanding of human existence and ourselves by investigating foreign cultures and civilizations".[1]

Since several publications - two of them available in English - exist already on the history of Islamic studies in Germany,[2] we thought this paper could more usefully offer a systematic approach to the subject. It will be discussed under the following headings:

1. The rise of Islamic Studies as part of Oriental Studies;
2. The principal German contributions to Islamic Studies;
3. Some characteristics of German Islamic Studies in general;
4. The present situation of Islamic Studies in Germany;
5. "Islam" in German Islamic Studies.

1. The Rise of Islamic Studies as Part of Oriental Studies

After the expansion of Classical Studies in Europe in the sixteenth century, the rise of Oriental Studies can be dated to the nineteenth century, although the scholarly study of Arabic goes back at least to the sixteenth century, if not earlier. Oriental Studies comprised the study of the languages, history and cultures of Asia and (North) Africa. Thcy were based on philology in the broad sense of the term, that is to say, knowledge of a culture through knowledge of its sources, in particular authoritative texts. Oriental Studies was patterned largely after Classical Studies, and was nearly always concerned with the past. The reasons why this expansion of Oriental Studies took place in the nineteenth century are complex and cannot be considered here in detail. The economic and political expansion of Europe into Asia and Africa was accompanied by a growing interest in their religions and cultures. Islamic Studies then arose as a distinct branch of Oriental Studies in the second half of the nineteenth century, at the time that the study of Oriental languages and literatures was recognized as an independent academic discipline at European universities. It took some time, however, before Islamic Studies in their turn constituted an independent field within the whole of Oriental Studies.

In Germany, up to the present day, studies of the languages, culture and religion of the heartlands of Islam have been pursued in what is known in the University as an *Orientalisches Seminar* (Oriental Seminar). Like Oriental Studies in general, Islamic Studies are independent of theology (including missiology) and unaffected by polemical and apologetical viewpoints. As a rule, Islamic Studies come under the Faculty of Arts, or one of the sections into which it has been divided, e.g., Cultural Sciences (*Kulturwissenschaften*) - and not that of Theology. The latter does not as a rule in Germany comprise Science of Religion (*Religionswissenschaft*) as an autonomous discipline, as is the case in, for instance, Sweden and Holland.

In the development of Islamic Studies everywhere in the West certain stages can be distinguished:

a) Islamic Studies presuppose an intensive study of Arabic as a language. An early German Arabist was Johann Jakob Reiske (1716-1774). Arabic Studies developed intensively in Europe from the beginning of the 19th century on, one of the masters in this field being the French scholar A.I. Sylvestre de Sacy (1758-1838).

b) Only on the basis of a solid knowledge of Arabic and other "Islamic" languages, such as Persian and Turkish, Urdu and Malay, could *textual* studies, including textual criticism and literary history, be carried out. Editions of texts are therefore considered a precondition for textual studies.

c) Familiarity with the study of the texts, in turn, is a prerequisite for the study of *history*. It includes the study of the earlier Muslim historians who wrote in Arabic, Persian and later also Turkish, and it demands a critical historical analysis both of the texts themselves and of the historical statements contained in them. The study of Islamic history may focus on the "inner" development of Islam, but it may also focus, for instance, on the "external" political, social and intellectual history of Muslim regions. The term "history of Muslim countries" is then preferable to "Islamic history".

d) Textual and historical research, in turn, prepare the way for the study of Islamic *culture* and *religion*. Among the many subjects covered by this may be mentioned the historical and philological study of religious texts; in the first place, the Quran and *hadīth*. It also includes the historical development of what may be called Islamic religion and culture, considered both as an "inner" development of ideas and practices throughout history and as part of the political, social and cultural history of the societies and cultures concerned. Such a study encompasses the understanding of the "Islamic" meanings of the phenomena, and pays attention to their implicit assumptions and explicit claims to truth.

e) The study of *larger Muslim cultural* areas forms an integral part of Islamic Studies, insofar as it takes the Islamic aspects of the cultures of these areas into account.

Much of the present state of Islamic Studies in the West becomes understandable against the background of this historical development of Islamic Studies. The history of Islamic Studies is a subject in itself; it may suffice here to refer to a monograph devoted to the subject and to a study which concentrates on five prominent Islamicists of the first hundred years of Islamic Studies.[3]

This general picture of the rise and further growth and development of Islamic Studies can be illustrated by what has happened on the German scene. German scholarship has indeed made important contributions to the development of Islamic Studies; a few scholars writing in German from other central European countries like Austria and Hungary are included here as well.

2. The Principal German Contributions to Islamic Studies until about 1950

German Orientalism in the field of Islamic Studies has a strong tradition. It is not unfair to a great number of younger researchers to state that the tradition would not be what it is now without the names of some early giants in the field. Of the first generation three names come to mind immediately: Theodor Nöldeke (1836-1930), Julius Wellhausen[4] (1844-1918) and Ignaz Goldziher (1850-1921), famous respectively for their research on the Quran, the early history of Islam, and the inner development of Islamic religion and culture. Of a second generation, the publications of Helmut Ritter[5] (1882-1971) on Islamic religious texts, and of Carl Brockelmann[6] (1868-1956) on the history of Arabic texts remain of outstanding value. Here also belongs the name of Hans Heinrich Schaeder (1896-1957) who was able to situate Islam within the broader framework of Near Eastern religious history, and of a world history no longer conceived on Eurocentric principles. Wide-ranging research was also carried out by Enno Littmann[7] (1875-1958) who studied many languages and kinds of literature of the Muslim world and produced, among other things, a translation of the *Thousand and One Nights*. Of this same second generation some great scholars, forced to emigrate in the Nazi period, influenced Islamic Studies abroad decisively: e.g. Joseph Schacht (1902-1969) through his studies of Islamic Law; Gustav Edmund von Grunebaum (Austrian, 1909-1972) through his studies of Arabic literature and Islamic history and culture; Richard Ettinghausen (1906-1979) through his studies of Islamic art; Richard Walzer (1900-1975) through his studies of Arabic philosophy. In Germany itself, Carl Heinrich Becker (1876-1933) and Jörg Kraemer (1917-1961) paid attention to the study of Islam within the framework of cultural history; Rudi Paret (1905-1982) is especially known for his translation and commentary of the Quran.

Names like those mentioned above stand for a special kind of "Islamological" culture, part of an elite "Orientalist" culture[8] occupying a recognized place in German life and society and enjoying an international reputation. Each one of these scholars was able to publish on many different subjects in the large field of Islamic Studies. They were personalities of intellectual strength, putting the highest demands on themselves as well as others; the more gifted the men, the higher the demands. Women at the time were virtually excluded from playing a significant role in the field, however. Research concentrated on the past rather than the present and personal involvement was avoided. The norms established by these first and second generations which had received their university education before 1933, have remained valid after 1945 in the work of German Orientalism in general and German Islamic Studies in particular.

Different university centres of Islamic Studies are the subject of special publications.[9]

A short survey of the main scholars who have made significant contributions to Islamic Studies, in particular before World War II, is appended at the end of this chapter, with their main publications indicated in English.

3. Some Characteristics of German Islamic Studies in General

In the German tradition, scholarship (*Wissenschaft*) requires a dedication which has sometimes had nearly sacred overtones. Being a scholar is not just a profession like others, and those who devote themselves to learning and scholarship adhere to the specific norms of this search for objective truth and cultivate an attitude of scholarly honesty. This, combined with great industriousness and self-discipline, has given German scholarship its formidable strength. Scholarship enjoys freedom provided it remains within its own autonomous field, keeping aloof from politics and religion. Those devoted to scholarship have enjoyed prestige and practical facilities, so that, for instance, a University Professor could have one or more assistants who would serve the discipline by research and teaching, later also administrative duties, and enable him to pursue his own projects. Scholars of repute constituted a guild which occupied a recognized and prestigious place in society. The period 1933-1945 constituted a serious break in this tradition.

In contrast to most other European countries except for instance England, Germany had and still has a decentralized system of public universities situated in the different states (*Länder*) and universities could develop their distinct traditions and "schools", competing with each other. Institutionally safeguarded as they have been, universities can stand as fortresses over against each other in academic disputes. Doctoral dissertations and *Habilitationsschriften* have practically always been published in some form or another and have been reviewed by leading scholars in prestigious academic journals. The university professor has always taken pride in educating his best students to carry out original research under his personal guidance and the relations between the scholar-teacher who enjoys great authority and his students can be much more immediate than the sometimes austere external forms would suggest. In his lectures, the university professor is wont to present the results of his own original research.

What has been said about German scholarship in general is still truer of the difficult and demanding field of Oriental Studies. In Islamic Studies, which are part of it, the general assignment has been to discover hitherto unknown facts and to bring to light new sources, in order to resurrect objectively and critically the almost lost worlds of the past - ancient cultures and civilizations. Those embarking on Islamic Studies can be likened to explorers sent out to discover new land, having undergone an extremely good and hard technical training. In this training the linguistic aspect has been foremost, in the three main languages of Islam (Arabic,

Persian and Turkish) and usually also some other Semitic languages like Hebrew, Syriac, and even Ethiopian or Akkadian.

From the beginning of this century Islamic Studies in Germany, thanks to Carl Heinrich Becker, were conceived as a cultural discipline (*Kulturwissenschaft*). They exhibited certain features and assumptions inherent to European culture at the time, like the superiority of western civilization and the pride of the scholar's national (in this case German) tradition of scholarship. Culture, including Islamic culture, was recognized as something in its own right, but differences between cultures, as between religions, were stressed. Consequently, Islamic culture was studied as basically different from European culture in general and German culture in particular. In the study of Islamic culture there was also a certain predilection for the "classical" period and for the "higher" cultural expressions of this civilization. The same holds true for other cultures studied in other branches of Oriental Studies.

In Islamic, like other Oriental Studies arising in the nineteenth century, the accent on texts and history was very marked, so that these studies for long concentrated on texts, historical facts and the casual connections between these facts. The ideal was and is specialization but without losing sight of the whole. Such specialization led to valuable, focussed and detailed studies, but the demand of having a view of the whole often came down simply to mastering an extraordinary mass of facts, rather than developing multiple perspectives, logical interpretations or keen insights. The preponderance of the study of facts gave Islamic Studies in Germany a "realistic" if not positivistic orientation. Religion too was studied along the same lines.

As is known, Germany only had colonies between 1884 and 1918, during which period it had Muslim populations in its African territories. This colonial situation led to an increased interest in the contemporary Muslim world at the time, and as a result a Seminar for Oriental Languages (*Seminar für orientalische Sprachen*) was opened in Berlin in 1887. In 1908 a Colonial Institute (*Kolonialinstitut*) was founded in Hamburg, with a special seminar for the History and Culture of the Orient. Such Seminars had corresponding professorial chairs. In 1912 a German Society for the Study of Islam was founded to study contemporary Islam and since 1914 it has published the journal *The World of Islam* (*Die Welt des Islam*, *Le monde de l'Islam*), which gives much attention to contemporary developments. In 1910 the scholarly journal *Der Islam* was founded as a journal for the history and culture of the Islamic Orient.

After World War I German Orientalism ceased to be influenced by problems arising from colonial policies, but it sometimes was perceived to be useful to improve relationships between German and particular Muslim countries. Although national feelings were not absent among German Islamicists and made themselves palpable for instance during World War I when Turkey was German's ally, German scholars collaborated in important international scholarly projects like the *Encyclopaedia of Islam*, the first edition of which also appeared in German, in five volumes (1913-1939), and the *Concordance et indices de la tradition musulmane* (8 vols, 1936-1988).

The painful period in Germany between 1933 and 1945 took its toll on Islamicists too. Some of Jewish descent like Paul Kraus, S.D. Goitein and Helmuth Plessner could emigrate, but many lives were lost, some professional libraries (e.g. that of the Hamburg Seminar) were destroyed and academic freedom ended. Not only were German Islamicists affected; the versatile Hungarian born scholar S.M. Stern, for instance, was also forced to flee. Between 1933 and 1945, a *Deutscher Orient-Verein* existed in Berlin. After World War II German Oriental Studies both in the Eastern and in the Western part of the country, as well as in Austria, had to begin anew.

4. The Present Situation of Islamic Studies in Germany

This subject is subdivided into the following themes:

a. University Institutions

b. Oriental Studies in general
c. Library Collections
d. Institutions and Organizations Outside the Universities

a. University Institutions

In 1960 a report was published by the German Research Association (*Deutsche Forschungsgemeinschaft;* D.F.G.) on the situation of Oriental Studies in the Federal Republic.[10] It stated that at that time all German universities except that of Saarbrücken had a Chair of Oriental Studies, adding that there were hardly any Oriental Studies outside the universities. Of the total number of 35 Professorial Chairs of Oriental Studies at the time, 12 were for Semitics and Islamic Studies, which were usually combined; there were moreover two holders of Extraordinary Professorships working in this field. On the basis of this report, the German Science Council in November 1960 recommended the establishment of 32 new Chairs of Oriental Studies, taking it for granted that each university should have four such chairs. It also recommended that Islamic Studies should be separated from Semitics.

Twelve years later, in 1972, the German Oriental Society (*Deutsche Morgenlaendische Gesellschaft;*D.M.G.) complained in a report that of the 32 recommended new Chairs for Oriental Studies only 21 had been instituted up to that moment and of these only three were for Islamic Studies.[11] The report also complained that Islamic Studies had not been separated from Semitics, that no independent Chairs had been created for Turkish, modern Persian, and the History of the Islamic world, and that there was an almost total neglect of Islamic art and of the history of Islam in Afghanistan, Pakistan, India and Indonesia. Since 1972 the situation has improved slightly. Turcology, Indian Islam and African Islam have been instituted at the less than twenty-odd Universities in the German Federal Republic, but measures have been taken to concentrate specific specializations at particular universities, both for research and teaching. The study-programmes of Islamic Studies at the different German universities are not uniform, and very much depends on the particular specialization and interests of the person holding the Chair at a particular time. A comparison of the different programmes at German universities falls outside the scope of this article and we merely take as an example the particular programme of Islamic Studies which existed at the Albert-Ludwigs University in Freiburg in Breisgau in 1981.[12]

The programme concerns Islamic Studies in the Philosophical Faculty, though at the time Islam was also taught in the Faculty of (Catholic) Theology by Richard Gramlich, a well-known specialist who moreover had been theologically trained. Islamic Studies in the Philosophical Faculty comprise the culture and history of the Muslim peoples. They are taught on a philological basis (with Arabic, Persian and Turkish as languages) and as a *geisteswissenschaftliche Disziplin* (as part of the humanities), which requires the study of written sources in the original languages and a general knowledge of the literature existing in the three languages mentioned. Islamic Studies constitute one section of the whole of Oriental Studies, the other sections being *Altorientalische Philologie* (ancient Near Eastern Languages), Near Eastern Archeology, Judaic Studies, Indology, Japanology and Sinology.

Among the aims of Islamic Studies, explicit mention is made of the *Überwindung des europazentrischen Weltbildes* (overcoming the Eurocentric view of the world). Islamic Studies can be chosen either with the accent on Arabic or with the accent on Persian and Turkish, but generally a speaking knowledge of all three languages is required.

The programme consists of a basic programme (*Grundstudium*) of four semesters (two years) and a main programme (*Hauptstudium*) also of four semesters for the M.A. degree. A full study programme of Islamic Studies including the doctoral dissertation comprises in any case 12 semesters or six years. In the basic programme all stress is on learning the three main languages of Islam and developing a reading knowledge of English and French. The speaking and writing of the "Islamic" languages is emphasized. In these two years students attend three introductory seminars (*Proseminare*: "Introduction to Islamics" (*Islamwissenschaft*), "Religion and culture of Islam" and "History of the Islamic peoples".

The main programme contains one main subject (*Hauptfach*) and two subsidiary topics (*Nebenfächer*). Here a combination of the accent on Arabic and lesser knowledge of Persian and Turkish (or the other way around) is mandatory, except if ancient Near Eastern languages (*Altorientalische Philologie*) are chosen as subsidiary subjects besides Islamic Studies with Arabic as a main subject. In that case the student does not have to take Persian and Turkish; in all other cases they are obligatory. If Islamic Studies are chosen as a subsidiary, only two languages are required: Arabic and either Persian or Turkish. It is safe to assume that in practice nearly all students whose main subject is Islamic Studies study Arabic, Persian and Turkish.

While engaged in their main programme, students are required to attend regularly the principal seminar, focussing on sources (*Arbeit mit Quellen*), take the course "Modern Orient" and attend seminars where modern texts in the Islamic literary languages are read. They also follow language courses in Arabic grammar, Persian and Turkish, and, when preparing to write papers, participate in the seminar on "Problems of Research in the Field of Islamics". Attending the lectures on various thematic topics is also strongly recommended. Students are advised to participate in excursions and to spend some time in the Muslim world. They can begin work on a dissertation before their M.A. as soon as they are capable of carrying out research themselves.

Besides the Islamic Studies programme at the University of Freiburg we should also mention the Institute for Islamic Studies (*Institut für Islamwissenschaft*) at the Free University of Berlin. It is unique in several respects: it has carried out research not only on the Islamic past but also on contemporary Islam, and it has integrated the study of religion and culture in its research and teaching programmes. Moreover, it has engaged in interdisciplinary research devoting attention to modern social, political and economic developments in the Near East and North Africa.

The Volkswagen Foundation has developed since 1970 a special programme to support research on the modern Near and Middle East, and made possible the establishment of two new Chairs at the Free University of Berlin, one for the Politics and Contemporary History of the Near East, and the other for the Economics of the Near East.

In Germany until recent times it was necessary for anyone intending to follow a scholarly career to submit a specific study (*Habilitationsschrift*) after his or her doctoral dissertation. From a bibliographical listing prepared by Klaus Schwarz[13] it appears that between 1885 and 1978, a total of 5,050 doctoral dissertations and *Habilitationsschriften* were submitted in the whole of Germany, Austria and German speaking Switzerland at universities on the area of the Near East, including Islam in the former USSR and China but excluding Pakistan, India, Indonesia and Africa south of the Sahara. Of this total number:

89 dealt with Christians in the area
42 dealt with Jews in the area
795 dealt with history including cultural history
40 dealt with philosophy
175 dealt with religion and theology

Most of these dissertations and *Habilitationsschriften* have been published and are accessible for research purposes.

b. Oriental Studies in General

During the 1960s and 1970s powerful incentives were offered for the development of German Oriental Studies. We mentioned the 1960 Report by the German Research Association (D.F.G., see n. 10) on Oriental Studies, which appeared as part of a whole series of reports on the situation of different fields of scholarship in the German Federal Republic. This Report also drew attention to the special problems which arise out of the tension between the established historical-philological tradition of Oriental Studies and the increasing interest in the contemporary problems of Asian and African countries, stimulated by political, economic and cultural developments. It made recommendations to improve the situation of teaching and research personnel and expand the necessary material facilities in universities, libraries, museums and collections.

The 1972 Report by the German Oriental Society (D.M.G.) on Oriental Studies in the 1970s mentioned above (see n. 11), formulated ten propositions. They may be summarized here since they are of particular interest to our theme:

1) The discipline of Oriental Studies (subdivided into about 20 sections) comprises the academic study of the languages and cultures of Asia and Africa from the earliest time until the present day and forms part of the humanities (*Geisteswissenschaften*);

2) Its subject matter encompasses: ". . . Sprachen, Literaturen, Geschichte, Religionen und Philosophien, Recht und Gesellschaftsformen, Probleme aus Zeitgeschichte und unmittelbarer Gegenwart kommen in immer stärkerem Masse hinzu. Selbstverständliche Voraussetzung für wissenschaftliches Arbeiten auf allen diesen Gebieten ist eine gründliche sprachliche Ausbildung" (p. 3/4).

3) The relevance of Oriental Studies to society is explained as follows: ". . . they deepen our understanding of the peoples of Africa and Asia, especially at the present time, in view of their discovery of themselves in different ways and of the changes taking place in their cultures. They contribute to the overcoming of traditional Eurocentric thinking and the misrepresentation of the world to which such thinking can easily lead. The role of the Orientalist is that of an irreplaceable intellectual mediator (*unersetzlicher geistiger Mittler*) without imperialistic or colonialist links".

4) After a relatively favorable development in the Federal Republic of Germany, Oriental Studies are threatened as far as academic posts are concerned.

5) At present, major tasks together with concomitant responsibilities, confront Oriental Studies and there are important themes to which research should devote itself.

6) Among such tasks and themes are:

"-Untersuchungen zu Gegenwartsproblemen Asiens und Afrikas,
-Sicherung gefährdeten Materials - jeder Art - zur Kultur der Völker Asiens und Afrikas (das oft gerade durch ihre heutigen sozio-ökonomischen Wandlungen gefährdet ist),
-die Erschliessung von Quellen zur Kultur-, Sozial-und Geistesgeschichte,
-die Rolle der Religionen und Denksysteme im Kulturwandel,
-die Entwicklung von Lehrmaterial und ehrprogrammen,
-vergleichende Untersuchungen von Kulturen und Gesellschafts strukturen,
-die Übersetzung bedeutender, repräsentativer literarischer und wissenschaftlicher Werke aus orientalischen Sprachen,
-die Mithilfe bei der Erarbeitung gegenwartskundlicher Hand bücher. Für die unaufschiebbare Auseinandersetzung mit den Problemen einer immer enger zusammenwachsenden Welt hält die Orientalistik unentbehrliche.
Informationen und Erkentnisse für Wissenschaft und Praxis bereit. Sie weiterhinungenützt zu lassen, wäre nicht zu verantworten" (p. 4-5).

7) Oriental Studies can develop subsidiary programmes (*Nebenfach-programme*) in the fields of history, economics and social sciences, while retaining their own fields of concentration (*Schwerpunkte*).

8) Only Oriental Studies offer a well-founded knowledge of the peoples and cultures of Asia and Africa.

9) There is a need for planning both research and the education of future specialists (*Nachwuchsbildung*):

-by an expansion of existing research institutes outside the universities,
-by developing special research areas (*Sonderforschungs-bereiche*)

A new central Institute for special research tasks should be founded, in so far as such tasks cannot be carried out at existing universities.

10) Planning of research in the section of Oriental Studies should not be at the expense of the possible creative initiative of the researchers themselves.

The 1972 Report further recommended that universities established in the future should also include Oriental Studies in their programmes, and that Oriental Studies should not be restricted to some universities only. It also dealt with the problem of future job opportunities for those who had finished their programme, recommending that they ought to have an applied subsidiary specialty to enable them to enter into the job market. It recommended that Oriental Studies concentrate much more on present-day problems than had been the case until now. Research institutes should be established in Asia and Africa, in addition to the Institute of the German Oriental Society which was set up in Beirut in 1961.

As far as the definition and status of Islamic Studies at universities are concerned, two expert opinions (*Gutachten*), which are anonymous and must date from the early seventies, are noteworthy. The first makes it clear that there is no generally accepted definition of the discipline of Islamic Studies, that its borderlines are not clearly fixed, and that there are no uniform and generally accepted programmes and examination demands. It constitutes a field of studies employing various disciplines. Within this field there is a line separating the purely linguistic subjects (including the learning of languages) on the one hand and the field of philology, literature and culture (*Kulturphilologische Fächer*) on the other. Co-operation with other disciplines should be left to private initiative and not be institutionalized, since the field of concentration (*Schwerpunkt*) of Oriental Studies should not be imposed from the outside. It would be helpful - as a kind of model - to consider all Departments (*Seminare*) of Islamic Studies in Germany as branches of one great "Near and Middle Eastern Centre" of the Federal Republic. A basic programme (*Grundstudium*) in the field should be available at all universities; on top of that, students should be able to pursue a special discipline. The special demands of each particular discipline within Islamic Studies should be met; the knowledge of languages alone was not sufficient.

The second expert opinion makes it clear that no scholar nowadays can survey the whole of Islamic Studies, and yet no more than one Chair has been allocated for this field in any one university. Islamic Studies should be disconnected from Semitics, Turkish and Persian; separate Chairs are therefore needed. There is a need for Chairs of Islamic history since significant regions of the Islamic world are neglected in research and teaching. An important observation is that since Islamic Studies constitutes a young discipline, "positivistic" tasks - assuring the preservation of manuscripts, the development of the tools to study them, and the putting on record of threatened languages and dialects - should have precedence:

> “Die Aufgaben der Forschung sind Legion. Da die Islamkunde und Arabistik - etwa im Vergleich zur klassischen Philologie - junge Wissenschaften sind, haben positivistische Aufgaben besonderen Vorrang: Erfassung, Sicherung und Katalogisierung der Handschriften, Texteditionen, Lexikographie, Aufnahme der Dialekte, die durch den Einfluß der Massenmedien nivelliert werden und zum Teil aussterben”.

c. Library Collections

Two libraries in the Federal Republic are particularly famous for their manuscript collections in Oriental Studies: the Bavarian State Library in Munich (founded in 1558) and the West German Library (the old Prussian State Library founded in 1661) in Marburg. The Niedersächsische Staats- und Universitätsbibliothek in Göttingen should also be mentioned for its manuscript holdings. Many other libraries possess manuscripts as well, and since 1957 a project has been carried out to catalogue those manuscripts (around 25,000) which do not figure in the existing Oriental manuscript catalogues in Germany.

There are about seventeen specialized library holdings at German universities, two of which should be mentioned here. The Near and Middle East Collection at the University Library in Tübingen, for instance, has a number of very old printed Arabic books.[14] After World War I it received special funds for the acquisition of books on Oriental Studies and after World War II it was chosen - in the terms of a programme initiated by the German Research Association (D.F.G.) in 1952 and involving 33 libraries - to develop a special subject collection (*Sondersammelgebiet*) in the fields of Near and Middle Eastern Studies and Indology, as well as, for instance, science of religions (*Religionswissenschaft*) and theology. This means that the Tübingen Library has the task of acquiring all materials published in the world about or in the Near and Middle East (except in the field of the natural sciences) with special funds provided by the German Research Association (D.F.G.). Tübingen was also designated the home for a large number of Arabic manuscripts which before 1945 had belonged to the collection in Berlin.

A second specialized library holding belongs to the Department for the History and Culture of the Near East at the University of Hamburg.[15] It had to be completely rebuilt after its destruction and loss of holdings in World War II and has now a stock of more than 40,000 volumes. In addition, the State and University Library in Hamburg has its own holdings including microfilms in the field of Islamic Studies.

d. Institutions and Organizations outside the Universities

Four kinds of institutions deserve mention here because of their importance for Islamic Studies in the wider sense of the word:

1) The Academies of Sciences (*Akademien der Wissenschaften*) of the different States (*Länder*) of the Federal Republic, and in particular the Committee for Orientalism (*Orientalische Kommission*) of the Academy of Sciences and Literature in Mainz, stimulate research, but they do not provide posts. They are able, however, to publish scholarly communica-

tions.

2) The German Research Association (*Deutsche Forschungsgemeinschaft*, D.F.G.) is an official body created to support and stimulate scholarly research in the Federal Republic. It is able to allocate funds to carry out research projects in the field of Islamic Studies at German universities, but such allocations are given for a limited period only.

3) The German Orient Institute (*Deutsches Orient-Institut*),[16] an independent foundation in Hamburg, is active in research on present-day developments in the Middle East. It is connected with another foundation in Hamburg, the German Overseas Institute (*Deutsches Übersee-Institut*). The German Orient Institute has an extensive Newspaper and Journal Collection, supports research and has several publications:

   -the series *Mitteilungen des Deutschen Orient-Instituts*
   -a series of books
   -a series of offprints

The German Orient Institute is closely connected with a documentation centre on the modern Orient. This *Dokumentations-Leitstelle Moderner Orient* has several publications under the umbrella of the German Orient Institute. These publications include different kinds of bibliographies and bulletins with information on current topics and events.

The German Orient Institute is also connected with the publication of the well-known journal *Orient* which is devoted to the contemporary history of Muslim countries and is formally published by the Near and Middle East Association in Hamburg. It also publishes articles in English.

4) The *Seminar für Orientalische Sprachen* which was founded in Berlin in 1887 has been mentioned above. It ceased to exist in 1935 but was reopened in Bonn in the fall of 1959. Its task is to teach the most

important living Oriental languages for practical use in a four-year study programme and to give instruction in the culture and society of different peoples in the East. The main *organizations* and *publications* in Germany of interest for Islamic Studies are listed in Appendix B.

The unification of East and West Germany in 1991 has added several centres of Islamic Studies to those existing in the Federal Republic. Special mention should be made of the Humboldt University in Berlin and the Universities of Leipzig and Halle. In Halle there is also the precious library of the German Oriental Society (D.M.G.).[17]

5) "Islam" in German Islamic Studies

Finally, the question should be asked: how does Islam look when studied in German Orientalism? The same question should be put with regard to studies in France and Britain - and for that matter the U.S.A., the former Soviet Union, and other countries.

In Germany, as elsewhere, a number of scholars prefer to speak either of Oriental Studies in general or of Middle Eastern Studies rather than of Islamic Studies. They stress the fact of studying specific culture zones in regional or geographic terms. Others choose a disciplinary approach and speak of the historical, anthropological or sociological study of specific societies and of the study of the literatures in specific languages. Others again consider Islam to be the determining factor in these societies and are inclined to pay special attention to it, its history, contents and variations, preferring to speak of "Islamic" Studies (*Islamwissenschaft*). This term, by the way, should not be used for the study of language and literature only. But whatever the name, the way the facts are studied is largely the same, so that the discussion about the name of the discipline has a mainly academic character, largely dependent on the attention one wants to give to the Islamic aspects of the subject-matter. Indeed, the ascertainment of facts and casual connections between such facts constitutes at present the main imperative of Oriental Studies in Germany as elsewhere. And the

"Oriental" visitors or readers may very well feel that their society, culture and religion are being reduced entirely to facts, and may wonder what contributions the technicalities of scholarly engineering can make to an understanding of the values by which people live. They may even protest against what might be seen as a degradation of social and cultural hopes and aspirations and the living faiths of people.

Scholarly discussions among German Orientalists are mostly of a highly technical nature and mainly concern specific linguistic, literary and historical problems. Islamic Studies are no exception; here, too, fundamental revisions of current research problems, methods and procedures, or the exploration of essentially new, interpretations, hypotheses and theoretical frameworks are relatively rare. To be sure, there were scholars like Carl Heinrich Becker[18] and Jörg Kraemer [19] who discussed broader issues of Islamic culture and the place of Islam in cultural history. But their theoretical concerns found little following among specialists who held facts, rather than their interpretation, that is to say constructed meaning, to be decisive in research.

The same tendency can be ascertained in German studies of Islam as a religion. It cannot fail to strike the observer that German Islamicists have hardly ever carried on any discussion about how to study the religious aspects of Muslim societies or the internal developments of the religion of Islam, taking into account the way in which these aspects or developments may have been conditioned by outside factors or whether they are the result of Islam as a spiritual, dynamic faith. Curiously enough, the history of religions as a discipline apparently has generated hardly any impulse so far among German Islamicists to articulate new ways to study Islam as a religion, except by studying Sufi or other religious texts.

This seems to hold true in particular for the study of the religion and culture of Islam in modern times. The studies of W. Braune[20] and R. Wielandt[21] are until recently the only major works on the subject by professional Islamicists and they cannot be considered as being inspired by the methodological concerns of modern *Religionswissenschaft*.[22] Besides the reticence shown towards interpreting religious aspects of Islam, the classical literary and historical concerns of German Orientalism seem to stand in the way of a new and original vision being reached of what has been going on in the Muslim world in the last hundred years and what this has meant to Muslim groups and societies. The work of Annemarie Schimmel has been a real breakthrough in this respect.

When we compared German Oriental Studies with the explorations made by scientific discoverers, we meant to hint at such points. Discoverers are assumed to be well-trained and equipped and when they begin, they need not necessarily have very clear perceptions of their own presuppositions and values: their first task is to discover new data and establish facts with the help of reliable procedures. What is difficult to explain in Oriental Studies, however, is that at a later stage so little intellectual effort has been made to put relevant questions, to integrate and correlate the collected data and enquire into the meanings they have for the people concerned.

The situation is the more astonishing since German culture has always had a speculative bent and German scholarship is reputed for its creative theoretical thought. Why precisely this German genius has been largely absent in the field of Islamic Studies is a problem. Should it be seen as a defense of pure scholarship against ideological aberrations and subjective engagement? The passion for the accumulation of factual data, the radical separation of facts and values (including the interpretation of the facts), the failure to question certain basic assumptions and procedures applied in the study of Muslim cultures and societies, a certain lack of communication with different kinds of Muslim intellectuals, their problems and their views of Islam today: all of this points to a certain rigidity in Islamic Studies in Germany. To the present writer who tries to combine both fields, it is for instance unclear why there has been so little creative interaction between the kind of questions put in the study of religion (*Religionswissenschaft*) and the kind of questions put in the study of Islam (*Islamwissenschaft*). Is scholarly research not primarily moved by questions rather than by amassing facts? Is true scholarship not characterized by continuously making self-corrections and readjustments to the subject matter studied?[23]

What kind of Islam is mirrored in Islamic Studies in Germany and elsewhere is such a question. A fresh look needs to be taken at the work of so many brilliant scholarly minds to discover what they saw as "Islam", and whether they all saw it differently - or had difficulty in seeing it at all.[24]

Things may change of course with a new generation of scholars who have personal experience of Muslim societies and have developed a sensitivity to their human dimensions. In this respect the German Orient Institute in Beirut and Istanbul can make an important contribution.

Notes

1. Rudi Paret, *The Study of Arabic and Islam at German Universities. German Orientalists since Theodor Nöldeke*. Wiesbaden: Franz Steiner Verlag, 1986, p. 5.
2. In addition to Paret's work, see also Johann Fück, *Die arabischen Studien in Europa bis in den Anfang des 20. Jahrhunderts*. Leipzig: Otto Harrassowitz, 1955. Islamic studies in the former German Democratic Republic and developments since 1991, have pending further analysis, been left out of consideration here.
3. Jean-Jacques Waardenburg, *L'Islam dans le miroir de l'Occident*. The Hague: Mouton, 1961, 3rd ed. 1970. Maxime Rodinson, *La fascination de l'Islam. Les étapes du regard occidental sur le monde musulman. Les études arabes et islamiques en Europe*. Paris: Maspero, 1980.
4. Kurt Rudolph, *Wellhausen als Arabist* (Sitzungsberichte der Sächsischen Akademie der Wissenschaften zu Leipzig. Philologisch-historische Klasse, Band 123, Heft 5). Berlin (Ost): Akademie-Verlag, 1983.
5. Ernst A. Bücher, "Verzeichnis der Schriften von Helmut Ritter", *Oriens*, XVIII-XIX (1965-66), 5-32. Also as a separate publication published by E.J. Brill, Leiden.
6. Otto Spies, *Verzeichnis der Schriften von Carl Brockelmann*. Leipzig: Otto Harrassowitz, 1938.
7. Anton Schall, "Enno Littmann, 1875-1958," in *Bonner Gelehrte. Beiträge zur Geschichte der Wissenschaften in Bonn: Sprachwissenschaften* (150 Jahre

Rheinische Friedrich Wilhelms-Universität zu Bonn, 1818-1968). Bonn: Bouvier & Rohrscheid, 1970, pp. 338-344. For a list of Littmann's publications, see the book mentioned in Note 8, pp. 139-195.

8. For an understanding of typical Orientalist culture, see for instance, *Ein Jahrhundert Orientalistik. Lebensbilder aus der Feder von Enno Littmann und Verzeichnis seiner Schriften*. Zum achtzigsten Geburtstage am 16. September 1955 zusammengestellt von Rudi Paret und Anton Schall. Wiesbaden: Otto Harrassowitz, 1955.

9. See for instance, Gernot Rotter (ed.) *Deutsche Orientalisten am Beispiel Tübingens*. Tübingen & Basel, 1974; Peter Heine, *Geschichte der Arabistik und Islamkunde in Münster*. Wiesbaden: Otto Harrassowitz, 1974; Paul Kahle, "Das Orientalische Seminar," in *Geschichte der Rheinischen Friedrich-Wilhelm-Universität zu Bonn am Rhein*. Band 2: *Institute und Seminare 1818-1933* (Bonn am Rhein: Friedrich Cohen Verlag, 1933), pp. 173-177; "Erlangen - ein Zentrum moderner Orient-Forschung," *Unikurier* (Zeitschrift der Friedrich-Alexander-Universität Erlangen-Nürnberg), Nr. 35/36, 7. Jahrgang, April 1981, pp. 20-26. Compare also in the book mentioned in Note 8 the commemorations (*Nachrufe*) of Georg Wilhelm Freytag, 1788-1861 (pp. 293-295, by Johann W. Fück), Carl Heinrich Becker, 1876-1933 (pp. 330-337, by Helmut Ritter), and Max Horten, 1874-1945 (pp. 327-329, by Otto Spies).

10. *Denkschrift zur Lage der Orientalistik.* Im Auftrag der Deutschen Forschungsgemeinschaft und in Zusammenarbeit mit zahlreichen Fachvertretern herausgegeben von Prof. Dr. Adam Falkenstein. Wiesbaden: Franz Steiner Verlag, 1960.

11. *Deutsche Orientalistik der Siebziger Jahre: Thesen, Zustandsanalyse, Perspektiven*. Deutsche Morgenländische Gesellschaft, n.d. (1972). Cf. Dietrich Seckel and Anton Schall, "Die sogenannten 'Kleinen Fächer' an den Universitäten. Memorandum zur Hochschulplanung," *Ruperto Carola*, Vol. 54 (1975), p. 11-15.

A survey of all centres of Oriental Studies in Germany with research interests in contemporary developments around 1974 is given in Rainer Buren, *Gegenwartsbezogene Orientwissenschaft in der Bundesrepublik Deutschland*. Göttingen 1974.

12. Albert-Ludwigs-Universität, Freiburg im Breisgau, *Studienpläne: Islamwissenschaft. Studienplan fur das Gesamtfach Islamwissenschaft*. Freiburg: Hochschul Verlag, 1981.

13. Klaus Schwarz, *Der Vordere Orient in den Hochschulschriften Deutschlands, Österreichs und der Schweiz. Eine Bibliographie von Dissertationen und Habilitationsschriften (1885-1978)* (Islamkundliche Materialien, Band 5).

Freiburg im Breisgau: Klaus Schwarz Verlag, 1980.

14. Walter Werkmeister, "The Near and Middle East Collection of the University Library of Tübingen," *Bulletin of the British Society for Middle Eastern Studies*, IX (1982), 82-87.

15. A. Hartmann, "The Library of the Department for the History and Culture of the Near East, Hamburg," *Bulletin of the British Society for Middle Eastern Studies*, VIII (1981), pp. 139-146.

16. *Orient-Institut der Deutschen Morgenländischen Gesellschaft in Beirut*. Herausgegeben anlässlich des 20-jährigen Bestehens. Beirut, 1981.

17. To what extent the unification of East and West Germany will influence German Oriental Studies in general and Islamic Studies in particular is impossible to say. Whereas in the former D.D.R. the role of Islam as a *religion* was left out of consideration, that of Islam as a *social factor* was stressed, and correctly so.

18. J. Van Ess, “From Wellhausen to Becker: The Emergence of Kulturgeschichte in Islamic Studies”, in Malcolm H. Kerr (ed.), *Islamic Studies: A Tradition and its Problems* (Georgio Levi della Vida Biennial Conference 7). Malibu, Calif.: Undena Publications, 1980, pp. 27-72.

19. See for instance Jörg Kraemer, *Das Problem der islamischen Kulturgeschichte*. Tübingen: Max Niemeyer Verlag, 1959.

20. Walter Braune, *Der islamische Orient zwischen Vergangenheit und Zukunft*. Berlin, 1960.

21. Rotraud Wielandt, *Offenbarung und Geschichte im Denken moderner Muslime* (Akademie der Wissenschaften und der Literatur. Veröffentlichungen der Orientalischen Kommission, Band 25). Wiesbaden, 1971.

22. Jacques Waardenburg, “Islamforschung aus religionswissenschaftlicher Sicht”, in *Ausgewählte Vorträge, XXI. Deutscher Orientalistentag*, 24. bis 29. März 1980 in Berlin (Supplement V der *Zeitschrift der Deutschen Morgenländischen Gesellschaft*). Herausgegeben von Fritz Steppat. Wiesbaden: Franz Steiner Verlag, 1982, pp. 197-211. Reprinted in J. Waardenburg, *Perspektiven der Religionswissenschaft* (Würzburg: Echter Verlag & Altenberge: Oros Verlag, 1993), pp. 181-195.

23. “Considering the mass of material to be mastered and the boundless mass of, mainly secondary, literature, the scholar must reconsider his position from time to time and ask himself whether he is not driving himself into an isolated position, and whether his specialized studies are not becoming an end in themselves”. Rudi Paret, *The Study of Arabic and Islam at German Universities* (Wiesbaden: Steiner Verlag, 1968), p. 69.

24. For bio-bibliographical data of German scholars of Islam during the nineteenth and twentieth centuries, see Erika Bär, *Bibliographie zur deutschsprachigen*

Islamwissenschaft und Semitistik vom Anfang des 19. Jahrhunderts bis heute. Wiesbaden: Dr. Ludwig Reichert Verlag, 1985 (Three volumes appeared until 1994.)

Appendix A
Some Prominent Scholars

1. Arabic Language Studies

Heinrich Leberecht Fleischer (1801-1888), pupil of the French scholar A. I. Sylvestre de Sacy. Founder of Arabic philology in Germany.

Georg Wilhelm Freytag (1788-1861), compiler of the famous dictionary *Lexicon Arabico-Latinum* (1830-1837).

Albert Socin (1844-1899), compiler of an elaborate card system for an exhaustive Arabic-German Dictionary. This card system is one of the sources of the dictionary of the Classical Arabic Language into English and German which is in course of publication now (*Wörterbuch der Klassischen Arabischen Sprache*).

2. Textual studies

Gustav Flügel (1802-1870), compiler of a text edition and Concordance of the Quran (1834) and editor of the *Kitāb al-Fihrist* by Ibn al Nadīm.

Josef von Hammer-Purgstall (Austrian, 1774-1856), famous for his Turkish, Persian and Arabic literary studies.

Jozef Horovitz (1874-1931), author of studies on the Quran and Muhammad, initiated a card system on ancient Arabic poetry which is at present at the Hebrew University of Jerusalem. He collaborated with other German scholars in the edition of Ibn Saʿd's *Tabāqāt*.

Theodor Nöldeke (1836-1930), famous for his History of the Quran (1860). A new edition appeared in three volumes (1909, 1919 and 1938) with revisions made by Friedrich Schwally (1863-1919), Gotthelf Bergsträsser (1886-1933) and Otto Pretzl (1893-1941). Bergsträsser started a project for the edition of an *apparatus criticus* to the Quran text.

Gustav Weil (1808-1889), author of an introduction to the Quran and a biography of Muhammad.

Ferdinand Wuestenfeld (1808-1899), editor of Ibn Hishām's *Sīrat al-Nabī* (1858-1860) and of Ibn Khallikān's *Wafāyāt al-ayān*.

3. Historical studies

Biographies of Muhammad were written by Gustav Weil (1808-1889) in 1843, Aloys Sprenger (1813-1893) who published his book in three volumes between 1861 and 1865 (1869), and Hubert Grimme (1864-1942) who described Muhammad foremost as a social reformer in 1892. Abraham Geiger (1810-1874) was the author of a well-known book entitled *What did Muhammed retain from Judaism?* (1833, Engl. tr. 1902)

Carl Heinrich Becker (1876-1933) whose historical papers, also treating the development and character of Islamic culture and religion, were brought together in his *Islamstudien* (2 vols., 1924-1932).

Carl Brockelmann (1881-1965), also known for his Semitic, especially Arabic Studies and his inventory of Arabic manuscript texts; compiled a well-known history of the Islamic peoples (1939).

Gustav Edmund von Grunebaum (Austrian, 1909-1972), migrated to the USA where he carried out a number of studies on Arabic literature, Islamic history and civilization, also with theoretical interests.

Richard Hartmann (1881-1965), contributed a number of historical studies, including some on contemporary developments of Muslim countries and Islam.

Alfred von Kremer (Austrian, 1828-1889), whose works include: studies on Ibn Khaldūn (1859 and 1879), a history of the dominant ideas of Islam (1868), and a cultural history of the Orient under the Caliphs (2 vols., 1875-1877).

Adam Mez (Swiss, 1869-1917), a private scholar in Basel, author of a well-known study of the Renaissance of Islam in the 10th century (1922).

August Müller (1849-1892), author of a study on Islam in the Occident and Orient (2 vols., 1885-1887)

Bertold Spuler (1911-1990), author of studies on Islamic history, e.g., early Islamic Iran (1952), the Mongol period in Iran (1939) and on the history of the Christian churches in the Near East (1964). Editor of the *Handbuch der Orientalistik* in many volumes.

Julius Wellhausen (1844-1918), author of several historical studies on early Islam:

Muhammad in Medina (al-Wāqīdi's *Kitāb al-maghāzi*, 1882).
Relics of Arabic paganism (Ibn al-Kalbī's *Kitāb al-asnām*, 1887, 1897).
Pre-Islamic Medina, Muhammad's Constitution of Medina,
Writings of, and missions to Muhammad (1889).
Prolegomena to the earliest history of Islam (1889).
The religio-political opposition parties in early Islam (1901).
The Arab Empire and its fall (1902).

4. Studies of the Religion of Islam

Ignaz Goldziher (Hungarian, 1850-1921), wrote extensive studies in German on many subjects of Islamic culture and religion, e.g.,
The Zāhirites (1884).
Muslim Studies (2 vols., 1889-1890); including a famous study on *hadīth* literature in Vol. 2).
Lectures on Islam (1910).
The tendencies of Islamic Quran interpretation (1920).

Richard Gramlich (Swiss, Basel), studies on Islamic mysticism and Shīʿa thought.

Max Horten (1874-1945), studies on Islamic theology and philosophy.

Fritz Meier (Swiss, Basel), studies on Islamic mysticism.

Helmut Ritter (1892-1971), wrote many studies of Islamic religious texts.

Annemarie Schimmel (Bonn), numerous studies on Islamic literatures, mystical texts and Islamic religion from a phenomenological perspective.

Rudolf Strothmann (1877 -1960), studies on the Shīʿa.

5. Studies of Islamic Law:

Gotthelf Bergsträsser (1886-1933), specialist of Islamic law.

Eduard Sachau (1845-1930). This scholar is also known for having brought to light some major works of al-Bīrūnī.

Joseph Schacht (1902-1969) emigrated to Egypt, England, Holland and then the USA. Well-known for his studies on Islamic law, the origins of Muslim jurisprudence and provenance of *hadīth* materials in legal texts.

6. Bibliographical Work and Cataloguing of Manuscripts

Wilhelm Ahlwardt (1828-1909), composed a classic 10-volume Catalogue of Berlin Mss (1887-1899).

Carl Brockelmann (1881-1965), well-known for his inventory of Arabic manuscript texts, in 5 vols. (1898-1902 and 1937-1942).

Georg Graf (1875-1955, working in Rome), well-known for his inventory of Christian Arabic manuscipt texts, in 5 vols. (1944-1953).

Moritz Steinschneider (1816-1907), well-known scholar of medieval Arabic texts written by Jewish authors (1902), author of an inventory of medieval polemical literature in Arabic.

APPENDIX B

Institutions and Publications

I. Institutions

1. The German Oriental Society (*Deutsche Morgenländische Gesellschaft*), founded in 1845, is the organization of all German Orientalists, with its headquarters in Mainz. It organizes regular conferences (*Orientalistentage)* every two or three years, publishes the journal *Zeitschrift der Deutschen Morgenländischen Gesellschaft* and the book series *Abhandlungen für die Kunde des Morgenlandes*.

It supervises the German Orient Institute in Beirut which was founded in 1961. This Institute stimulates research by German scholars, keeps track of publications appearing in Lebanon and Syria, and inventories modern Arabic literature. It publishes a series of text editions, the *Bibliotheca Islamica*, and a series of monographs, the *Beiruter Texte und Studien*. An earlier local branch (*Nebenstelle*) of the German Oriental Society in Istanbul, which Helmut Ritter had headed during his work there from 1927 until 1949, developed to a full-fledged Institute in Istanbul in the 1970s, as a branch of the Institut in Beirut, with attention being paid to Turkey and the Turkic-speaking part of the Muslim world.

2. Institutions and persons working on the contemporary Near and Middle East have organized themselves into a working group: *Arbeitsgemeinschaft Vorderer Orient für Gegenwartsbezogene Forschung und Dokumentation* (AGVO). It publishes regular communications (*Mitteilungen*) which contain details about research in progress on the present-day Near East and which give practical information about current developments, conferences, publications, etc.

3. The Near and Middle East Association (*Nah-und Mittelost-Verein*) in Hamburg publishes its own annual surveys (*Jahresberichte*), and also, in association with the German Orient Institute in Hamburg, the quarterly journal *Orient*.

4. The International Society for Oriental Research (*Internationale Gesellschaft für Orientalistische Forschung*), founded by Helmut Ritter, with its headquarters in Frankfurt, publishes the annual journal, *Oriens*.

II. Publications

1. Periodicals

Zeitschrift der Deutschen Morgenländischen Gesellschaft, since 1855, the official journal of the German Oriental Society, with special issues as Supplements. A General Index was published in 1955, covering the articles which appeared during the first 100 years of publication. This journal covers the whole field of Oriental Studies.

Der Islam, founded by C.H. Becker, since 1910. This is the leading journal in Germany for the historical study of Islam.

Die Welt des Islam/The World of Islam/Le Monde de l'Islam, since 1914; a new series number started in 1951. This journal covers the modern and contemporary history of Muslim countries and Islam.

Die Orientalistische Literaturzeitung (Leipzig), from 1898 until 1944, and again since the 1950s. This journal contains elaborate book reviews and surveys in the field of Oriental Studies, including Islamic Studies.

Oriens (Frankfurt), since 1948. See I,3.

Orient (Hamburg), since 1959. See I,3.

Mundus, since 1965. This journal contains reports in English on recent German publications concerning Asia, Africa and Latin America.

Bulletins and Bibliographies on the present-day Middle East are published by the Dokumentationsdienst *Moderner Orient* mentioned above, in Hamburg.

2. Book series

Abhandlungen für die Kunde des Morgenlandes, since 1859, under the auspices of the German Oriental Society (D.M.G.)

Bibliotheca Orientalis, since 1929. Some 30 text editions have appeared. (Not to be confused with the journal of the same name published in Leiden!).

Beiruter Texte und Studien, since 1964. Some 60 volumes have appeared up to now.

Islamkundliche Materialien and *Islamkundliche Untersuchungen*, since 1971 (Klaus Schwarz Verlag, Berlin). More than 160 books have appeared up to now in a practical offset edition.

III. Special Projects and International Cooperation

Of the many items falling under this heading a few may be mentioned at random.

Since 1948 a number of volumes of the *Handbuch der Orientalistik*, written by specialists from different countries and supervised by Bertold Spuler, have appeared, with many books in the field of Islamic Studies.

Since 1957 a large project of cataloguing Oriental manuscripts in the Federal Republic has been under way and several volumes of the *Verzeichnis der orientalischen Handschriften in Deutschland* have appeared already. A special project for the conservation and cataloguing of Oriental manuscripts elsewhere, funded by the Cultural Section of the German Foreign Office, is underway.

The major project of the *Tübingen Atlas of the Near and Middle East* (TAVO) has been in progress since 1969. It concerns not only the topography and geography but also the economy, social structure, architectural and other aspects of the region throughout history. A number of volumes have appeared already. A research project on *minorities* in the Islamic world has led to the publication of several volumes on the subject.

German scholars contribute to the *Encyclopedia of Islam* (New Edition) and participate actively in the Congresses of the *Union Européenne d'Arabisants et d'Islamisants*, the congress of 1974 having been held in Göttingen. In 1986 the International Congress on Asian and North African Studies - formerly called the International Orientalist Congress - was held in Hamburg.

Mohammed Arkoun

The Study of Islam in French Scholarship

I would like, from the beginning, to make clear that French Orientalism is represented by a wide spectrum of activity not restricted to Arabic Studies and Islamology. Far Eastern cultures, languages and civilizations are also included in the field called Orientalism; but this chapter is concerned only with Arabic and Islamic Studies. It deals initially with some historical information about French Orientalists, followed by a more personal perspective, based on my experience as a Professor of History of Islamic thought at the Sorbonne since 1961. I hope to avoid any value judgements about French Orientalists and about Orientalists in general, since my purpose is to create a climate of solidarity between Muslim and Western scholars wherever they work, and to avoid all the ideological disputes which have been carried on for too long and have recently been revived in America, especially after the work of Edward Said. From a historical point of view, I think we can describe French Orientalism (and also other forms of Orientalism) as a continuous movement from at least the sixteenth century until 1962 - a long period. The reason for choosing 1962 is that this year marks the end of the Algerian war. This is important because the Algerian war is of major historical significance not only for French Orientalism, but also as a watershed in the history of the French nation. The Fifth Republic, which is now the régime of France, was created in 1958 during the Algerian war. This simple fact illustrates one aspect of the importance of this event; but unfortunately, this event has not yet been evaluated and studied by French scholars in all its aspects.

From the general point of view, French, as well as British Orientalism, can be said to have been linked, though not necessarily caused by the colonial strategy of domination; and this situation explains many of the characteristics of Orientalism. I think it is not necessary to go as far back in history as the sixteenth century because I have already covered the earlier period elsewhere. In France, the first Chair devoted to Arabic teaching was created for Guillaume Postel in the *Collège de France* in 1539; thus we may consider the work of Orientalists, from an academic point of view, to have begun from this date; and since then, Arabic teaching was confined to the *Collège de France* until the creation of *l'Ecole Nationale des Langues Orientales* in 1793.

The first Professor nominated to teach Arabic at this school was Sylvestre de Sacy. During the eighteenth century, when de Sacy was teaching Arabic Studies, another approach to the study of Oriental societies was inaugurated by a famous traveller: Volney (1757-1820) who travelled to Syria and Egypt and wrote a very important account of these two countries. Jean Gaulmier has emphasized the significance of this particular approach to identifying Oriental societies through social observation rather than academic research.[1] One method was based on direct contact with people, the other merely relied on philological readings of ancient texts. These two trends will converge, as we shall see, among some scholars in North Africa, during the colonial period. But the philological method remained dominant because the major focus of academic training in the universities (including the preparation of theses) encouraged it.

The French conquered Algeria in 1830, Tunisia in 1881 and Morocco in 1912. Thus, from 1830 to 1962 the field was open to anyone who wanted to go to North Africa, to discover the society and to live there as long as they wished. This generated a vast number of studies in the field. This North African school started to publish an important review, called *La Revue Africaine*, in 1880, which was published without interruption until the 1950s. This review reflects work done by several kinds of individuals - not all of them scholars, because they included army officers, writers, journalists, politicians, etc. Within the colonial military administration, officers who had administrative responsibility pursued the study of society. As a result, the main interest developed by this school was a kind of ethnographic description of the society and the study of dialects. The name which immediately springs to mind is that of the great Arabist William Marçais. His work has had a very important impact on Arabists in France like René and André Basset, and he has contributed greatly to the study of colloquial Arabic, especially the study of Berber dialects. This interest in the dialects shows us one new field of research which developed during the late nineteenth century. But there were also historians and geographers like Emile Felix Gautier, a brilliant theoretician of North African society drawing from Ibn Khaldūn and the cognitive framework currently used during the nineteenth century. The literature accumulated during this period, much of which was hastily published after independence, is called "Colonial Science". In recent years, with increasingly detachment, one can appreciate the importance of this earlier research on North African society, because it preserved a great deal of first-hand information.

Many famous scholars started their careers in North Africa. For example, Louis Massignon acquired his interest in Islamic Studies with Lyautey as an officer during the conquest of Morocco. Jacques Berque also was a highly placed administrator in the Atlas where he prepared his thesis. E. Lévi Provençal, R. Blachère, R. Brunschvig, Georges and Philippe Marçais, M. Canard, J. Lecerf, R. Le Tourneau, Ch. Pellat and others, all started their careers in North Africa.[2] It was a rich movement, but it was a product of the colonial process which had little impact on the Maghribi population itself. Very few Algerian students were interested in studying "Arabic" at the University of Algiers until independence in 1962; they preferred to study law or medicine, according to the ambitions of their social origins. When I started myself my Arabic Studies in 1969, we were not more than five students attending courses.

Another characteristic of this "colonial science" is the ethnographic perspective reflected in the study of religions. Such studies tended to describe the superstitions, magical beliefs and practices among the peoples of North Africa rather than Islam. It is true that North African society in Morocco, Algeria and Tunisia in the nineteenth century was yet to be deeply influenced by the West. One should also add that many parts of this society were as yet untouched by Arabic language and culture, and a genuine Maghribi way of life flourished in these parts before it was fully exposed to the impact of the West or the impact of modern Arabic culture - influences that only became fully evident after the independence of these countries. For this reason it was natural that those individuals who discovered and described this society concentrated initially on the more visible aspects: what they called, in the language of the time, superstition and magic. They studied what we would call "popular", as opposed to "learned", religion. But these scholars were dominated by the positivist definition of progress, rationalism, science and civilization, all of which were contrasted with the primitive mentality (as reflected in the work of Lucien Lévy-Bruhl). The concept of primitive societies was basic to colonialist ideology because it gave a "scientific" legitimation to the domination of African and Asian societies by the conquering Western civilization. The positivist dogma which had developed in the nineteenth century was taken as axiomatic. Nobody questioned this and everyone thought and worked within its intellectual and scientific assumptions.

An interesting example is the work done by A. Hanoteau and A. Letourneux who were engaged as administrators in Kabylie. Kabylie lies in the northern region of Algeria where only Berber was spoken, and only Berber (*tamazight*) law and not the *Sharīʿa* was applied. As a result, these administrators, according to the politics decided by Napoleon III, started to look at the customs and the laws of the Berbers, and they compiled a large and magnificent corpus entitled *La Kabylie et les coutumes kabyles*.[3] The importance of the North African school is also shown by the fact that the other approach, the scientific and philological method, which developed in Paris in the School of Oriental Languages, was linked to the North African milieu. For example, E. Lévi-Provençal (1894-1956), who was one of the leading Arabists in France, started his career in the Institut des Hautes Etudes in Rabat. Then, he spent time at the University of Algiers; and when he went to France after the Second World War, he founded the Institut d'Etudes Islamiques which still exists at the Sorbonne. Thus, the study of Arabic at the Sorbonne started only - it is important to note - after the War, with the Chair given to Lévi-Provençal. It was not until 1952 that a second Chair at the Sorbonne, the Chair of Arabic philology and literature, was established and held by R. Blachère. It is noteworthy how slowly Arabic studies developed in spite of the French colonial experience in North Africa, Lebanon, Syria and Muslim West Africa.

The development of modern Arabic studies in North Africa itself really dates from 1880 when the University of Algiers was founded (initially as a School of Humanities). At this school, the two approaches I have described co-existed: the ethnographic and the philological and were represented by Professors René Basset, William and Georges Marçais and Henri Pérès. All of the professors, concentrated in the Institute of Oriental Studies at the University of Algiers, left after 1962. Roger Le Tourneau started at this date to found a similar centre in Aix-en-Provence, renamed, the Centre de Recherches et d'Etudes sur les Societes Méditerranéennes (CRESM). It is today one of the most important in France, a centre of research for specialists in political and social sciences, which publishes the *Annuaire de l'Afrique du Nord* and many other monographs on the Contemporary Middle East and North Africa.

After 1962, R. Le Tourneau at Aix continued to provide it with leadership. The heritage of Algiers University was concentrated in the centre at Aix, and it was here that the official archives of Algeria since 1830, were transferred. These archives aroused a long and bitter polemic between the Algerian government and the French government, each claiming the right to have it as a sign of sovereignty. In fact, the real academic significance of this debate was enhanced by the increasing importance of Arabic Studies at the Sorbonne where E. Lévi-Provençal was succeeded on his death in 1956 by Régis Blachère, who retired in 1968, to be followed by Charles Pellat who taught until 1979. A third centre was created in Bordeaux under Professor R. Brunschvig who moved to Paris in 1954, and a fourth was created in Lyons, under Henri Laoust, the son of Emile Laoust who started his career in Morocco. Another centre was created later in Strasbourg in 1967 under Professor T. Fahd. Claude Cahen began in Strasbourg where he was teaching medieval history and introduced under this rubric, the economic and social history of the Muslim East. He came to the Sorbonne in 1960 and retired in 1979. You may say that 1980 marks the end of a generation, the generation of Régis Blachère, R. Brunschvig, R. Arnaldez and Henri Laoust.

Another point worth mentioning in connection with this period after 1962, is that many North Africans, Tunisians, Moroccans and Algerians, had emigrated to France as workers, so that at present, there are over three million people from North Africa living in France. This created the necessity of developing within the secondary schools the teaching of Arabic as a foreign language, a feature unique to France, because I believe nothing comparable exists in any other European country. At present, Arabic is taught together with English, German and other foreign languages. The teaching of Arabic has developed significantly in the last five or six years because there is increasing pressure from the North African population to provide their children with the opportunity of studying Arabic. This has led to a new demand in universities to train teachers to teach Arabic in secondary schools, which in turn has created a new situation for Arabic Studies in the Universities.

Finally, I would like to discuss the situation with regard to the new generation, if I may use this expression, because, as we shall see, from the scientific point of view, no major changes have occurred. There are now many other centres in France where Arabic and Islamic Studies may be pursued. Very briefly, I must mention the *Ecole Pratique des Hautes Etudes* (IVe-V^{e} et VIe Sections, specializing respectively in philology, religious sciences, and the social sciences) and the *Collège de France*, where there is only one Professor of Arabic, André Miquel, since the late Professor Jacques Berque's retirement. A predecessor of Berque was Robert Montagne who, like him, had been an officer and administrator in Morocco before he came to the *Collège de France*.

The other universities in which Islamic Studies are offered as part of the curricùlum are Nancy, Clermont-Ferrand, Toulouse, Rennes and Lille. Some other universities are also starting to show an interest, and it should be added that the then Minister of Education, Alain Savary, officially decided in 1983 that Arabic Studies were to be considered a national priority in France. In the following year, despite an economic crisis, he took the extraordinary decision to create five new posts in this area of studies at the level of assistant professor, not full professors.

What are the disciplines represented in Arabic Studies in France? There is a desperate shortage of professors in all disciplines. To illustrate our present shortcomings, let me say that when the late Claude Cahen retired, it was impossible to find one competent professor to replace him, and his Chair at the Sorbonne (Paris I) has remained vacant until now, although Professor Dominique Sourdel continues to teach at the Sorbonne (Paris IV). One reason for this state of affairs is that previously, with Professors R. Blachère and E. Lévi-Provençal, few French students had shown an interest in attaining the level of doctorate, and therefore, very few academics became qualified to be recruited as professors. This is the present predicament.

The most dominant contemporary trends in Arabic Studies are Linguistics, History and Political Science. The most popular of these trends is Linguistics, partly because of the general fashion for this subject in the French universities, and partly because Sociology and Anthropology require fieldwork, whereas a theoretical linguist can do research in the libraries of Paris, Lyons or Strasbourg. Besides, there is an ideological component in all Social Sciences because they raise delicate problems for local governments. Field trips are always strictly controlled. The difficulties encountered by the CRESM in Aix-en-Provence have already been mentioned. With regard to the Social Sciences, one may begin with reference to the now famous article published by Claude Cahen in 1955 in *Studia Islamica* which was a kind of manifesto. The title was in itself eloquent "Economic and Social History of the Medieval Muslim Orient".[4] What he argued in his article was that very few Arabists working on the history of Oriental societies were trained as historians. They were trained as philologists. They had learned Arabic according to the approach introduced by William Marçais at the beginning of the twentieth century, but that in itself was hardly adequate. Claude Cahen himself was basically an historian, not an Arabist. He was sufficiently conversant with Arabic to read very technical texts (finance, economics, law) and applied to Arabic Studies with great success the "new history" developed in France since

1930 under the name of "*L'Ecole des Annales*"[5] without adhering fully to all the trends of that school.

Another, but less important, event, was the publication of an article entitled "Perspectives" by Robert Brunschvig to launch the new journal *Studia Islamica*. In this article, he outlined some new approaches for Islamicists or Islamologists, defining them in the light of history, because R. Brunschvig was first of all an historian famous for his work on the Maghrib. As time went on, he turned to the study of Muslim jurisprudence. His essays, collected in *Etudes d'Islamologie* (2 vols., Paris: Maisonneuve et Larose, 1976), opened rich new ways for the study of Islamic thought linked to social and cultural issues. Unfortunately, these ways have not been pursued, and today, we have no specialist to teach Islamic Law in French universities.

The situation has been changing since the seventies. The new methods and problematics in Linguistics, Semiotics, Sociology, Ethnology, Anthropology, History, and Literary Criticism are being applied to Arabic and Islamic Studies. Historians, anthropologists, sociologists, philologists, and literary critics in this domain of studies are still few in number, especially if one considers the tremendous work which needs to be done in these fields. The demands of students coming each year from Arab universities to prepare theses in France are not met sufficiently and the problem is likely to get worse in the coming years. My own experience at the Sorbonne, where each year the demand increases, has convinced me that we are not adequately prepared to face the problem. I know, of course, that many theses are presented each year in several universities in France; but it is well-known that many professors who supervise these theses are neither Arabists, nor Islamicists and the results leave a lot to be desired.

As far as Islamic Studies are concerned, I wish to mention here an important issue. The present political concerns associated with militant forms of Islam has led to an increasing interest in its study in the West. Little interest has, however, been focussed on the study of Islam as a religion. Most studies are related to the methods of Political Science, and an impressive number of monographs have been published. Thus, it can be argued that there has been a failure in the effort to understand Islam in all its dimensions - religious, social, political, anthropological, psychological and cultural. My own efforts to balance this trend are illustrated by what I have termed "applied Islamology".[6] It has two aims:

1. A critical re-reading of the exhaustive Muslim Tradition, free from the dogmatic definitions of the existing literature on schools and sects, leading to a new mode of religious analysis and thinking that will integrate all modern knowledge and sciences.

2. The historicizing of contemporary Muslim discourse, which has been characterized by ideological references, concerns and slogans. The criticism of ideologies is thus a major task of applied Islamology. One can discern that such an approach is lacking in the present scholarship on Islam and Muslim societies; most studies being limited to descriptions, reports of what Muslims themselves say about their religion and societies. The further distortions reflected in the presentation of Islam in the mass media also exacerbate the problem of a correct understanding of the field.

Philological analysis is still necessary but is no longer sufficient as many scholars have pointed out. And we know that all these sciences are not sufficiently taught or practiced in the new universities founded in Muslim countries. That is why I insist on considering all the social, historical, political and cultural questions which have been neglected either because they have been overlooked or because they have seemed implausible. The history of neglected, eliminated, forgotten aspects of Islamic thought remains to be written. The lack of interest in so-called minor thinkers, heterodox schools or trends, popular beliefs and habits has always been imposed by the ruling classes of the time using the argument of "orthodoxy". Some Orientalists have paid attention to "sects" or schisms (in purely descriptive terms), like H. Laoust in his book *Les Schismes dans l'Islam* (Paris: Payot, 1965). Islamic Studies today needs to develop a modern critical analysis about the central issues disputed between the schools and the sects during the formative and classical period. But there are still some scholars who are not prepared to combine several methods with a critical epistemology; they prefer to practice cumulative scholarship as represented by the well-known, and in a laudable sense, the German philological tradition.

I do not wish to disparage the value of philological erudition; we need it more than ever, especially for Arabic Studies, where a large number of manuscripts or badly edited works have to be critically presented. But it is time to develop new fields of research like semantics, religious sociology, cultural anthropology, critiques of ideologies, historical psychology (the history of imagination, myth, rational, irrational, conscious, unconscious, natural, supernatural, sacred, etc.). All these domains of knowledge are particularly relevant to the ideological "birthlag" which characterizes Islamic thought since the sixties.

Professor Van Ess has shown in his *Zwischen Hadīth und Theologie* how the *Hadīth* were manipulated for ideological purposes in the Ummayad period; we can start from his philological analysis to study how *hadīth* became a specific expression of "*social*" imagination (*l'imaginaire social*) rather than a historically established subject-matter.

Islamic Studies, aided by this new epistemological framework, may also enable us to raise problems concerning Judaism, Christianity and other religious traditions that too might be approached from the perspective of religious anthropology. In order to go beyond traditional, closed, theological systems which have been, for centuries, a basic legitimation for "religious" wars, we need to revise epistemological attitudes hitherto assumed in the study of religions.

Of course I am aware of the difficulties inherent in such an undertaking, particularly in societies dominated by a growing demand for mobilizing collective activities, as well as for mobilizing and legitimizing discourses. We must remember that Orientalists, removed from the ideological premises which exist in Islamic societies, cannot feel the same need to be engaged epistemologically. For this reason, they cannot see the intricate relationship between epistemology and politics. This is, from my own experience, the biggest issue in the future collaboration between Muslim and Western scholars.[7]

Accurate description must precede interpretation; but interpretation cannot be attempted today without a rigorous analysis using linguistic, semiotic, historical, and anthropological tools. This aspect is missing in the major part of Orientalist production in general. In this production, substantial differences are to be found according to the language and the cultural tradition in which each scholar is raised and ideologically involved. This problem, or epistemological obstacle, is not even considered or recognized as such by many well-known Arabists and Islamicists. It is also neglected if not altogether denied by many contemporary Muslim scholars who nevertheless claim to be in a superior position to interpret correctly Islamic thought and culture. Only a major, continuing effort can take us beyond polemical and apologetic concerns and revitalize Islamic Studies as an academic discipline, which is not divorced from the actual needs of Muslim societies.

Notes

1. Jean Gaulmier, *L'Ideologue Volney, 1757-1820, Contribution a l'histoire de l'orientalisme en France*, Beirut: Impr. Catholique Le Deux, 1951.
2. To appreciate the importance of French Orientalist scholarship, with special reference to North Africa, the following works may consulted: Pessah Shinar, *Bibliographie selective et annotée sur l'Islam maghrébin contemporain. Maroc, Algérie, Tunisie, Libye (1830-1978)*, Paris: Centre National de La Recherche Scientifique, 1983; J.C. Vatin, *L'Algérie politique. Histoire et société*, Paris: Foundation National des Sciences Politiques, 1974; and the *Revue de l'Occident Musulaman et de la Mediterranée* (Association pour l'étude des Sciences humaines en Afrique du Nord, Archives d'Outre-Mer, Aix-en-Provence). 3

vols., Paris: Impr. Nationale, 1872-73 (rev. edn, Paris: Challonel, 1893).

3. A. H. Hanoteau and A. Letourneux, *La Kabylie et les coutumes Kabyles*, Paris: Impr. Nationale, 1872-3.

4. "L'histoire economique et sociale de l'Orient musulman medieval", *Studia Islamica*, III (1954-55), 93-115.

5. This school of thought was initiated by two major historians, Marc Bloch and Lucien Febvre, who reacted against what they called "l'histoire événientielle", that is to say, the mere description of political and military events and the succession of dynasties.

6. *Lectures du Coran*: 1982; 2nd edition, Tunis: Aleef, 1991; *Pour une Critique de la Raison Islamique* (Islam d'hier et d'aujourd'hui, 24), Paris: Maisonneuve et Larose, 1984; *Penser l'Islam aujourd'hui*, Alger 1993. *Rethinking Islam, Common Questions, Uncommon Answers*, Boulder, Co.: Westview Press, 1994.

7. I do not mean at all that Muslim scholars are more prepared than Orientalists to respect principles of epistemological criticism; on the contrary, many of them do not even rely on precise philological criticism, because they are too much influenced by ideological commitments. I should insist more on the generation of French Orientalists which replaced the one I presented after 1980. But this would require a special development because of the diversity of positions, disciplines, trends, institutions which need to be described. I confess that I do not feel easy to evaluate the work of friends and colleagues with whom I use to collaborate in many fields and opportunities.

   To have an idea of the diversity and increasing numbers of specialists since 1980, one can read the *Lettre d'information de l'Association français, pour l'etude du Ronde Arabic et Musulman* (AFEMAM), Annuaire des chercheurs et enseignants, (numbero 8), November 1993.

I refer also to my study on the work of Claude Cahen: "Transgresser, Déplacer, Dépresser," in *L'oeuvre de la Cahen: Voies nouvelles et revisions hélenaires*, Arabica, (special issue), Brill: Leiden, 1995.

C. E. Bosworth

The Study of Islam in British Scholarship

The history of Islamic Studies in Britain cannot in its earliest stages be divorced from the history of these studies in medieval Christendom as a whole, of which the British Isles were an integral part, with England at least bound ecclesiastically to Rome since the days of Pope Gregory the Great and St. Augustine of Canterbury. These medieval centuries were the ones when Islam and Christendom faced each other as two inexorably hostile worlds. Each was convinced that it had a monopoly on divine truth, and only by strict adherence to its creeds and laws could the respective adherents achieve salvation. There was thus little scope in the Middle Ages for cultural interaction, although it seems likely that in such regions as Spain and Sicily, where Muslims and Christians were in forced contact over periods of several centuries, there arose a certain amount of respect for the other side's artistic and cultural achievements, where these could be divorced from religion. But the normal state of affairs between the two world civilizations was one of periods of open warfare or guerilla activity along frontiers punctuated by cessations of hostilities which were regarded, at least under Islamic law, as periods of truce only.

Once it had rallied from the initial shocks of the expansion of the Arabs at the outset of Islam, Christendom became for long engaged in the *reconquista* in the Iberian peninsula and was for a while able to take the offensive in the Levant under the vigorous line of Macedonian emperors of Byzantium and the Frankish Crusaders, without, however, making much more than a dent in the fabric of Islam there in the East. Islam had early reached a state of fair stability in the Mediterranean basin once the initial momentum of Arab energy had spent itself, but it embarked on a fresh wave of expansionism under the Ottoman Sultans, when the long-coveted prize of Constantinople fell to the Muslims, and the Turks, having gobbled up the Greek and Slavonic Balkans, seemed poised to overrun Hungary, Central Europe and Italy, Only from the eighteenth century onwards did Islam slowly have to recognize that the conversion of the *Dār al-Kufr* would have to be postponed from historic to messianic times.

It was natural that such unreasoning attitudes should engender a bitter and protracted polemical battle between the two sides, one which can be amply documented from both the Muslim and Christian sources. Thus a fourteenth century *fatwā* from Mamlūk Egypt states that:

> It is known that the Jews and Christians are branded with the marks of wrath and malediction of the Lord because they gave Him associates and stubbornly denied His signs. God has taught His servants the prayers which they are to use in addressing Him. He has commanded them to march in the direction of those on whom He has showered His grace, in the path of His prophets, the righteous, the martyrs and the virtuous among men; He has also commanded them to keep away from the path of the profligate from whom He has withdrawn His mercy and whom He has debarred from Paradise. Those that roused His wrath and those that have gone astray are fraught with His vengeance and His curse. Now, according to the text of the Quran, the people of the wrath are the Jewish people, and the people led astray by error are the trinitarian Christians who adore the Cross.[1]

Christian publicists were equally vehement in their denunciations of their opponents, and a distorted image of Islam, its Prophet and its Holy Book emerged from the pens of medieval ecclesiastics. Islam was depicted as a maleficent force, sprung from Christian heresies like Arianism and then helped along by Nestorian or Jewish renegades. Muhammad was either an insensate idol or else a deluded, diseased fanatic, to be equated with Satan or the Antichrist, and the Quran was viewed as an incoherent jumble put together by the Prophet and his human aides out of the lucubrations of their own minds or the whisperings of the Evil One.[2]

Perhaps the earliest mention which a British author made of the Muslims is that of the Venerable Bede, writing in his monastery at Jarrow just before his death in 735, who commented in his *Ecclesiastical History of the English Nation* on recent events, "At that season, that most grievous pest, the Saracens, wasted and destroyed the realm of Gaul with grievous and miserable carnage; but they soon after received and suffered the due punishment of their perfidy."[3] He must have been alluding to the Arab incursions into the western parts of Merovingian Gaul which were checked by Charles Martel near Poitiers in 732 in the battle known to the Spanish Muslim Chroniclers as that of *Balāt al-Shuhadā*'.

Although the Crusades were of little significance for cultural interchange, the securing by the Franks of footholds on the Levant coast, and the accelerated progress of the *reconquista* in Spain from the end of the eleventh century onwards, stimulated a widespread craving in the East for knowledge about Islam, if only so that warfare with the Muslims could be carried on at the intellectual level as well as the military one. As Rodinson has observed:

> . . . the Crusades created a vast and eager demand for a full, entertaining and satisfying image of the opponents' ideology. The man in the street desired an image that would both show the hateful character of Islam by presenting it in crude terms and would also be such as to satisfy the literary taste for the wonderful which strikes one so strongly in all the works of that time; the average person wanted a picture of the most outstanding of the exotic traits that had struck the Crusaders in their dealings with the Muslims.[4]

One of the great figures of the twelfth century is Peter the Venerable, Abbot of Cluny (d. 1156), who through the network of Cluniac houses in Spain had acquired a first-hand knowledge of the requirements for a firmly-based Christian apologetic for use against the Moors. Hence in Spain he financed a band of translators who produced both original theological and polemical works of their own in Latin and who also undertook the translation into Latin of a series of Arabic texts, always with an unswerving conviction of the rightness of their views, yet with efforts at an objectively-based, scientific conception of Islam, hence infused with a charitableness and calmness of mind unusual for the age. Amongst his helpers was the Englishman Robert of Ketton (from the village of Ketton in Rutlandshire, long famous for its stone quarries), for whom Peter the Venerable commissioned a translation of the Quran (not that this was to be the only Latin translation to be produced at the time, since another, more literal version was made independently by Mark of Toledo), the autograph manuscript of which still exists in the *Bibliothèque de l'Arsenal* in Paris. Ketton's approach was that of aiming at an intelligent paraphrase; the result was a less faithful rendering of the sense of the Arabic than Mark of Toledo's but a more comprehensible one. Be this as it may, it was Ketton's translation of 1143 which achieved the wider circulation in the later Middle Ages and, through its publication in 1543 by the humanist Theodore Buchmann or Bibliander, in the Renaissance and Reformation periods, so that the Dutch jurist Grotius was still citing it in the early seventeenth century.[5] Towards the end of the medieval period, increased diplomatic and political contacts with the Ottoman Empire and, above all, commercial relations between the Muslim powers controlling the Syro-Palestinian-Egyptian and Black Sea coastlands on the one hand, and the Italian and Catalan trading ports on the other, created a secular, as opposed to a religious, motivation for the study of Islam and its languages. It was true that, parallel to the theological clash with Islam, there had been taking place a peaceful process of the reception by the West of the philosophical, scientific and medical heritage of the scholars of Islam, and behind them, of the ancient Greeks, so that it could be said of the physician whom Chaucer met at the Tabard Inn in Canterbury around 1390:

> Wel knew he the olde Esculapius,
> And Deyscorides, and eek Rufus,
> Old Ypocras, Haly and Galyen,
> Serapion, Razis and Avycen,
> Averrois, Damascien and Constantyn,
> Bernard and Gatesden and Gilbertyn.[6]

It was this approach to the secular knowledge of the East which really gave an impetus to the birth of Orientalism in the West as we know it today. The humanism and cosmopolitanism of the Renaissance; the search for new frontiers in knowledge; the realization from the great discoveries that a Eurocentric conception of the universe was no longer valid; above all, the decline of religious passions as the Wars of Religion burnt themselves out, all contributed to a more dispassionate study of Islam.[7] The ability to print in Arabic was a most important stimulus to the growth of Oriental Studies in the West, for it meant that printed texts could be passed around and utilized as bases for study; e.g., for the compilation of histories of the Islamic lands by the scholarly community in Europe. Surprisingly, the first complete Arabic text of the Quran was, however, not printed until the Protestant pastor Abraham Hickelmann's text appeared from Hamburg in 1694, perhaps an indication that the secular aspect of Arabic literature - history, science, philosophy, *adab* - was now considered of greater interest in this post-Reformation period when the tide was in any case beginning to turn against Ottoman expansionism.[8] His printing of Oriental and Arabic texts was a slow process, and aside from the technical considerations, very soon surmounted, it could only proceed on a basis of the collections of Hebrew, Syriac, Arabic and other Islamic manuscripts which now began to be assembled by western princes and other great men.

Here, England was specially to the fore. The commercial interests already mentioned above supplied a catalyst for this zeal to accumulate manuscripts. In 1581, Queen Elizabeth had granted a charter to a group of London merchants trading with the East, the origin of the Levant Company of London; an English ambassador (whose salary was actually paid by the Company) was appointed to the Ottoman capital Istanbul, and a network of factories or trading establishments set up in the Aegean region and the Levant, including at Chios, Smyrna and Aleppo.[9] Thus a continuing basis for peaceful contacts with the Islamic lands was set up, one which English scholars were not slow to exploit. Levant Company merchants were commissioned to obtain Arabic, Persian, Turkish, Syriac, Hebrew and Samaritan manuscripts. Thus in 1624 Archbishop Ussher sent to the Levant Company's factor in Aleppo, Thomas Davies, for manuscripts but received a discouraging reply from Davies about the difficulties of purchasing Arabic, Syriac and Hebrew ones: "to effect business of this nature," he wrote back, "requires time, travell being very taedious in these countries." Ussher's successor in the seat of Canterbury, William Laud, was more determined and more successful in this quest. In 1634 he obtained a letter from King Charles I to the Levant Company requiring that each of their ships returning from the eastern Mediterranean should bring back one manuscript, and in the same year he established at Oxford what was the second Professorship of Arabic in England, the Laudian Chair, primacy in the instituting of an Arabic Chair having gone to the City of London cloth merchant Sir Thomas Adams, who had endowed a Chair at Cambridge two years previously. Laud's manuscripts, presented to the Bodleian at Oxford in 1639-42, formed the nucleus of that Library's great collections of Arabic and Hebrew manuscripts; it is only regrettable that we know so little of their provenance.[10]

The Levant Company was, however, to prove an even more significant stimulus for Arabic studies in seventeenth and eighteenth century England in that it began in 1630 the policy of sending out to its factories, in particular to Aleppo and Istanbul, Anglican clergymen to act as chaplains to the English merchant communities there and, it was hoped (largely in vain, as it happened), in order to carry on Protestant missionary work as the Roman Catholic religious orders were doing in Lebanon, Syria, Iraq, etc., among the Oriental Christians. Only clerics who already had a keen interest in Oriental Studies were likely to accept these posts, but it was for several of these a heaven-sent opportunity to live and work in an Arab environment and to learn the language and culture from native scholars, things which were not otherwise easy for Westerners to achieve at that time. It was thus that Edward Pococke (1604-91), the greatest English Arabist of his age, was able to vastly improve his knowledge of both written and spoken Arabic, one begun as an academic studying at the University of Oxford in the years 1626-1629 under a German refugee scholar from the devastations at Heidelburg of the Thirty Years' War,

Matthias Pason, who taught Hebrew, Aramaic, Syriac and Arabic there and who delivered an inaugural lecture entitled "A Plea for the Study of Arabic" (*Oratio pro linguae arabicae professione*). Pococke remained for six years in Aleppo, learning Arabic there from a certain Fath. Allāh, a skill put to practical use decades later, in the latter part of his long life: he wrote panegyric verses in Arabic to greet the restoration in 1660 of King Charles II and elegies at his death in 1685; in 1668 he translated a letter in Arabic sent by Sultan Mawlāy al-Rashīd of Morocco to Charles II in connection with England's acquisition of Tangier as part of the dowry of his wife, the Portuguese princess Catherine of Braganza; and in 1682 he greeted at Oxford the ambassador of Sultan Mawlāy Ismāʿīl al-Samīn with a speech of welcome in Arabic.[11] (The translation of state documents emanating from the Arab lands, and especially from Morocco, was one of the not infrequent tasks of Arabists at this time; the Cambridge scholar Simon Ockley, Sir Thomas Adams Professor, 1711-1720, was employed in 1714 to translate official papers relating to the release of Christian captives by Mawlāy Ismāʿīl and to the conclusion of a trade treaty.)[12]

More important for the future of Arabic scholarship, Pococke began in Aleppo the literary studies which were to put England in the forefront of contemporary Arabic historical studies. He transcribed a manuscript of al-Maydānī's great collection of ancient proverbs, the *Amthāl al-ʿArab*, translated it into Latin (the learned language of the time) and provided it with a commentary (the work still survives in manuscript, but was never printed). He doubtless also began to supply Archbishop Laud with Oriental manuscripts and started amassing a significant collection of his own which later passed to the Bodleian too. In 1636 he returned to Oxford to become the first holder of Laud's new chair of Arabic and began to lecture on, amongst other things, the aphorisms attributed to the Caliph ʿAlī and the *Maqāmat* of al-Harīrī. A second trip to the Near East in 1636-1641, covering Istanbul and Egypt, enabled him further to add to his own manuscript collection. His fortunes suffered an eclipse during the Civil Wars and Interregnum period, but at the restoration, as a confirmed royalist, he gained the Regius Chair of Hebrew at Oxford.

It was during these decades of the 1640s and 1650s, when he had to maintain a low profile, that Pococke began the publication of a long series of Arabic texts and their translations into Latin or English, which were to be used a basis for the composition in the West of accounts of the life of Muhammad, the unfolding of the faith of Islam, and the course of medieval Islamic history for some two centuries. These works on Arabic authors included a long-edited excerpt from, and a Latin translation of, Abū l-Faraj Ibn al-ʿIbrī or Barhebraeus's *Mukhtasar taʾrīkh al-duwal*, enriched with what was for its time an incredibly erudite commentary and with notes in which Pococke showed himself scientific and dispassionate enough to ridicule and refute many of the erroneous ideas about Islam which had been fixed in Western minds since the early Middle Ages, e.g., that Muhammad's body was suspended in an iron coffin between two magnets in the mosque at Mecca.[13] He also produced a remarkable English translation of the philosophical romance by Ibn Tufayl about the autodidact Hayy b. Yaqzān, which is largely lost but which clearly antedated the publication of an independent English translation in 1718 by Ockley; a translation of the whole of Saʿīd b. al-Biṭīq or Eutychius's *Nazm al-Jawhar*; and an edition and translation of al-Tughrāʾī's poem, the *Lāmīyat al-ʿAjam*; and he began work on ʿAbd al-Laṭīf al-Baghdādī's history of Egypt, the *Kitāb al-Ifāda waʾl-Iʿtibār*, but never completed it.[14]

Holt has characterized the significance of Pococke's work as being, first, that together with his continental colleagues, the Dutchmen Erpenius and Golius, he began the process of changing the image of Islam in Western minds, a process continued in eighteenth century England by scholars like Ockley, Sale and Gibbon; and second, that by his publications in the field of Islamic history, he demonstrated the general educational value to the scholarly world of a study of Islamic civilization.[15] Other Levant Company chaplains in Istanbul and Aleppo interested themselves in a study of the Greek and Oriental Christian Churches and in the other great Islamic languages of Persian and Turkish, as did academic Orientalists back in England. Thus Pococke's successor in the Chair at Oxford, Thomas Hyde (d. 1703), was primarily concerned with Persian and in 1700 published a book on the religion of ancient Persia, *Historia religionis veterum Persarum eorumque Magorum*.[16]

The growth in the eighteenth century of calmer religious attitudes, with more rational forms of religion like Socinianism and Deism becoming influential and with latitudinarianism affecting the established church in England, began to have a certain cooling effect on men's religious passions and, consequently, on western attitudes towards Islam. The military threat from the Ottoman Turks began to recede after occupied Hungary had been restored to Christian control in the later seventeenth century and Belgrade became a frontier town, whose control oscillated between the Hapsburgs and the Ottomans. Already in later seventeenth-century England, a curious work called the *Account of the Rise and Progress of Mahometanism with the Life of Mahomet and a Vindication of him and his Religion from the Calumnies of the Christians* had been written, probably in the 1670s by the scholar and physician Henry Stubbes, in which the author had attempted a favorable description of the Prophet, emphasizing his essential rationality, had surveyed the Quran and tried sympathetically to understand the tenets of Islam, and had endeavored to prove that Islam was not a militaristic religion dedicated to the extirpation of Christianity and other faiths. Although religious passions were, as noted above, beginning to die down a little, this book was still strong meat for its age, and although Stubbes' work circulated in manuscript, it was never published until a group of Turkish and Indian Muslims undertook this in 1911.[17] It may nevertheless have been as a refutation of this work that Humphrey Prideaux, Dean of Norwich, composed his violent attack on Islam and the person of the Prophet, *The True Nature of Imposture Fully Displayed in the Life of Mahomet. With a discourse annexed for the vindication of Christianity from this charge. Offered to the consideration of the Deists of the present age* (1697). Prideaux used the historical works of Pococke and Erpenius, and apparently not the recently-published Arabic text of the Quran by Hinckelmann but the ancient Latin version of Robert of Ketton. Prideaux's great aim was to expose the errors of Islam and to contrast the origins of Islam with those of Christianity, thereby strengthening the latter against

Deism, which he considered to be a dangerous force in his time; but he was still credulous enough to regurgitate much of the legendary material which had accreted around Muhammad's life.[18]

A much more solid contribution to historical knowledge of Islam was made by Ockley in his two volumes, *The Conquest of Syria, Persia and Egypt by the Saracens* (1708) and *The History of the Saracens* (1718), landmarks in that they included the first attempt to write a continuous history of the Arabs, extending from the Caliphate of Abū Bakr to that of ʿAbd al-Malik. He was carrying on from where Prideaux had left off and would doubtless have carried his narrative further had not penury and death supervened; the second volume was produced from Cambridge Castle, where the author was imprisoned for debts of 200 pounds. The great merit of these volumes arises from the fact that Ockley not only used the printed historical texts already available but also unpublished texts which he found in the Bodleian's collection of manuscripts, the resources of Oxford being at that time far richer than those of Cambridge. Hence he used above all the *Futūh al-Shām* attributed, probably apocryphally, to al-Wāqidī in his account of the expansion of the Arabs, but he also cited from manuscripts such varying authors as al-Tabarī, Ibn ʿAbd Rabbih, Ibn al-Athīr, Abū ʼl-Fidāʼ, al-Suyūtī and Mujīr al-Dīn al-ʿUlaymī (the latter for the history of Jerusalem). Of secondary sources, D`Herbelot's invaluable *Bibliothèque orientale* (1697), which has been called an early attempt at an *Encyclopaedia of Islam*, was pressed into service, especially for the information from Persian writers. Ockley was still prisoner enough of prejudices of the age to regard Muhammad as "the great Imposter" and the Arab conquests as "that grievous Calamity," but does not display Prideaux's virulence. He was obviously much more interested in Arab history as a secular record rather than as a backcloth for ecclesiastical controversies, and in this wise, his works mark a step forward.[19]

The eighteenth century was notable for the production of an accurate English translation of the Quran, one far better than that of the Scotsman Alexander Ross (1649), made from an intermediate translation into French by the Sieur du Ryer.[20] This was the translation of George Sale (?1697-

1736), a lawyer by training and the first major English Arabist who was not a cleric, although Sale did much work for the SPCK and helped produce Arabic versions of the Psalter and New Testament. Meanwhile, he was working on his Quran translation, whose publication in 1734 was a remarkable achievement for the age. It proved of such value as to be reprinted frequently well into the present century. Much of its value arises from Sale's detailed annotation of the text from the Muslim commentators, above all from the commentaries of al-Baydāwī and al-Suyūtī. Sale cannot be given a prize for original scholarship, it is true, since he seems to have drawn heavily on the sources used by the Italian monk Lodovico Maracci in his *Alcorani textus universus*, with its Latin translation (1698), as he freely confesses in his preliminary "To the reader," adding, however, that the great value of his own book is that it is in English and not in Latin. Still worthy of consultation as giving an easy conspectus in English of traditional Muslim scholars' views on the Jāhiliyya in Arabia, Arabian paganism, Quranic doctrines, the development of the Islamic sects and Islamic eschatology, is Sale's lengthy "Preliminary discourse", which not only draws on a wide range of classical Arabic authorities from the historians to heresiographers like al-Shahrastānī, but also cites extensive parallels from Biblical, Rabbinical and Mishnaic Hebrew and the testimony of recent European writers on the contemporary Islamic world, such as Sir Paul Rycaut on the Ottoman Empire and the traveller Sir John Chardin on Safavid Persia. Sale's great virtue was thus his insistence on the vital importance of native Arabic authors, from Quran commentators to historians, for elucidating the course of Islamic history and for expounding the doctrines of the Quran. His work complemented the purely historical achievement of Ockley, and both these authors were to be the standard sources informing British minds about Islam and early Islamic history till the second half of the nineteenth century.[21]

The rational spirit of the eighteenth century Enlightenment looked at Islam through new spectacles, and though it still found in Islam much to condemn of fanaticism, credulousness and superstition, it was at the same time disposed to search for more favorable elements, if only to buttress a rationalist and deist appreciation of orthodox, revealed Christianity. However, the men of the Enlightenment found these good points hard to discern; thus Voltaire in France estimated the fanaticism of contemporary Christianity, as exemplified in the savagery of the Roman Catholic Church against the Huguenot Calas, to be exactly on a par with that of Islam, which he depicted in his treatment of the Prophet in his play *Le Fanatisme oú Mahomet le prophete* (1741).[22] Others of the period recognized Muhammad as one of the world's great legislators, and there was much argument over the question of Muhammad's personal sincerity. Was he a genuine prophet, even if perhaps led astray by others, e.g., renegade Christian monks or Jewish rabbis, into paths of hypocrisy and deception? Edward Gibbon (whose tutor John Kirby had in 1745 published a *Life of Automathes*, with the full title of *The Capacity and Extent of the Human Understanding Exemplified in the Extraordinary Case of Automathes, A Young Nobleman, who was accidentally left in his infancy upon a desolate island and continued nineteen years in that solitary state separate from all human society*), obviously inspired by the thesis of Ibn Tufayl's *Hayy b. Yaqzān* that the truths of natural religion were apprehendable by the unaided human intellect,[23] in his *Decline and Fall of the Roman Empire* (1776-1788), rather inclined to this view of an initial sincerity and enthusiasm, which had however to be compromised in the interest of statesmanship and the founding of a new world-empire. He could not believe that a sincerely religious figure could at the same time be a successful politician and military leader.[24]

The full recognition of Muhammad's essential sincerity, a novel concept for its time, came only in the following century and not from an Orientalist but from the Scottish thinker and publicist Thomas Carlyle. In 1840 he delivered one of his course of lectures *On Heroes and Hero-Worship* on the subject of "The Hero as Prophet", dealing with Muhammad; W. Montgomery Watt has called this "the first strong affirmation in the whole of European literature, medieval and modern, of a belief in the sincerity of Muhammad". Carlyle admired Goethe and was aware of the poet's appreciative attitude towards Muhammad and the Quran as shown in the notes to the *West-östlicher Diwan*. He read Sale's translation of the Quran, and though he found it heavy going, was imaginative enough to construct for himself a view of the Prophet's inner struggle, as one who had grappled with the great questions of human destiny and existence. He concluded that no human being could have achieved so much and could have changed the course of history so decisively without a burning conviction of the righteousness of his call from God and his mission to awaken mankind to their sole path to salvation.[25]

We are now on the threshold of the nineteenth century, the age of scientific Orientalism, signalled on the continent by the French Revolutionary Convention's setting up in 1795 the *École des Langues Orientales Vivantes* in Paris and by the careers of outstanding scholars like A. I. Silvestre de Sacy (1758-1838) in France and Josef von Hammer-Purgstall (1774-1856), founder of the first specialist Oriental journal in the West, the *Fundgruben des Orients* (1809-18), in Austria. The actual term "orientalist" seems to occur in England around 1779, with a connotation at that time of someone primarily concerned with India, the part of the Orient on which British attention was then focussed. In 1823 the Royal Asiatic Society of Great Britain and Ireland was founded, two years after the *Sociéte Asiatique* in Paris, but these events had been antedated in the previous century by the foundation of the Asiatic Society of Bengal (1784) and the publication by it of the series of *Asiatique researches*.[26]

These last are bound up with the commanding figure of Sir William Jones (1746-1794). Jones was a linguist of prodigious talent, who early mastered Arabic, Persian (he produced a Persian grammar in 1771) and Turkish, embarked also on Chinese and then, when appointed to a judgeship in Bengal, tackled Sanskrit and published important translations of Indian poetic and legal texts. Amongst his achievements here too was his recognition of the relationship between Sanskrit and the later-developing Indo-European languages. But his main claim to our attention is his pioneer aesthetic appreciation of Arabic, Persian and Turkish literature as such, above all, of poetry, hardly touched upon by earlier scholars who had been largely concerned with historical, legal and theological texts for polemical, didactic or practical purposes, and who, if they had occupied themselves with Arabic poetry, had viewed this basically as a philological exercise. His *A Persian Song* introduced Hāfiz to the Western literary world, but he had already achieved fame with his *Poesis Asiaticae commentarium libri sex* (1774) in which he glanced at such exotic fields as Chinese and Ethiopic poetry, but was primarily concerned with Islamic poetry and prosody, dealing with the metres, poetic tropes and stylistics, and which contained translations of Arabic, Persian and Turkish *qasīdas* and *ghazals*, e.g., of Ibn al-Fārid, Firdawsī and Mesīhī. As was the fashion of the age, Jones strove hard to assimilate these poetic themes and metres to classic Greek and Roman equivalents, and such somewhat futile exercises remained influential in Western Orientalism till the opening of the present century, since when Islamic poetry has been judged and appreciated on its own distinctive merits as *sui generis*. The climax of Jones' work here was his translation of the seven *Muʿallaqāt* (1782). Unfortunately, his legal duties in Calcutta prevented him from ever writing the promised critical commentary and account of the beliefs and customs of the ancient Arabs (this was in fact supplied a generation or so later by A. P. Caussin de Perceval in his *Essai sur l'histoire des Arabes avant l'Islamisme*).[27]

Within the nineteenth century proper, Islamic Studies in Britain tended to lag behind those of Germany and France in scientific rigour and, above all, in the application of the canons of higher criticism which evolved, in Germany in the first place, as a tool for Biblical criticism, but which were eventually, in the hands of scholars like Goldziher and Wellhausen, to serve equally for elucidating the origins and early development of Islam. Hence the very necessary task of producing critically-edited texts of classical Arabic works of grammar, history, geography, exegesis, belles-lettres, poetry, etc., continued to be mainly undertaken by French, German and Dutch scholars. Nevertheless, there were certain British scholars who participated in this work, such as William Wright (1830-1889), who produced excellent editions of the *Rihla* of Ibn Jubayr (1952) and the *Kāmil* of al-Mubarrad (1864-1874), and from the next generation, A. A. Bevan

(1859-1933), who published a monumental text of the Naqā'id of Jarīr and al-Farazdaq. Scholars like these tended to have close connections with the German Orientalist world; the publication of the *Kāmil* was indeed undertaken by the *Deutsche Morgenländische Gesellschaft*.[28] The comparative dearth in Britain of scholars with an exact philological training is shown by the fact that no British scholars participated in such international ventures as the editing of the Leiden editions of al-Tabarī and Ibn Saʿd.

The strength of British Orientalism at this time came rather from personal experience of and/or prolonged residence in various parts of the Islamic world, whether as a private citizen in Cairo like E. W. Lane (1801-1876); as a British consul in Damascus like Sir Richard Burton (1821-1890); or as administrators in India like Sir William Muir (1819-1905), Governor of the North-West Frontier Province before he returned to Scotland to become Principal of Edinburgh University, and Sir Charles Lyall (1845-1920), for eighteen years resident in the Subcontinent as a member of the Indian Civil Service.

Lane's years in Cairo during the late 1820s and early 1830s gave him the material for his perspicacious and at times not unsympathetic portrayal of Egyptian traditional society on the eve of the modern age, *The Manners and Customers of the Modern Egyptians* (1836), and gave him a philological interest in Arabic which led him to acquire and to read the original lexicographical authorities. The product of this, in the remaining decades of his life, was the preparation of a dictionary of classical Arabic which would repair, by its completeness, the shortcomings of the earlier dictionaries of Golius (1653) and Freytag (1837). The result, published through the patronage and financial support of the then Duke of Northumberland, was his great *Lexicon*, alas not completed beyond the first part of letter *qāf*; only in our own time are the dictionaries of Blachère *et alii* and, above all, the *Wörterbuch der klassischen arabischen Sprache*, supplementing and completing it.[29]

Burton's exotic interests put him on the fringes only of Islamic Studies, although his travel books on the Hijaz and on the region of Midian in

Northwestern Arabia gave useful, first-hand topographical information, much of it not superseded till the journeys of Musil and others over half-a-century later.[30]

Burton's pseudonymous production of a long ode in English, allegedly inspired by the fatalistic strain of certain pre-Islamic Arab poets, *The Kasîdah of Haji Abdu El-Yezdi, A Lay of the Higher Law* (1880), was apparently an attempt, though Burton vehemently denied it, to cash in on a mood of gentle pessimism and resignation popularized in later Victorian Britain by the resounding success (after a slow start; it was remaindered down to one penny and not reprinted for another ten years) of Edward Fitzgerald's renderings of the *Rubāʿiyyāt* of ʿUmār Khayyām (1859).[31]

Muir's interest in Islamic scholarship was that of a convinced Christian apologist (whilst in India he had actively encouraged the Christian missionary centre at Agra and was especially concerned with the Quran's relationship to the Bible) and of a historian hoping to throw light on the early centuries of Islam.[32] His contemporary, the Austrian A. Sprenger (1813-1893), was also working until 1856 in the British service in India and was producing in German a life of Muhammad based on such original sources as Ibn Hishām's recension of the *Sīra* and on historians like al-Wāqidī and al-Tabarī (1861-1865), but no such work had been produced in English since the age of Prideaux and Ockley. There was now a place for such a work, one written in conformity with the demands of the flourishing nineteenth-century British historical tradition. This lack Muir set out to remedy with his *Life of Mahomet* (1861), utilizing the same sources as Sprenger, whilst he carried forward the story of the course of early Islamic history in what was eventually called *The Caliphate, its Rise, Decline and Fall* (lst ed. 1858-1861. 2nd ed., under this title, 1891), basing this essentially on the chronicle of Ibn al-Athīr, available in the Swedish scholar Tornberg's edition since the third quarter of the century. Noteworthy was the inclusion in the first of these two books of a lengthy study "Sources for the biography of Mahomet. The Coran and tradition," in which Muir attempted to disentangle what he styled the legendary, the historical and the traditional elements, and adopting a rather more severe attitude towards Islamic tradition than Sprenger did.[33] The two books, both undergoing various editions, remained standard works in English on their subjects for a long time to come. His biography of the Prophet was not really replaced, for English readers, till the appearance of D. S. Margoliouth's *Mohammed and the Rise of Islam* (1905) and, more particularly, of W. Montgomery Watt's two volumes, *Muhammad at Mecca* and *Muhammad at Medina* (1954-1956), and his history of the early Caliphate was only fully replaced by Hitti's *History of the Arabs* (1937). As observed above, Muir's attitude was that of a committed Christian apologist, and his historical techniques were orthodox enough not to excite the *odium theologicum* which his fellow-Scottish Arabist colleague, W. Robertson Smith (1846-1894), had aroused in Aberdeen as a result of his imbibing in Germany the heady wine of the higher Biblical criticism.[34]

The career of Sir Charles Lyall illustrates a continuing component of British Orientalism: the fact that highly significant work has come from the pens not only of university-based scholars enjoying a leisured and cloistered life such as ought in theory at least to be conductive to productive scholarship (and indeed, the provision for academic Orientalists in British universities until the First World War was very meager, provoking a scholar like E. G. Browne to inveigh against his country's neglect of academic Orientalism compared with the ample facilities and the official encouragement available in France, Germany, Austria and Russia),[35] but equally from the pens of busy men of affairs, whose principal careers have been in the public service, civilian or military, but have nevertheless in their free moments been able to make valuable contributions to Orientalist knowledge. The tradition is perhaps almost dead in our own more hectic post-Second World War society, but was still living up to a generation or so ago and was perfectly exemplified in the achievements of Sir Gerard Clauson (1891-1974), Colonial Office functionary and then businesses tycoon, but also the premier British Turcologist of his age, whose *Etymological Dictionary of Pre-Thirteenth Century Turkish* (1972) is unlikely to be superseded in the foreseeable future.[36] Lyall interspersed his days in the Bengal Civil Service and then at the India Office, first with the preparation of his *Translations of Ancient Arabian, Chiefly Pre-Islamic Poetry* (1885), which still remains one of the most erudite and at the same time fairly readable anthologies of this difficult and allusive verse (Lyall tried to imitate the metres of the original Arabic of the poems, substituting stress for vowel length, and noting that a favoured metre like *tawī l* already existed in English prosody as a form of the anapaestic metre). But his supreme monuments of exact scholarship are his editions of the *Muʿallaqāt* with al-Tibrīzī's commentary (1981-1894) and, above all, his text and translation of the *Mufaddaliyyāt* anthology (1918-1921), which follow the models of Wright and the German and Dutch philologists in rigorousness of method.[37]

The focus of study for all these British Islamicists, with the possible exception of Sir William Jones, was Arabic. The study of Persian was still a requirement for those British personnel in India, who, despite Macaulay's reforms in education, had to deal with the more educated levels of the Muslim population and, to a certain extent also, of the Hindus, amongst all of whom Persian had long been the language of polite society,[38] whilst a literary tradition at home extending from Jones through Morier to Matthew Arnold and Fitzgerald encouraged a romantic if hazy view of Persia and the Persians. Yet in the realm of serious scholarship, the momentum of Sir William Jones's Persian studies had been largely lost. But now the figure of E. G. Browne (1862-1926) came on the scene. Originally fired by an enthusiasm for the Sultan's cause in the Russo-Turkish War of 1877, when he reacted against the cant of the Gladstonians and other partisans of the Greeks and Slavs and felt that "he would have died to save Turkey," he passed on to a study of Arabic and Persian. A year's travel in Persia in 1887-1888 gave him an empathy with the land and its people, including with the Babis/Bahais, about whose origins and the development of whose faith he was later to write. Back in Cambridge, eventually as Sir Thomas Adams Professor of Arabic, he not only threw himself into work on Persian texts and their translation and produced what is still the most readable of all books on Persian literature, *A Literary History of Persia* (1908-1924), but also involved himself tirelessly in Persian political and social causes, for the first quarter of this century saw Persia plunged into unparalleled political and constitutional upheavals. Undoubtedly, therefore, Browne merits recognition as the principal begetter of the present British interest in Persian studies.

Turkish studies in 19th century Britain were almost as exiguous as Persian ones, although the continued presence in diplomacy of the "Eastern Question" and the Crimean War, when British troops passed through Turkey and Turkish troops fought side-by-side with those of Britain and France in the Crimea, kept up a certain interest. Two names only are of significance, those of Sir James W. Redhouse (1811-1892) and E. J. W. Gibb (1856-1901), but their books have stood the tests of time and are still much used. Redhouse was a good Arabic and Persian scholar, and his translation of the South Arabian historian of the Rasūlids, al-Khazrajī, was issued posthumously (1906-1908), but he was above all the commanding figure of his age in Britain, and perhaps in Europe also, for Ottoman Turkish grammatical and lexicographical studies. By profession he was a diplomat and interpreter, originally employed by the Sublime Porte in Istanbul; he acted frequently as intermediary and translator in negotiations over Turkish questions, and in 1854 became Oriental Translator to the Foreign Office in London. His *Grammaire raisonnée de la langue ottomane* (1846) is a model of clarity, and in 1855 he produced very hurriedly, for the use of military and naval personnel then involved in the war in the East, a *Vade-mecum of Ottoman Colloquial Language*. But above all, Ottomanists are eternally grateful to him for his massive (Ottoman) *Turkish-English Dictionary* (1890), which seems unlikely ever to be replaced.[39] Finally, one should mention the all-too-brief career of Redhouse's pupil E. J. W. Gibb of Glasgow, who wrote in his comparatively short life the five volumes of his *History of Ottoman Poetry* (published posthumously 1905-1908), adorned with elegant verse translations and with a penetrating introductory volume on Sufism. It was in his memory that the Gibb Memorial Trust was founded for the publication, from 1905 onwards, of texts and translations in the three great Islamic languages.[40]

Our survey has taken us approximately to the time of the First World War. From this point onwards, British national policy became, with the foundation in 1917 of the London School of Oriental and African Studies,[41] more aware of the need to encourage study of the East. Islamic Studies in the West became in many ways widened in attitude (though the self-imposed isolation of Russian scholars under Communism subtracted them from the community of Orientalists), with a greater awareness of the achievements of, and a greater recognition of the need of cooperation with, indigenous scholars in such Islamic countries as Egypt, Syria, Turkey, Persia and India. Hence a new phase begins, one whose evaluation we are not yet perhaps in a position to undertake, but in which greater objectivity and empathy with the Islamic world are seen as ideals for Western Orientalism.

Notes

1. A good example of these polemics against the Christians, a peak in the period after the Crusades and the Mongol invasions had exacerbated Muslim-Christian relations, is seen in the Mamlūk tract examined by M. Perlmann in his "Notes on Anti-Christian Propaganda in the Mamluk Empire", *BSOAS*, X (1940-1942), pp. 843-61.
2. See on this image in general, the detailed study of N. Daniel, *Islam and the West, the Making of an Image*, Edinburgh: Edinburgh University Press, 1960. Rev. ed. Oxford; New York: One World, 1993.
3. Cited by M. Rodinson in his chapter "The Western Image and Western Studies of Islam" in *The Legacy of Islam*, 2nd ed., ed. J.Schacht and C.E. Bosworth, Oxford: Clarendon Press, 1974, p. 9.
4. *Ibid.*, p. 13.
5. Cf. J. Kritzeck, *Peter the Venerable and Islam*, Princeton: Princeton University Press, 1964, pp. 62-65, 94-100; M. T. d'Alverny, "Deux traductions du Coran au Moyen Age", *Archives d'histoire doctrinale et littéraire du Moyen Age*, XXII-XXIII (1947-1948), pp. 69-131; Rodinson, in *Legacy of Islam*, pp. 14ff.

6. *The Canterbury Tales*, Prologue, ll.429-34.
7. Cf. C.E. Bosworth, "Orientalism and Orientalists," in *Arabic Islamic Bibliography, the Middle East Library Committee Guide*, ed. D. Grimwood Jones et al., Hassocks: Harvester Press, 1977, p. 149.
8. Chr. F. Schnurrer, *Bibliotheca arabica*, Halle: I.C. Handelii, 1811, pp. 402-4, 410-412, nos. 367, 376, who already discounted a widespread belief that a text of the Quran had been printed by moveable type at Venice nearly three centuries before; cf. also Y. Safadi, "Arabic Printing and Book Production," in *Arabic Islamic Bibliography*, pp. 223-4.
9. A.C. Wood, *A History of the Levant Company*, London: Oxford University Press, 1935, pp. 7ff.
10. P.M. Holt, "Arabic Historians in Seventh-Century England," *Studies in the History of the Near East*, London: Cass 1973 (originally in *BSOAS*, XIX [1957], pp. 444-55, 128-32); Bosworth, "Orientalism and Orientalists", *loc. cit.*
11. P. M. Holt, "An Oxford Arabist: Edward Pococke (1604-91)," in *Studies in the History of the Near East*, pp. 3-26.
12. A.J. Arberry. *Oriental Essays, Portraits of Seven Scholars*, London: Allen and Unwin, 1960, pp. 36-8.
13. This firmly-rooted legend of the suspension of the Prophet's coffin is discussed specifically by S.C. Chew, *The Crescent and the Rose, Islam and England during the Renaissance*, New York: Oxford University Press, 1937, pp. 387-451.
14. Holt, *Studies*, pp. 10-19; *idem*, "Arabic Historians in Seventeenth-Century England," pp. 33-36.
15. *Ibid.*, pp. 36-37.
16. *Ibid.*, pp. 27-46.
17. P. M. Holt, *A Seventeenth-Century Defender of Islam. Henry Stubbe (1632-76) and His Book*, Friends of Dr. William's Library, Twenty-sixth lecture, London, 1972; C. E. Bosworth, "The Prophet Vindicated: A Restoration Treatise on Islam and Muhammad," *Religion, a Journal of Religion and Religions*, VI (1976), pp. 1-12.
18. P. M. Holt, "The Treatment of Arab History by Prideaux, Ockley and Sale," in *Studies* (originally in *Historians of the Middle East*, ed. B. Lewis and P.M. Holt, London, 1962, pp. 390-402, 50-4.
19. *Ibid.*, pp. 54-7; Arberry, *Oriental Essays*, pp. 28-34, 42-5.
20. For these early versions, see Daniel, *Islam and the West*, p. 284; J.D. Pearson, "Al-Kur'ān: 9. *Translation of the Kur'ān*". *Encyclopaedia of Islam* (2nd ed.), Vol. V, pp. 429-30.
21. Holt, *Studies*, pp. 57-60.

22. Cf. Daniel, pp. 289-9; Rodinson, pp. 38-9.
23. Edward Gibbon, *Memoirs of My Life*, ed. G. Birkbeck Hill, London: Methuen, 1900, pp. 32-4.
24. Cf. Daniel, pp. 291-2.
25. W. Montgomery Watt, "Carlyle on Muhammad," *The Hibbert Journal*, LIII (1954-5), p. 247.
26. Rodinson, *idem*, pp. 45-6.
27. Arberry, pp. 48-86; *idem*, *British Orientalists*, London: W. Collins, 1943, pp. 16, 29-30; J. Fück, *Die arabische Studien in Europa bis in den Anfang des 20 Jahrhunderts*, Leipzig: Harrassowitz, 1955, pp. 129-35.
28. *Ibid*. pp. 206-207, 278-9.
29. *Ibid*, pp. 168-70; Arberry, *Oriental Essays*, pp. 87-121; Leila Ahmed, *Edward W. Lane. A Study of his Life and Work and of British Ideas of the Middle East in the Nineteenth Century*, London and Beirut: Longman, 1978.
30. See Fawn M. Brodie, *The Devil Drives. A Life of Sir Richard Burton*, London: Eyre and Spoltiswuade, 1967, pp. 96-106, 281-3.
31. *Ibid*, pp. 276-9; C. E. Bosworth, "The Influence of Arabic Literature on English Literature," *Azure, The Review of Arab Literature, Arts and Culture*, London, no. 5 (Spring 1980), 17-18.
32. One of Muir's shorter works was an English translation of *The Apology of al Kindy written at the Court of al Mâmûn...in defence of Christianity against Islam*, published by the SPCK, London, 1881, with the prime object, so he stated, of placing the work "in the hands of those who will use it in the interests of the Christian faith" (Preface, p. 7). Note the also the title of the tract mentioned by Fück, *Die arabische Studien* p. 181, n. 462.
33. *Ibid*, pp. 181-2.
34. Smith was deprived of his chair of Oriental Languages and Old Testament Exegesis at the Free Church College there in 1881 because of what were regarded by his church as unorthodox views; see J.S. Black and G.B. Chrystal, *The Life of William Robertson Smith*, London: A. and C. Black, 1912.
35. See his strictures on British indifference in his Introductory chapter of *A Year Amongst the Persians*, 3rd ed., London: A. and C. Black, 1950, pp. 2-5.
36. See the obituary by C. E. Bosworth, in *British Society for Middle Eastern Studies Bulletin*, I (1974), pp. 39-40.
37. Fück, pp. 279-80.
38. Cf. Arberry, *British Orientalists*, p. 18.
39. See E.G. Browne's Editor's preface to Redhouse's *The Pearl-Strings: A History of the Resúliyy Dynasty of Yemen*, I, Leiden-London: E.J. Brill, 1906, pp. xxi-xxv.

40. Arberry, *British Orientalists*, p. 19.
41. See J.D. Pearson, *Oriental and Asian Bibliography. An Introduction with Some Reference to Africa*, London: Lockwood, 1966, pp. 35-47.

Jacques Waardenburg

The Study of Islam in Dutch Scholarship

Holland is a small country bordering the North Sea which has carried on extensive international trade since the seventeenth century and for more than a century governed a colonial empire in South East Asia. Oriental Studies in Holland have developed in a specific context and acquired their own style and characteristics. Though they cannot be measured against the massive achievements of Oriental Studies in much larger countries like France, Germany and the United Kingdom, which each have their own traditions of culture and scholarship and their particular relationships with the world of the "Orient", they have nevertheless made their own contribution to international scholarship. This contribution will be examined here, together with some specific features of Islamic Studies as they evolved in the Dutch context:

1. Historical Development of Islamic Studies
   a. The Period until World War I
   b. The Colonial Interlude and Oriental Studies
   c. Developments since World War I

2. Some Features of Dutch Islamic Studies
   a. Study Programmes
   b. Features of Study and Research
   c. Individualism

3. The Present Situation
   a. University Institutions and Library Collections
   b. Institutions and Organizations outside the Universities
   c. Publications and International Cooperation
   d. New Developments and Areas of Research Interest

4. Conclusion

1. Historical Development of Islamic Studies

a. The Period until World War I

The rise of Islamic Studies in the Netherlands, as elsewhere, presupposed the development of Arabic Studies and a familiarity with Arabic, Persian and Turkish texts. Soon after the University of Leiden was founded in 1576, Arabic was taught by such well-known scholars as Thomas Erpenius (1584-1624), author of a famous Arabic grammar, and Jacobus Golius (1596-1667) who was an accomplished scholar in several fields. At that time Arabic was studied together with Hebrew and other Semitic languages like Syriac, not only in Leiden but also at several other institutions of higher education elsewhere in the country.

The seventeenth century has rightly been called the Golden Age of the Netherlands, which developed trade relations with Muslim countries like Morocco, the Ottoman Empire, Safavid Iran, Moghul India and several Indonesian islands which were just undergoing a process of Islamization at the time. Commercial and diplomatic interests encouraged the study of Arabic, Turkish and Persian. For example, Levinus Warner (d. 1665) lived for more than twenty years in Istanbul, where he held the office of Netherlands Resident from 1654 on. He combined his practical duties with pursuing Oriental Studies and collecting a number of precious manuscripts which were later to become part of the rich collection of the Leiden University Library. Diplomats and travellers showed an increasing interest in Muslim ways of life, as is reflected in many accounts of travellers from the seventeenth century onwards.

The first objective history of Islam as a religion was written at the beginning of the eighteenth century by Hadrianus Relandus (1676-1718), a scholar attached to the University of Utrecht (founded in 1636). A French translation of the Latin original was published in 1731. This work by Relandus, who may be seen as an early Enlightenment figure, set the stage for further Islamic Studies both in Holland and beyond. The interest in history was to develop into a critical academic discipline in the nineteenth century and contribute to the growth of Oriental studies within a historical framework. The private scholar Reinhart P. Dozy (1820-1883) is still known for his history of the Muslims of Spain, based on Arabic sources, as well as for his dictionaries: that of Arab articles of clothing and above all his famous two-volume supplement to the Arabic dictionaries.

Indispensable for any study of Islam, historical or otherwise, were critical text editions. One of the internationally reputed masters in this field was Michael Jan de Goeje (1826-1909) who was Professor of Arabic in Leiden and who edited, besides the complete History of al-Tabārī, an important series of Arab geographers, both projects being carried out in cooperation with scholars abroad. It may not have been an accident that it was in Holland that Arab geography was rediscovered, given the interest in travel accounts which Holland shared with the medieval Muslim geographers.

b. The Colonial Interlude and Oriental Studies

In Holland, too, the nineteenth century saw the rapid rise of Oriental Studies. Besides Islam and the study of certain Muslim regions, these comprised primarily Indology and the study of Indonesian languages and cultures, and they were centered on the University of Leiden. Hendrik Kern (1833-1917), one of the masters of his time in the fields of Sanskrit, Pali and Indo-European languages in general, plus Javanese, left seventeen volumes of Miscellaneous Writings (*Verspreide Geschriften*) as well as several books, among them a valuable history of Buddhism in India and a manual of Buddhism. With J.Ph. Vogel, Indological interests expanded into Indian archaeology and art history.

But it was in particular in the field of Indonesian studies that Dutch Orientalism expanded by the end of the nineteenth century. Scholars like H.N. van der Tuuk (1824-1894), who worked on Indonesian languages, were employed either as "linguistic officers" by the Netherlands Indies Government or as "delegates" by the Netherlands Bible Society. Archaeological research on Java was initiated by J.L.A. Brandes (1857-1905) and continued by N.J. Krom (1883-1945), who organized the Archaeological Service in the Netherlands Indies which was set up in 1913. Anthropologists like G.A. Wilken (1847-1891), A.W. Nieuwenhuis (1864-1953) and J.P.B. de Josselin de Jong (1886-1964) worked among different peoples in the Archipelago while Cornelis van Vollenhove (1874-1933) initiated and developed the study of *ʿādāt* law.

There is of course a connection between the rise of this branch of Oriental Studies and the establishment of the Netherlands Indies as the principal Dutch colony at the same time. For younger Dutchmen who felt confined in an increasingly overpopulated territory with relatively small and traditional horizons, the discovery and study of a wider world offered emancipation and perhaps even personal liberation. Studying and discovering the East, both past and present, presented a challenge for certain members of the Dutch intelligentsia. Islamic Studies profited from the situation in various ways. For the colonial administrators a certain knowledge of Islamic law was needed, and in that context Th. W. Juynboll wrote a standard work on the Shāfiʿī school of law, which was the current one in Indonesia. The book was first published in 1903. Colonial administrators, besides their practical fields of expertise, needed to be familiar with Islamic law and institutions and these subjects were taught first at two special institutions in Delft and Leiden where future colonial administrators received their training. This training was later transferred to the University of Leiden so that they could also acquire a basic knowledge of Arabic and Islamic doctrines within a proper university curriculum and thus be better qualified for their future work. As a result, Arabic and Islamic Studies in Leiden, where C. Snouck Hurgronje became Professor in 1906, were pursued by a relatively large number of students who either had a scholarly or intellectual interest in the field or were preparing to become civil servants in the colonial administration; or in some cases, missionaries. In 1925 a similar training course for future colonial administrators was established at the University of Utrecht on the initiative of some oil companies and larger businesses, which wanted to encourage a more conservative orientation than the liberal one pervading the instruction in

Leiden. In Leiden, a clear distinction was made between scholarship, entailing freedom of research, thought and expression on the one hand, and colonial administration, where all kinds of interests were entangled.

The colonial policy and the guidelines of colonial administration were formulated at the Ministry of the Colonies in the Hague, and were, of course, dependent on parliamentary consent. Formally there was a clear separation between "science" or scholarship, pursued at the universities, and policies formulated by the government. With a few exceptions, those Dutch Islamicists who did not pursue a career in the colonial administration were not involved with colonial problems and colonial or foreign policy. They were mostly interested in research on texts and history. There were, however, some scholars in Leiden who were sensitive to the hopes and national longings of the Indonesian students studying there and the interests of the Indonesian people generally; for instance, Cornelis van Vollenhoven seems to have been sympathetic to the Indonesian nationalist movement which started before World War I. There were tensions between these knowledgeable, independent scholars and the politicians and civil servants who executed the colonial policies, though they kept to their respective domain of responsibilities. Such tensions increased when the so-called "ethical" phase of the colonial policies in the first two decades of this century was replaced by a more reactionary phase between the two World Wars.

It is against the complex background of the expansion of Islamic Studies in Holland, the establishment of a colonial empire with a large majority of Muslim inhabitants by the end of last century and the empire's decline after World War I that the life and work of Christiaan Snouck Hurgronje (1857-1936) should be situated. Thanks to the untiring efforts of P.Sj van Koningsveld, many new facts about the biography of this intellectual giant have come to light: his critical historical research, his formal acceptance of Islam and subsequent stay in Mecca in 1884-85, to become better acquainted with Muslims from Indonesia resident there; his two successive marriages to Muslim women of the Javanese nobility; and his work first serving, then guiding and finally protesting against the colonial policies of his country at the time.

His case, like that of Louis Massignon and Jacques Berque in France and T.E. Lawrence and H.St. John Philby in England, reveals something of the intricate problems and even the ethical conflicts involved, when Orientalists with their specialized knowledge of Islam and Muslim people took up positions different from, and sometimes opposed to those of their governments. This became acute when they did not confine themselves to fulfilling the role of interpreter or bridge between Islam and the West, like several of their colleagues, but became committed in their loyalties to a certain Muslim people, or to Islam itself. When moving beyond what was held to be permissible in the Dutch, French or British ruling society of their times, they ran the risk of becoming "distinguished" outlaws. In a way they responded to certain problems of their time, and we can arrive at a better knowledge of the world in which they lived precisely by taking them seriously as witnesses to it.

Snouck Hurgronje is a case in point. He started out in the 1870s following the Leiden tradition of enlightened critical scholarship with historical work; his dissertation concerned the origin of the Muslim pilgrimage, the *hajj*. In the early 1880s, however, he became interested in Islam in the colonies and the problems and challenges it posed the Dutch administration. While continuing historical work, he went to the Netherlands East Indies at government expense, studying Indonesian languages and doing anthropological research on the spot. He soon became an official adviser to the Netherlands Indies Government on colonial administration and policies. Whenever these policies touched on Islam his advice was called on, but he could also give advice on his own initiative. After the end of his Indonesian period (1889-1906) and his return to the University of Leiden as professor of Arabic and Islam, a position he held from 1906 to 1927, he was a salaried official adviser to the Ministry of the Colonies on matters relating to Islam.

In this advisory capacity and by educating a generation of colonial administrators Snouck Hurgronje was able to win for Islam, at least in theory, a degree of comprehension and perhaps, in some cases, even respect in the colonial administration. This was an achievement in itself, since Islam was a bogey to Dutch public opinion and politicians, after several wars of fierce resistance to the Dutch colonial advance had been waged under the banner of Islam on Sumatra and Java in the course of the nineteenth century. Over against the prevailing facile idea that Islam was the major obstacle to Dutch colonial authority and should be curtailed as much as possible, Snouck Hurgronje formulated an alternative view.

The government should respect Islam on the basis of the freedom of conscience and religious expression guaranteed by the Constitution, but it should not allow Muslims to engage in political activities referring to Islam. This projected Islamic policy was part of a broader colonial policy devised by certain liberals, which was directed against crude economic exploitation of the population but curbed free political expression and intended to offer educational and other facilities to the Indonesian leadership with a view to its assimilation into western, that is to say Dutch culture. Over against the "economic" policy of the nineteenth century this became known as the "ethical" policy. It started to take effect at the beginning of Queen Wilhelmina's reign in 1898, when ideas of renewal were in the air and the political scene in Holland made such a change of policy possible. The new policy was not intended to lead to the independence of Indonesia. On the contrary, the assimilation to Dutch culture envisaged by Snouck Hurgronje aimed gradually to emancipate the Indonesian Muslims from the traditional structures of their society and forge links of a more permanent nature between the Indonesian and the Dutch part of the kingdom. Snouck Hurgronje developed his ideas on the basis of the traditional Islam he had known during his stay in the East Indies and virtually ignored or underestimated the movements of Islamic reform and renewal which started there in 1910 when he had left. His thinking on the future of Islam was formulated before World War I, at a time when the colonial powers of Europe were legitimating their rights to the colonies they had been able to acquire.

Instead of allowing far-reaching changes in the established power formations in Asia and Africa, they tried to impose themselves even more forcefully.

Snouck Hurgronje's ideas, activities and recommendations lead to negative reactions at the Hague and in Batavia. Oil and big business as well as the Christian and liberal political parties wanted to follow tougher lines in colonial policies and, after a glimmer of hope immediately after World War I, his ideas as well as any prospect of at least some democratic participation by Indonesians in policy decisions came to nothing. His ideas may even have provided a certain focus for the reaction which became more vigorous in the years of the Depression. Dutch colonial policies in the thirties were of the most shortsighted kind imaginable. Besides the official advice memoranda (*Ambtelijke Adviezen*) to the Government, a selection of which has been published by his pupil E. Gobee in three volumes, the scholarly work of Snouck Hurgronje is contained in a number of books and seven volumes of Miscellaneous Writings (*Verspreide Geschriften*). Another disciple in government service, able to note down his observations of Dutch policies for some twenty-five years, was D. van der Meulen. His private notebooks and other documents still need to be studied as a valuable source for the period between about 1925 and 1950.

c. Developments since World War I

Snouck Hurgronje's pupil and successor Arent Jan Wensinck (1882-1939) was an eminent Semiticist who was familiar not only with the Old Testament and its historical setting, but also with Syriac and its religious literature, and especially Arabic and the early and medieval Islamic texts. He also carried out comparative research in the field of Semitic religious ideas and practices, and he was able to situate the early history of Islam within the broader context of the history of religions. International scholarship is particularly indebted to Wensinck on two scores. First, he brought the first edition of the *Encyclopaedia of Islam* to a successful conclusion. The idea of an encyclopaedia had already been launched by

Ignaz Goldziher in 1895 and the first volume, under the editorship of the Utrecht professor of Arabic and Islam M. Th. Houtsma (1851-1943), appeared in 1913. From 1922 onwards the project was carried out under the auspices of the Royal Netherlands Academy of Arts and Sciences; Wensinck became the official secretary in 1924 and in 1938 the last (Supplement) volume appeared. The second edition of the *Encyclopaedia of Islam* was launched after World War II, again under the auspices of the Netherlands Academy; this edition is expected to be completed after the turn of the century. The second project of international scholarly collaboration resulted from Wensinck's initiative in 1916 to publish a *Concordance and Indices of Islamic Traditions*. This was completed in eight volumes in 1988, some fifty years after his death in 1939. Both the *Encyclopaedia* and the *Concordance* have been of lasting significance for the progress of Islamic Studies.

Wensinck's successor to the Chair of Arabic and Islam, now enlarged to include Persian and Turkish as well, was J. Hendrik Kramers (1891-1951), a distinguished scholar in a number of fields including Arabic geography. Kramers may be considered to have been the last Dutch scholar to cover the whole range of Islamic Studies (except South East Asia and Africa south of the Sahara) on the basis of a solid knowledge of the sources in the three main languages. During World War II he made a Dutch translation of the Quran in a somewhat archaic prose style, which was published posthumously. After his death Joseph Schacht occupied the chair of Arabic and Islam in Leiden for a few years and gave a powerful impetus to the new edition of the *Encyclopaedia of Islam*. Because of local opposition he chose to accept an offer to join Columbia University in New York. Another internationally known scholar, E.O. Jahn, a Czech by origin and Professor of Persian and Turkish in Utrecht and Leiden, left some fifteen years later for similar reasons.

Outside Leiden, Arabic has been taught at other Dutch universities as well. The name of M. Th. Houtsma (1851-1943) in Utrecht has already been mentioned; his successor was Th. W. Juynboll (1866-1948). In Amsterdam T. J. de Boer (1866-1942) wrote a history of Aristotelian philosophy in Islam. In 1956 an Institute for the Study of the Modern Near East was officially opened at the University of Amsterdam, its first director, G.F. Pijper, who had worked in Indonesia, occupying the Chair of Arabic, Semitics and Islam from 1954 until 1965. This Chair was later occupied by Stefan Wild, from 1973 until 1977.

The existence of the Institute of Social Studies at the Hague was to benefit Islamic Studies in an unexpected way. This Institute was founded in the early fifties and then staffed with researchers, the majority of whom had returned from Indonesia. It was meant to offer training courses for foreign students, notably from developing countries, in the Social Sciences, specifically directed towards problems of development. C.A.O. van Nieuwenhuijze could here develop his approach to the study of Islam and the Middle East within a sociological framework, paying due attention to the dimension of development. This gave Islamic Studies a dynamic perspective and provided a fresh impulse for new kinds of research.

2. Some Features of Dutch Islamic Studies

a. Study Programmes

The programme of Islamic Studies belonged to the Faculty of Arts. It involved the study of the three main languages of Islam (Arabic, Persian and Turkish) and required fluency in at least one of them; knowledge of the main European languages, ideally including a reading knowledge of Italian, Spanish and sometimes Russian, was assumed. Such a study implied familiarizing oneself with the Quran and the Hadīth literature and with texts of the Islamic religious sciences: *tafsīr* and *'ilm al-hadīth*, *fiqh*, *kalām* and *tasawwuf*. It also demanded a broad knowledge of the "secular" history of the Muslim regions, of Islamic cultural history, the Islamic arts and the effects of the Greek heritage on medieval Islam. To complete the programme of studies, which could last some seven years or more, the student was required to present a substantial paper based on original sources and thus demonstrate an ability to treat such sources independently and carry out innovative research leading to a doctoral dissertation.

Islamic Studies conceived in this way represented the culmination of a solid philological and historical programme. The high regard for the study of Islam as a religion and culture reflected itself in demands which in fact only exceptional students were able to meet and which were comparable to those in other European centres of Oriental Studies like Oxford and Cambridge, Tübingen and Berlin, Paris and Uppsala, Naples and Rome.

There has, however, been an alternative way of studying Islam. The course of studies in the Faculty of Arts sketched above might very well produce experts in Islamic Studies whose training was chiefly philological, but such experts were not necessarily interested in the intricacies of religious thought in Islam or the categories of faith and ritual, ethics and law, and "religion" in general. Neither did this programme of the Faculty of Arts offer knowledge of other religious traditions than Islam or pay much attention to comparative studies in the realm of religion and culture. Since 1876 the discipline of "history of religions" has been part of the Faculties of Theology in the Netherlands and here it has been possible to develop an approach to the different religions, including Islam, where they are studied in a scholarly way as part of the methodology of the history of religions. One advantage was that students of Theology were, until recently, thoroughly familiar with Hebrew besides Greek and Latin, and that they had already obtained a general view of the history of religions at the beginning of their studies. This alternative way of studying Islam in the Faculty of Theology makes considerable demands on the students. They are supposed to be familiar with the history of the religion of the Hebrew Bible in its context and with that of Christianity, and they should master the field of history of religions and comparative religion through handbooks and other secondary sources. When they choose Islam as their field of specialization, they should be familiar with Arabic, able to read certain Islamic texts in the original and be knowledgeable in matters of Muslim doctrine, institutions and history.

Since the late sixties some important developments have taken place at the universities in Oriental Studies in general and Islamic Studies in particular. They may be summarized as follows:

1. The concept of the region of Islamic Civilization (*Islamitisch cultuurgebied*) has found acceptance and led to what is called an area studies approach. Islam is basically no longer conceived of solely as a doctrinal system but as a religion and culture showing a social pattern with many variations in which several original culture areas can be distinguished: Arab, Iranian and Turkish; the culture areas of South Asia, Central Asia, South East Asia, West and East Africa, and Europe and America, where Muslim communities live in a diaspora. In the Faculty of Arts the interest in Arabic, Persian, Turkish and Urdu language and culture has diversified and separate specializations have appeared. The resulting graduates are scholars of Arabic, Persian, Turkish or Urdu language and literature rather than experts on Islam. In the Faculty of Theology increasing attention has been paid to contextual factors conditioning religious expressions and the institutional setting of religion both generally and in the case of Islam. This brings history of religions closer to general history and to the social sciences of religion.

With the rise of the Social Sciences and of Asian and African history, students of history and political science, geography, sociology and anthropology, at least at some universities, have been able to choose the region of the Middle East or the Arab world as their field of specialization. This necessitates a certain knowledge of Arabic and Islam. This situation is comparable to that of students of history of religions taking Islam as their special field. At the University of Leiden opportunities have been created to develop on one hand more specialized studies in Indonesian, Indo-Pakistani and African Islam, and on the other hand a simpler programme of Islamic Studies in which no knowledge of languages is required. It is important to note, however, that the concept of interdisciplinary studies - for instance of the Middle East - has only rarely been carried through since the system of independent faculties has been one of the major obstacles. What is probably worse is that the same system stands in the way of developing integrated programmes of Islamic Studies of good quality. Scholarship in "Oriental" languages and literatures (Faculty of Arts), history of religions (Faculty of Theology) and non-western anthropology, sociology and political science (Faculty of Social Sciences) could contribute greatly to such a field.

2. There is a remarkable interest in the modern and contemporary scene of Muslim countries and Islam which cannot be satisfied by the established programmes of Islamic studies in either the Faculty of Arts or the Faculty of Theology. In particular, an understanding of modern and contemporary developments, "Islamicist" movements and current trends demands a specialization and particular techniques not foreseen by the classical programmes. As a result, a certain distinction has become apparent between those working on contemporary Islam and those working on other aspects of present-day Muslim societies.

3. The role of Islam in Muslim societies has been more critically assessed and increasingly attention has been paid to the more general economic and social history of these regions. Many of the existing tensions and conflicts are not due to Islam but may express themselves in Islamic terms. The variety of Islamic movements is stressed and current tendencies to stamp such movements as "fundamentalist" are resisted.

4. The presence of some 450.000 Muslim immigrants from Turkey, Morocco, Surinam and elsewhere has encouraged research on their way of life, culture and religion. Research funds have been made available for the study of religions of ethnic minorities in the country and this has resulted in some doctoral dissertations on the subject, mostly in the social sciences.

b. Features of Study and Research

Apart from the different programmes of Islamic studies at Dutch universities, which have recently undergone drastic change, we may speak now of some general features of studies and research in this field in Holland. To begin with, a distinction is made between those studies which take as their starting point the source material in the relevant Oriental languages and other forms of research and study which deem it sufficient to have a basic knowledge of the language concerned and utilize additionally good materials in translation. In both forms, however, the approach itself is strictly factually oriented, looking for the utmost precision and the least possible ambiguities. The very style of writing of scholars like Wensinck and Kramers (that of Snouck Hurgronje has more literary distinction) excels in clarity. We find here a basic attitude of what is scholarly modesty vis-à-vis materials which are neither easily accessible nor easy to interpret.

This kind of realistic scholarship has its strengths and weaknesses. On the positive side, it accepts limits as defined in advance, it aims to avoid mistakes and errors at all cost, and it is wary of generalizations and ideological bias. It shows its greatest strength in the study of texts and other kinds of subject-matter which are assumed to contain only a few unknown factors and the structure of which is so to speak relatively simple. On the negative side, however, this type of scholarship does not generate theoretical interests, is not keen on discovering general rules and is profoundly hesitant towards any hypothesis which does not lend itself to an immediate factual verification. It also shows little interest in the development of specific disciplines within Islamic studies, each with its own methodology, like the study of history, history of religions, literature, anthropology or sociology. Not being discipline-oriented or even discipline-conscious, it is little prepared for interdisciplinary research and sees its role mainly as that of studying facts from the history and present time of the world of Islam. There seems to be a certain fear of speculation or raising profound questions, an instinctive rebuttal of any reference or implication esteemed to be of a metaphysical nature, and a clear refusal to allow any subjective factors which might impose themselves on the subject-matter. The typical "puritanical" features of this type of scholarship are that it is overly critical and self-critical (to the extent of a fear of publishing anything imperfect), that its basic attitude to any scholarly publication is rather critical (even though the critic may be unable to write anything on the subject himself), and that in principle all those approaches that are held to be deviant are severely attacked (the attacker's own approach being mostly considered to be the right one). There is also a certain distrust of sharpening methodological knives and of a too critical questioning of the assumptions of the type of research being carried out. On the other hand, once the usefulness of an approach has been demonstrated on the basis of the concrete fruits which it has led to, this approach will be recognized as legitimate. This type of solid scholarship is very keen to avoid any ideological or theological issues in research.

As such, Dutch Oriental Studies, including Islamic Studies, have always been sensitive and open to what may lead to a real improvement of knowledge. This partly accounts for international contacts and scholarly cooperation. Its critical realism also provides the capacity to bridge existing oppositions between different schools of research, or between different approaches by non-Muslim and Muslim scholars, sometimes with good results. Fundamentally, a certain centrifugal force away from Dutch society which enhances the interest in other societies, cultures and religions, seems to be implied.

c. Individualism

An attentive observer cannot fail to see a rather individualistic attitude in Dutch Oriental and Islamic Studies. This cannot be explained exclusively by the demands incumbent on scholars working in this field, by the need for specialization or by the limited number of posts available. It may be due also to personality features and a certain style of intellectual life.

The institutional setting of the universities, which includes a somewhat diffuse hierarchy and excludes too much interaction, as well as the civil servant status of researchers leave much to individual initiative. In the seventies there still was a relatively easy procedure to obtain tenure, largely depending on the length of time that an appointment had been held, but this has changed with the increasing budget restrictions. At that time there were quite a few cases of a never-ending preparation for a doctoral degree and of the blocking of posts by people who were not the most brilliant. The modest experience which Dutch students formerly had in writing papers compared with their colleagues in most other countries, together with unhealthy forms of excessive self-criticism and anxiety, may have partly accounted for the comparatively modest scholarly output of Dutch Islamicists. And pedagogy at universities was poor. Fortunately, during the last twenty years certain things have changed and outside influences and incentives, such as international congresses, and the publication of papers have had a positive influence. Intellectual freedom is upheld and originality, also in debate, is increasingly appreciated.

3. The Present Situation

a. University Institutions and Library Collections

Arabic Studies can be pursued in the Faculties of Arts of all seven Dutch universities except one (Rotterdam), with Professorships of Arabic in each, except Groningen. Turkish and Persian, however, can be studied only in Leiden (with a Chair for Turkish and a special Chair for Persian), Utrecht and Nijmegen. The University of Leiden has a Chair in the Faculty of Theology for the history of Islam in Europe and the University of Amsterdam has a special Chair for Islamic law. The University of Utrecht during the last fifteen years has strengthened the research and teaching of languages and cultures of Turkic Muslim peoples and of Muslim immigrants in the Netherlands. Anthropology students from Dutch universities have been doing fieldwork in Muslim societies in North Africa and elsewhere. Islamic Studies are concentrated in particular at the Universities of Leiden, Utrecht and Nijmegen.

Some universities have specialized institutes. At the Institute for the Study of the Modern Near East (University of Amsterdam) specializations exist in Islamic law and the modern history, anthropology and political science of the Middle East. The University of Nijmegen's Institute for Languages and Cultures of the Middle East, which was opened in 1975, succeeding an older Semitics Institute, provides integrated programmes of the study of Islam and Islamic culture, encourages interdisciplinary approaches and attracts many students. The research pursued at the Africa Institute in Leiden includes the study of Islam in African countries; at the Institute of Anthropology due attention is given to Muslim societies. At present, posts for the teaching of Islam are located in the theological faculties in Leiden, Tilburg and Utrecht, the first two on a professional level.

This extension of Islamic Studies and the study of the basic languages of Islamic civilization cannot disguise some serious problems which have arisen as a result of the austerity programme imposed in the 1980s and subsequently by the Ministry of Education and Sciences, under whose competence the universities fall. The threat to eliminate one or more centres of Arabic and Islamic Studies seems to have been thwarted for the moment, but the freezing of posts which have fallen vacant still goes on. A separate chair of Islamic Studies at the University of Leiden had existed for some fifteen years and was abolished after the retirement of the Professor concerned.

There are two more critical developments, that deserve mention. First, all study programmes have been reduced to five years, so that the programmes of Oriental Studies as outlined above for Islamic Studies, which had existed for decades, could not be maintained. Second, the only kind of research officially permitted within working hours at the university, apart from preparing lectures, is that required by participation in accepted, well-defined projects, the quality and progress of which are continuously monitored and evaluated by research committees. For better or for worse, there is a system of increasing supervision and consequently, researchers cannot change their programmes at will. Senior researchers and professors are reputed to have normally time left only to supervise, organize and evaluate the scholarly research of others while they can scarcely develop their own research programmes let alone engender new research under the official guidelines.

The status of scholars as civil servants attached to Dutch universities was once a guarantee of security and freedom; it has now become a liability entailing involvement in activities which hinder teaching and research. Quite a few scholars, including those in the field of Islamic Studies (Hans Daibaer), have gone abroad. One positive result of these measures is that people have been forced to greater circumspection. A certain haughtiness which some Orientalists were guilty of, with regard to their colleagues, including Muslims, and which in fact was contrary to the scholarly tradition, has come to an end. Another positive result is that with the retirement of scholars over sixty years of age, younger scholars could be appointed, though at lower ranks and mostly without tenure. Considerable time will be needed for the revised university system to generate new forms of studying Muslim societies, cultures and Islam, which are capable of holding their own against sound scholarly criticism.

The largest Islamic manuscript collection in the country belongs to the University Library in Leiden, whose *Legatum Warnerianum* is internationally known; the Houtsma Collection in the University Library in Utrecht also deserves to be mentioned, though it is much smaller. The University Library in Leiden also has a valuable collection of manuscripts (Islamic and other) from Indonesia. Besides the holdings of the university libraries, important collections in the field of Islamic studies can be found at the libraries of the following institutions: the Institute for the Study of the Modern Near East of the University of Amsterdam, the Institute for Languages and Cultures of the Middle East of the (Catholic) University of Nijmegen, the Netherlands Near East Institute in Leiden, and the Institute of Social Studies in the Hague. The Department of Oriental Languages and Cultures of the University of Utrecht has an interesting collection of materials on the contemporary history of Iran and Central Asia as well as the history of Islam in the Netherlands.

b. Institutions and Organizations outside the Universities

The following institutions in Holland play a part in furthering Islamic Studies, including the historical and anthropological study of Muslim regions and peoples:

1. The Netherlands Research Organization (N.W.O., formerly Z.W.O.), founded after World War II, is a semi-official body able to fund research projects including those in the field of Islamic studies. All research on the Near East, including Islamic culture, is brought together in a specific research group (*werkgemeenschap*). At present scholarly research on Islam and the Middle East is financed exclusively from public funds, mainly through the universities and the above research organization N.W.O. but also through the Royal Academy of Sciences. There is evidence that these public sources will be insufficient to permit adequate research in the future, but if funds are provided from other sources there is a risk of strings being attached to the kind of research to be carried out.

2. The Netherlands Near East Institute (*Nederlands Instituut voor het Nabije Oosten*), founded in the early 1930s in Leiden, is a private institution. It originally encouraged research on the Ancient Near East but in the 1960s it extended its activities to the Islamic Near East. Since 1943 the Institute has published *Bibliotheca Orientalis*, (not to be confused with the German book series carrying the same name!) which contains mainly book review articles.

3. The Royal Institute of Linguistics, Geography and Anthropology (*Koninklijk Instituut voor Taal-, Land- en Volkenkunde*), also in Leiden, was founded in 1851 as an official institution with public funds, concentrating research on the former Netherlands East Indies. Since Indonesia's independence the Institute has broadened its research to Asia, Africa and Latin America. The Institute has published the journal *Bijdragen* (*Contributions*) since 1853.

4. The Oriental Institute (*Oosters Instituut*), founded in Leiden in 1917, is a private institution. It has a library and gives modest support for scholarly projects.

The *De Goeje Foundation* in Leiden gives financial support for publications in the field of Arabic studies. The *Houtsma Foundation* in Utrecht subsidizes research and publications in the field of Islamic Studies.

The following two institutions outside the Netherlands are intended to stimulate research in Islamic Studies as well as other related fields.

1. The Netherlands Institute for Archaeology and Arabic Studies in *Cairo* was founded by the University of Leiden in the late sixties and is now sponsored by several universities. It has a library and offers services and a residence for Dutch and other researchers and students doing research in Cairo. It also organizes seminars and meetings with Egyptian scholars.

2. The Netherlands Historical and Archaeological Institute in *Istanbul* is connected with the Netherlands Near East Institute in Leiden. It also has a library and offers similar services.

The following private, non-political organizations encourage research in the field of Islamic Studies:

1. The Oriental Society (*Oosters Genootschap*), founded in 1920 in Leiden, is the organization of Dutch Orientalists. Some of the lectures held here are published as separate fascicules.

2. The Netherlands Association for the Study of the Middle East and Islam (M.O.I.), founded in 1980, holds study-days on particular themes. It brings out several publications indicated below.

c. Publications and International Cooperation

The main Dutch periodical in the field of Oriental Studies is the already mentioned *Bibliotheca Orientalis*, published by the Netherlands Near East Institute in Leiden; the *Bijdragen*, published by the Royal Institute of Linguistics, Geography and Anthropology, includes contributions about Muslim regions in Asia and Africa.

The main Dutch book series in the field of Islamic Studies is a series of publications by the Netherlands Historical and Archaeological Institute in Istanbul, under the auspices of the Netherlands Near Institute in Leiden. The series *Verhandelingen* (since 1938) of the Royal Institute of Linguistics, Geography and Anthropology, has published a number of volumes on Islam and Muslim societies in Indonesia and elsewhere. A smaller series of publications (mainly in Dutch) are the so-called *MOI Publications* on specific themes (in Dutch) and the journal *Sharqiyyāt* with articles on various subjects (partly in English) which appear under the auspices of the Netherlands Association for the Study of the Middle East and Islam (M.O.I.); its annual *Encounter, on meetings between Europe and the Middle East*, appears in English. During the last thirty years a number of literary works have been translated from Arabic and other "Muslim" languages into Dutch. Needless to say that the presence of E.J. Brill Publishers in Leiden has given its own impetus to Islamic Studies in the country by providing publication possibilities.

The second edition of the *Encyclopaedia of Islam*, the editorial office of which is established in Leiden, is one of the major projects of international cooperation of Islamicists at the present time. Dutch researchers also contribute to other international projects like the on-going *Onomasticum Arabicum*, the *Aristoteles Arabicus*, or for instance, the *Bibliography of Contemporary Arab Culture*, prepared under the auspices of UNESCO and published in Paris in 1981. Dutch researchers participate regularly in the conferences of the Union Européenne d'Arabisants et d'Islamisants which are held every two years (in 1980 in Amsterdam, in 1990 in Utrecht). Many of them entertain contacts with scholars abroad both in non-Muslim and Muslim countries. Within the framework of Dutch-Indonesian cooperation a number of Indonesian students has spent a year in Leiden in order to become acquainted with Islamic Studies carried out in the West.

d. New Developments and Areas of Research Interest

Although a certain ideal of the scholar in Islamic studies still prevails, the preceding remarks will have made clear that, at least at the present day, its realization requires a lifetime instead of the seven years or so of study at a university. Specializations within Islamic studies together with new interests which have developed since the 1970s have led to new developments in Islamic studies in Holland, the most important of which are the following:

1) Institutionally, Islamic Studies are no longer concentrated exclusively in Leiden which develops a new programme attracting also graduate students from abroad. There has been an upsurge at the University of Nijmegen, which had the largest number of students of Arabic by the late eighties and concentrates on the Middle East as a cultural area in past and present. More recently there has been considerable extension at the University of Utrecht; at the University of Groningen research is carried out on Quran, *tafsīr* and Hadīth literature. At the Free University of Amsterdam research has been carried out into the Greek heritage in Islam and the meeting of different religious communities in the Near East. At the University of Leiden research projects are carried out on Arabic translations of Aristotle, historical relationships between Islam and Christianity in medieval Spain and in the former Netherlands Indies, and Islam in Europe. Most publications by Dutch researchers are now in English, whereas before World War II they were in German or French.

2) Since the fifties, Dutch researchers have developed more interest in the Arab world and the Middle East generally, whereas before World War II most research on contemporary Islam concentrated on Indonesia. The development of the Institute for the Study of the Modern Near East, in Amsterdam, with its involvement in historical and anthropological research on this region, is a case in point. This interest has also led to critical assessments of contemporary conflicts in the Middle East, and recognition for the rights of Palestinians and other minorities in the region. A growing interest has also developed in relations between groups, cultures and civilizations. This interest is reflected in studies on minority groups in the Middle East and on relations, for instance, between Islam and Christianity or between the Arab world and Europe. The same interest has also been pursued on a more theoretical level in cross-cultural studies, studies of the influences which play a role in relations between different groups, and mutual image formation. This has in turn stimulated a self-critical reflection on Orientalism and Islamic Studies generally, with a vivid interest in views held by the other side. In this area of research a sensitivity has developed

to the various kinds of impediments and barriers which impose themselves or are imposed in intercultural and interreligious relations.

There is considerable cooperation between Dutch researchers when compared to the situation of the early fifties. Since 1975 annual study-days on particular themes have been held and this led to the formal foundation of the Netherlands Association for the Study of the Middle East and Islam (M.O.I.) in 1980, This Association has counterparts in the United Kingdom, Scandinavia, France and some other European countries, as well as the United States. The study group called *Adab*, which existed for a few years at the end of the seventies, and where researchers in the field of Arabic literature (classical and modern) discussed scholarly contributions, can be regarded as an experiment preparatory to the organization on the European level of Conferences of teachers of modern Arabic literature (the EMTAR project). The first such conference was held in Nijmegen in 1993 and its papers have been published. The year 1983 saw the foundation of an Association for the Study of Law in Islam and in the Middle East (R.I.M.O.) which also pays attention to legal problems of Muslims living in the Netherlands. In 1984 a Dutch handbook for Islamic studies appeared, the fruit of cooperation between Islamicists from different universities; a third edition of the book appeared in 1994. A new scholarly Koran translation by Fred Leemhvis appeared in 1989.

3) The general interest in Middle Eastern and Islamic Studies is obviously increasing. Present-day developments in the Middle East, as well as the presence of some half a million second and third generation Muslim immigrants from Turkey, Morocco, Surinam and other countries, have not only awakened interest in Islam as a religion and way of life but also revealed the persistence of prejudices (ideologically or religiously expressed) and misconceptions about Islam in Dutch society. Here and there a stimulus from the grassroots can be seen, in which expert advice and reliable information about Muslims, Islam and the Middle East is being sought. Such an "upward" push to Islamic studies probably never took place before and it may give Islamic studies in Holland closer links with

both Muslims in the country and Muslim societies elsewhere, and a better view of current and future research tasks.

4. Conclusion

The untimely death of Professor J.H. Kramers in 1951 as well as the end of the Dutch colonial empire a few years earlier had raised the question of whether classical Orientalism in the Netherlands was perhaps at an end. Would there be the necessary funds and the expertise and, in particular, the necessary motivation for an impartial and even sympathetic study of Muslim societies, Islamic history, and the present role of Islam in Asia and Africa?

Judging by a bibliography of Dutch publications on the Middle East and Islam since 1945, one may conclude that the impetus for this kind of studies has been maintained. The number of researchers in this field is now much greater than in the pre-World War II period, which some consider to have been the golden age of Islamic studies in the Netherlands. It may be true that only a few major studies, generally dissertations of high quality, have been published by Dutch Islamicists since World War II, and that - at least for some time - quite a few foreign scholars in this field have been appointed at Dutch universities, some of whom left again after having worked in Holland for a time. It must be admitted, however, that during the last twenty-five years a considerable number of articles by Dutch researchers have appeared in international journals and that a much more specialized and diversified knowledge of Islam and Muslim regions of the world is now available in the country than some thirty years ago. Even if the passing of a heroic age of liberal scholarship and of elite scholars with encyclopedic knowledge may be regretted, our less romantic period has quite a number of researchers who have proved their scholarly potential and have a sense of what scholarly norms are. And in scholarship in the future, as in the past, the pace will be set by those who recognize these norms. They will now emerge, however, from a much broader basis than could be the case some fifty years ago.

We would like to close with three observations of a more critical nature on present-day Islamic studies in the Netherlands.

Compared to research carried out abroad, Dutch scholarship in this field appears to have been sensitive to Islam precisely as a religion and faith. This may have to do with the plurality of religions in Holland and the various roles they play in Dutch society. But this very sensitivity can also exaggerate the role of Islam and blind researchers to the fact that Islamic phenomena, studied in their contexts, have both religious and non-religious meanings. Religion, and certainly Islam, is not a domain besides others but rather a dimension or resonance of religious meanings behind the social and political ones. In many Dutch publications on Islam one still finds simplistic notions of what Islam as a religion is and an equally simplistic idea of how we can know it.

Second, although some scholars from Muslim countries have worked in Holland in the field of Islamic studies and Dutch researchers have private contacts with Muslim colleagues, it is unfortunate that there are still too few cases of close cooperation between non-Muslim Dutch and Muslim researchers. In this respect the Dutch situation compares unfavorably with that of France or Britain. This has to do in part, of course, with the language problem, and in part with the problem of how to attract qualified Muslim scholars. A welcome initiative in this sense was taken by the University of Amsterdam inviting Mohammed Arkoun in the early nineties. It is a requirement of the time that the interpretation of Islamic texts and the study of Muslim societies be carried out in cooperation between scholars from non-Muslim and Muslim societies, of the same academic level and free from suggestions of superiority.

Third, Oriental Studies in Holland as elsewhere have suffered from the legacy of a certain Eurocentrism and too much emphasis on the presumed *iʿjāz* of western scholarship. Fortunately, a fundamental revision of former attitudes according to which western orientalists were best placed to know people of the East can be discerned. Any ideology of the superiority of western scholarship tends to work against scholarship as the impartial quest for knowledge.

At a research symposium on "Orientalism" organized at Skopje by UNESCO in April 1974 - long before Edward Said published his book - the participants tried to find ways in which the old one-sided Orientalism could be replaced by mutual intercultural studies. Thus Japanese scholars would be able to study, say, French literature together with French specialists in France, and French Japanologists would be able to study Japanese literature with Japanese specialists in Japan. The same would be valid for the reciprocal study of western and Muslim traditions and cultures, not to mention the relations between their religions. Islamic Studies still have a long way to go, but they are moving in this direction.

References

A Bibliography of Dutch Publications on the Middle East and Islam 1945-1981, by A.H. de Groot and R. Peters, with the assistance of M. Bernards (MOI Publication Nr. 10). Nijmegen, 1981.

Brugman, J. "Arabic scholarship". *Leiden University in the Seventeenth Century: An Exchange of Learning*. Leiden: Univ. Press & E.J. Brill, 1976. 203-15.

Brugman, J. and F. Schroeder. *Arabic Studies in the Netherlands*. Leiden: E.J. Brill, 1979.

Fück, Johann. *Die arabischen Studien in Europa bis in den Anfang des 20. Jahrhunderts*. Leipzig: Harrassowitz, 1955.

Kilpatrick, H.M.D. "Middle Eastern Studies in the Netherlands". *Bulletin of the British Society for Middle Eastern Studies* IV (1977): 484-88.

Koningsveld, P.Sj. van. *Levinus Warner and his Legacy*. Leiden: E.J. Brill, 1970.

Koningsveld, P. Sj. van. *Snouck Hurgronje en de islam. Acht artikelen over leven en werk van een oriëntalist uit het koloniale tijdperk*. Leiden: Rijksuniversiteit Leiden, Faculteit der Godgeleerdheid, Documentatiecentrum Islam-christendom, n.d. (ca. 1988).

Pedersen, Johannes. *The Scientific Work of Snouck Hurgronje*. Leiden: E.J. Brill, 1957.

Pijper, G.F. *Islam and the Netherlands*. Leiden: E.J. Brill, 1957.

Shadid, W.A.R. and P.S. van Koningsveld (eds.,). *Islam in Dutch Society: Current developments and future prospects*. Kampen: Kok Pharos, 1992.

Snouck Hurgronje, C. *Oeuvres Choisies - Selected Works*, ed. by G.H. Bousquet and J. Schacht. Leiden: E.J. Brill, 1957. With a biography in French by G.H. Bousquet . xi-xxi.

Vogel, J.P. *The Contribution of the University of Leiden to Oriental Research*. Leiden: E.J. Brill, 1954.

Waardenburg, J.D.J. *L'Islam dans le miroir de l'Occident. Comment quelques orientalistes occidentaux se sont penchés sur l'islam et se sont formé une image de cette religion: I. Goldziher, C. Snouck Hurgronje, C.H. Becker, D.B. Macdonald, Louis Massignon*. Diss. Amsterdam, 1961. 3rd rev. ed. Paris-the Hague: Mouton, 1970.

Waardenburg, J.D.J. "Islamforschung aus religionswissenschaftlicher Sicht". *Ausgewählte Vorträge XXI. Deutscher Orientalistentag* (März 1980). Wiesbaden: F. Steiner, 1982. 197-211. Reprinted in the same, *Perspektiven der Religionswissenschaft*. Würzburg: Echter Verlag & Altenberge: Oros Verlag, 1993. 181-95.

Waardenburg, J.D.J. "Islamic Studies". *The Encyclopedia of Religion*. New York: Maccmillan, 1987, Vol. 7, 457-64.

Waardenburg, J.D.J. "Wensinck, Arent Jan". *The Encyclopedia of Religion*. New York: Macmillan, 1987, Vol. 15, 369-70.

Waardenburg, J.D.J. "Mustashrikûn". *Encyclopaedia of Islam*. New Edition. Leiden: E.J. Brill, 1993, Vol. vii, 735-53.

Dimitri Mikoulski

The Study of Islam in Russia and the Former Soviet Union: An Overview

The country now known as Russia has been known by many names, the Russian Empire, the Union of Soviet Socialist Republics, as well as the present day Russian Federation. Although predominantly Christian, Russia has been closely associated with the world of Islam. That is why Islamic Studies has played an important role in Russian and Soviet scholarship and, in a broader sense, in the culture in general.

Russia was influenced by Islam from the very beginning of its existence. One of the most important neighbors of Ancient Russia (or Rus as it was called at that time) was the Kingdom of Bulghar, situated in the Volga Basin. This Kingdom adopted Islam in the ninth century under direct influence of the Caliphate of Baghdad. Later the native population of the Kingdom of Bulghar became the ancestors of the Tartarian nation, who now represent the largest group of Muslim people in the Russian Federation. Since the eleventh century Russian princes and their warriors (made up predominantly of Scandinavian Vikings) invaded the areas of Transcaucasia, where, especially in Azerbaijan, Muslim influence had begun to spread since the second half of the seventh century. Extensive information about the ancient Russians and other Slavs can be found in Arabic historical and geographical works of the ninth and tenth centuries.

By the second half of the tenth century rulers of ancient Rus were facing the problem of adopting one of the world religions. In 988 the Russian Prince Vladimir selected Greek Orthodox Christianity. According to legend, representatives of other religions, Catholicism, Judaism and Islam, came to Kiev, the capital of Russia at that time, along with the Greek priests, and presented their creeds to Vladimir for adoption. Islam, it is said, was rejected because of its teachings prohibiting the use of alcohol. Prince Vladimir is reported to have said that "the joy of Rus is in drinking"!

Early Russian histories contain some information concerning Islam, borrowed mainly from Byzantine chronicles where Muslims were depicted as pagans and infidels, a perspective characteristic of Medieval Christian historical works.

In the thirteenth century, Russia was conquered by the Mongols. In the next century, Mongols established a state in Eastern Europe and the Golden Horde, as they were called, adopted Islam. Since then the struggle of Russia against Mongol domination acquired an anti-Islamic character. Christianity's victory over Islam was assured by the Russian victory over the Golden Horde at Kulikovo in 1380 and the subsequent liberation from Mongol dependence in 1480.

In the second half of the fifteenth century and later in the sixteenth century, Russia faced another Muslim adversary, the Ottoman Empire. In spite of the fact that Ottoman Turks were considered enemies because they had conquered Constantinople, which was greatly venerated in Russian historical consciousness and folklore, the strong centralized Ottoman state was considered a model political structure in Russia at that time. An author of the second half of the sixteenth century, Ivan Peresvetov, wrote about the Ottoman Empire and its Sultan Mehmet the Conqueror, glorifying the Sultan's strength and the obedience of his subjects to him, even the most noble ones. Some Russian scholars think that the name of Peresvetov was the penname of the Russian Czar Ivan the Terrible. However, references to Muslim themes are to be found in some of Ivan the Terrible's works as well as in those of Prince Audrey Kurbski, one of the Czar's most famous opponents, who emigrated to Poland because of political differences with Ivan the Terrible. Prince Kurbski took an active part in the conquest of the Kazan Khanate (1552), a Muslim Tatarian state, which was situated in the Volga region.

During the seventeenth century, especially during the reign of Czar Alexey Mikhailovitch, some West European works on history and geography were translated into Russian. These works contained descriptions of Mecca and Medina, the Ka'ba, the Tomb of the Prophet, Baghdad, Damascus, Constantinople and other Arab and Muslim cities. Under Peter the Great, Russia experienced several bitter clashes with the Ottoman Empire, organized an unsuccessful military expedition to the Bukhara Khanate and lead a victorious Persian expedition to the Caucasus in 1722-1723. The latter played an important role in the development of Islamic Studies in Russia because German experts, invited by Peter the Great, accompanied his army and copied down many Arabic inscriptions which were found in the Caucasus.

In 1711, Peter the Great returned to Russia after an unsuccessful campaign against the Turks in Moldavia, accompanied by the former Moldavian Prince Dimitri Hantemir (1673-1723), a highly educated person. After settling in Russia, Prince Hantemir wrote historical and philosophical works such as the *History of the Rise and Fall of the Ottoman Empire* and The *Book of System* which, for the first time introduced objective information on Islam into Russian culture. Dr. Hantemir was admitted in 1714 as a member of the Berlin Academy of Science in recognition of his outstanding scientific contributions.

In 1706, at the height of the reign of Peter the Great, Piotr Posnikov, a prominent diplomat and envoy to France, published a translation of the Quran, which was based on the seventeenth century French translation by De Rye. Since Posnikov was unfamiliar with the basic principles of Islam and did not know Arabic, his translation contains many inaccuracies and misrepresentations. During the same period, another, but anonymous Russian translation of De Rye's French translation was made, which is considered to be more accurate and therefore more reliable.

The decades following Peter the Great's death were marked by political instability, cruel tyranny and oppression which did not encourage any kind of academic studies. Government policy toward Muslims within Russia was hostile. However, Moscow University was established (1755) during the reign of Elizabeth, Peter the Great's daughter, and it later became one of the centers of Islamic Studies in Russia.

Islamic Studies were encouraged during the reign of Empress Catherine II. There are two reasons for this increase in interest. First, once again, just as in the reign of Peter the Great, Russia was confronting the Ottoman Empire. Vast territories such as the Northern coast of the Black Sea, the Crimean Peninsula and the Southern Ukraine had been conquered by Russia from Ottoman control. Secondly, many Muslims participated in the Pugatchev revolt (1771-1773), and the state wished to pacify them through adopting a new policy, which was based upon a proper knowledge of their faith and culture. That is why one of the decrees issued by the Empress pointed to the necessity of including Oriental languages, such as Turkish, Tatarian and Persian, into the curriculum of public high schools located in the eastern region of the country.

In 1787, for the first time in Russia's history, an Arabic edition of the Quran was published (with several reprints thereafter) in St. Petersburg. This edition was acknowledged throughout Europe as one of the best of its kind.

In 1789 the Spiritual Governing Body of Muslims was established in Kazan, whose task was the supervision of the religious life of the followers of Islam in Russia. Previously, Muslim religious leaders had been subordinated to local bishops of the Russian Orthodox Church.

The state paid great attention to the social, anthropological study of the peoples located within Russia, among them, Muslims. Several scientific expeditions were organized, the most important of which was the expedition carried out under the leadership of a German scientist Peter Simon Palast who explored Siberia, the Volga Basin Region, Northern Caucasus and Crimea between 1768-1774 and 1793-1794. Two new Russian translations of the Quran appeared at this time. The first and most successful one was carried out by a well-known poet of the time Michael Verevkin (1790). It is believed that the Quran translation made by M. Verevkin influenced some of the poetical works of Alexander Pushkin. Of course, Verevkin did not know the Arabic language and used the French translation of De Rye as his predecessor Piotr Posnikov had done. The other translation was carried out by a professional interpreter of the

Admiralty, A. V. Kolmakov (1792). This translation was based upon a contemporary English rendering of the Quran and was far less stylistic.

The reign of Catherine's grandson Alexander I was marked by the establishment of research and teaching institutions which would play an important role in the Islamic Studies in Russia. These acts were partly the result of Russia's active policy in the Black Sea Region and at the Balkans as well as Russia's quest for the conquest of the Caucasus. It began with the establishment of the Universities of St. Petersburg, Kazan and Kharkov. In 1815, in Moscow, a wealthy Armenian merchant family, the Lazarevs, founded the Lazarev Institute for Oriental Languages which included Near-Eastern languages and Islamic Studies. The Asian Museum was organized in St. Petersburg in 1818, designed to collect Oriental manuscripts, coins and books. By 1917 the Museum had become a unique research center and library where Islamic Studies were carried out by a number of outstanding scholars. The German-born Professor Christian Fen (1782-1851), one of the first scholars to address Islamic Studies in Russian, at Kazan and St. Petersburg, played an important role in the organization of the Asian Museum. The other outstanding personality of the time was another German, Professor Boris Dorn (1805-1881), who taught at Kharkov University and was especially interested in Iranian Studies. Among the early Russian experts on Islamic Studies was Ossip Senkowski (1800-1858), Professor at St. Petersburg University, who also gained fame as a creative writer of romantic works, borrowing plots of many of his works from Muslim life.

Mirza Muhammed Kazem-bek (1802-1870) was a Muslim and Persian by birth. He received a traditional Muslim education at home. Kazem-bek's family moved to Russia where he mastered the Russian language, converted to Orthodox Christianity and adopted the first name of Alexander. Later he became Professor at Kazan and St. Petersburg Universities. Kazem-bek was an interpreter at the negotiations between Czar Alexander II and the Emir of Bukhara who visited St. Petersburg. But his fame came from his writings on Islamic topics. Kazem-bek was among the first in Russia to publish on the subject of Islam in Iran.

The next generation of scholars in Islamic Studies is represented by two brilliant professors of the 1854 Oriental faculty of St. Petersburg University, Vladimir Girgas (1835-1887) and Victor Rosen (1849-1908), his student. Their successful collaboration resulted in the publication of *The Arabic Chrestomatie*. *The Arabic Chrestomatie*, which continued the tradition established by the French scholar Silvestre de Sacy, contained a large number of medieval Arabic Texts such as pre-Islamic and Islamic poetry, Hadīth, *tafsir*, abstracts from histories and geographies, and works on grammar. It is still used as a manual. In 1888, Professor Girgas's greatest accomplishment, the *Leide* was published. It dealt with an important Muslim work of history, Kitāb al-Akhbār al-Tiwāl (*The Book of Long Stories*) by the ninth century historian al-Dināwarī. Victor Rosen also collaborated in the international edition of al-Tabārī's *Annales*. Russian Islamic Studies owes much to him for introducing new, scientific methods of text criticism for the editing of Near Eastern texts. Girgas and Rosen were responsible for the development of Islamic Studies in Russia at the turn of the nineteenth century. Due to their contributions, a number of Islamicists pursued research and teaching under the Bolshevik regime and managed to transfer the traditions of Islamic Studies to a new generation of scholars.

New Russian translations of the Quran appeared in the second half of the nineteenth century. In 1864 an excellent translation by K. Nikolaev was published, based on the French version produced by Kazimirski. In 1871, General D. Buguslavski was the first to translate the Quran in Russian from the original text. However, his work has never been published. It was not until 1878 that a Russian translation of the Quran by G. Sablukov was published.

Perhaps the most outstanding of the disciples of Girgas and Rosen was Vasiliy Barthold (1869-1930). After graduating from St. Petersburg University he traveled to Central Asia and there published a number of scholarly works on the history of Central Asia which are considered classics and have been translated into several Western languages. In addition, Barthold wrote many articles and books on the classical period of Islam. He also edited journals such as, *The World of Islam* (1912-1913) and *The Muslim World* (1917). After the Bolshevik revolution he was one of the organizers of the Central-Asian University (1918) and took part in the introduction of new alphabets to the Muslim nations of the new Union of Soviet Socialist Republics.

Alexander Schmidt (1871-1939) was a graduate of the same Oriental Faculty of St. Petersburg University as Barthold. Later he became Professor of Arabic Philology at St. Petersburg University, but focused most of his attention on Islamic Studies. His main works in this field are: *An Overview of Islam as a Religion* (1912) and *Some Traits of the History of the Sunni-Shiite Relations*. Schmidt also contributed to the transmission of modern Islamic and general Oriental Studies to Central Asia. For example, in 1920-1924 he was Rector of the Turkestan Oriental Institute and from 1924 up to his death, he was Dean of the Oriental faculty of Tashkent State University which was created on the model of the latter Institute.

Finally, the last in this tradition of these scholars is Ignatiy Kratchkovski (1883-1951). The majority of his scholarly interests were dedicated to the study of Arabic and the history of Arabic literature, but he was also responsible for the first Russian scholarly translation of Quran which was published in 1963 by his disciples. While the latter represent the St. Petersburg School of Russian Islamic Studies, the Moscow School of that field has also produced a number of outstanding scholars connected with the Lazarev Institute of Oriental languages.

The most multi-faceted and brilliant of them was Aghafangel Krimski (1871-1942) who was not only an Orientalist, but also a Ukranian novelist and poet of note. As Professor at the Lazarev Institute, Krimski published, among other things, such outstanding works as *History of Islam* (1903-1904) and *History of the Arabs and their Literature, Lay and*

Spiritual (1911-1913). In 1939 Krimski was arrested on charges of being a Ukrainian nationalist and died in a prison camp.

At the Lazarev, later called Moscow Institute of Oriental Studies, two outstanding scholars emerged as representatives of the new Soviet regime - Eugeny Bertels and Eugeny Beliaev. Bertels became famous because of his research in the field of Iranian Studies, but he also wrote a classic work *Sufism and Sufi Literature*. Beliaev, who was a brilliant lecturer, wrote at least two books which still remain among the most prominent Russian manuals on Islam: *Muslim Sects* (1957) and *The Arabs, Islam and the Arab Caliphate in the Early Middle Ages* (1966, published in Moscow posthumously). In the latter work Beliaev promulgated a new theory of the origins of Islam. He tried to prove that Islam emerged on the basis of the transition of the Bedouin society of Arabia from a patriarchal base and slavery. Later he argued, that the Arabs made a transition to feudalism, influenced by the nations they conquered.

Beliaev's scholarly work is based upon a careful study of sources and scholarly literature. This cannot be said, however, of Lutzian Klimovitch who, in his infamous volume *Islam*, takes a purely unscholarly stand and denies even the historical existence of Muhammad, just as Soviet atheistic scholarship used to deny the historical existence of Jesus Christ. In this work, as well as in other books and articles by Klimovitch, there can be found aspects of how Islam was represented in the official scholarship of the former Soviet Union.

In the period from the 1960s to the 1980s, reforms which had started under Khruschev created a new epoch for Russian society as well as for academic study, including Islamic Studies, because the changes created an atmosphere more favorable to intellectual activity. New centers for Islamic and Oriental Studies were established: the Institute of Oriental Languages (later called the Institute of Asian and African Countries) at Moscow University and the African Institute at the Academy of Sciences of the U.S.S.R. in Moscow. Activities in that field continued at the older centers of Islamic Studies at Leningrad (now St. Petersburg) University and the

Institute of Oriental Studies which possesses branches in Moscow and St. Petersburg (at that time Leningrad).

A new theory on the appearance of Islam was constructed by Professor Leon Nadiradze of the Institute of Oriental Languages (now Professor at Tiflis University). Nadiradze attributed the appearance of Islam to the birth of feudal relations in Arabia, examples of which he observed in the management of the Khaybar oasis by the Prophet Muhammad.

Special attention should be paid to the monograph of the late I. P. Petrushevski (Professor at the Oriental faculty of Leningrad (St. Petersburg) University), *Islam in Iran in the VIIth-XVth Centuries* (Leningrad, 1966). The author shows here the cultural background of Islam as a religion not only in relation to Iran, but to the entire Middle East region. Valuable studies were also published by R. Polonskaya, M. Batunski, B. Shidfar, I. Filshtinski, A. Ionova, A. Vasiliev, A. Ignatenko, and A. Sagadeev.

Marietta Stepanyantz framed a new approach to Islam in *Reformist Islamic Movements of the XIXth-XXth Centuries* (Moscow, 1976, new edition, 1982) in which, for the first time in Soviet Islamic Studies, notions of Islamic traditionalism, modernism and fundamentalism were applied to contemporary Islamic movements.

Qasim Kerimov also wrote during this period. His main work, *The Social Essence of the Muslim Sharia* (1978), is very important because it was one of the few Russian language works written during the Soviet period, which treated the foundations of the Islamic juridical system.

The majority of the above-mentioned authors dedicated their efforts to the study of Islam outside the Soviet Union. The Communist government did not encourage objective studies on Islam within its borders, because Islam was considered to have no merits of its own and was only studied as part of the "remains of the past". However, there were a few authors who contributed significantly to the field at the time. Among the most important of them are Abdulla Nurullaev, Talib Saidbaev and Vladimir Basilov.

The scholarly tradition of classical Islamic Studies was preserved at the branch of the Institute of Oriental Studies at St. Petersburg. Important scholars of older and middle generations as Anas Khalidov, Piotr Gryaznevitch, Mikhail Piotrovski, Stanislav Prozorov, Irina Mikhailova, are still active. They trained a number of scholars of the younger generation, such as Dimitri Ermakov, Alexander Knysh and others.

Moscow continues to be the site of active, classical Islamic Studies. Among the most important works should be mentioned the translation of al-Ghazālī's *The Revival of the Sciences on the Faith*, carried out by Vitaly Naumkin (Moscow, 1980). One of the most important gains of the "Perestroika" and "Post-Perestroika" for Islamic Studies was that it became possible to study Islam in Russia and in the other former Soviet Republics, with greater freedom and openness.

Thus in 1985-1988 the Institute of Scientific Atheism (later the Institute of the Study of Religion) of the Academy of Social Sciences (neither institution exists today) carried out a sociological study of Islamic religion in the main Muslim regions of the former Soviet Union. The research was carried out under the guidance of Dr. Remir Lopatikin, at that time the Head of the Department of Sociology of Religion of the aforementioned Institute. Later the results of the research were published in a collective monograph *The State of Atheistic Activities and Religiousness in the Muslim Regions of the USSR* (Moscow, 1990). In spite of its rather ideologized attitudes, the monograph managed to show the dynamism not only of Muslim beliefs, but of the traditional social structure that survived in the Muslim regions of the former Soviet Union in spite of all the persecution and pressure under Communist rule.

A significant study for the understanding of Islam was a book by a renowned scholar of Central Asia, Sergei Poliakov, *Traditionalism in Contemporary Central Asian Society* (Moscow, 1989). Professor Poliakov managed to show vividly that in spite of the assumptions of the Soviet propaganda about the construction of a monolithic socialist society all over the Soviet Union including the Muslim regions in Central Asia, the traditional way of life managed to survive Soviet and Communist institutions. A prominent Turkologist, Dimitri Eremeev, showed in a monograph *Islam: A Social Anthropological Approach* (1990) the influence of nomadic institutions of the Bedouin Arabs and the nomadic Turks upon Muslim doctrine and societies in the Middle Ages and in contemporary Muslim societies.

The essence of the Soviet tradition of Islamic Studies is represented in *Islam: An Encyclopaedic Dictionary* (Moscow, 1991) which was edited mainly by scholars of St. Petersburg, with the support of some scholars from Moscow. This work, the first of its kind in the Russian language, is in many respects similar to the *Shorter Encyclopaedia of Islam* but reflects thought current among Soviet scholars of the time.

At present, the majority of Russian experts on Islamic affairs are concentrating on the study of Muslims in Russia. Among the most prominent are Vitaly Naumkin, Alexey Maleshenko, Olga Bibikova, Alexey Kudravtsev, Georgi Miloslavki, Ludmila Polonskaya, and Alexander Ignatenko. There is considerable scholarly potential in this field in Russia and, no doubt, the future of Islamic Studies will depend, in spite of all temporary hardships, on further work, to sustain one of the most developed branches of Humanities in Russia.

This study has concentrated mainly on research in Moscow and St. Petersburg. However, major efforts in this field were also carried out in Baku, Tiflis, Erevan, Tashkent, Alma-Ata, Dushanbe and Bishkek, but that is the subject of another study. Such an analysis will need to pay particular attention to the role of scholars of Muslim background and their attempts to revitalize Islamic and cultural studies in their new environments.

References

Allworth, Edward, ed. *Muslim Communities Reemerge: Historical Perspectives on Nationality. Politics and Opposition in the Former Soviet Union and Yugoslavia*. Translated by Caroline Sawyer (Durham: Duke University Press, 1994).

Bennigsen, Alexandre. *Muslims of the Soviet Empire: A Guide* (Bloomington: Indiana University Press, 1986).

Bennigsen, Alexandre. *Mystics and Commissars: Sufism in the Soviet Union* (Berkeley: University of California Press, 1985.).

Bennigsen, Alexandre, et al. *Soviet Strategy and Islam* (Basingstoke: Macmillan, 1989).

Bennigsen, Alexandre, and Chantal Lemercier-Quelquejay. *Islam in the Soviet Union*. Translated by Geoffrey E. Wheeler and Hubert Evans (New York: Praeger, 1967).

Carrere d'Encausse, Helene. *Islam and the Russian Empire: Reform and Revolution in Central Asia*. Translated by Quintin Hoare (Berkeley: University of California Press, 1988).

Cudsi, Alexander and Ali E. Hillal Dessouki, eds. *Islam and Power* (Baltimore: Johns Hopkins University Press, 1981).

Eickelman, Dale, ed. *Russia's Muslim Frontiers: New Directions in Cross-Cultural Analysis* (Bloomington: Indiana University Press, 1993).

Lemercier-Quelquejay, Chantal, et al., eds. *Turco-Tatar Past, Soviet Present: Studies Presented to Alexandre Bennigsen* (Louvain: Editions Peeters, 1986).

Malik, Hafeez, ed. *Central Asia: Its Strategic Importance and Future Prospects* (New York: St. Martin's Press, 1994).

Malik, Hafeez, ed. *Domestic Determinants of Soviet Foreign Policy Towards South Asia and the Middle East* (New York: St. Martin's Press, 1990).

Ramet, Pedro, ed. *Religion and Nationalism in Soviet and East European Politics* (Durham: Duke University Press, 1984) .

Troyanovsky, Igor, ed. *Religion in the Soviet Republics: A Guide to Christianity, Judaism, Islam, Buddhism and Other Religions* (San Francisco: Harper San Francisco, 1991).

Zenkovsky, Serge A. *Pan-Turkism and Islam in Russia* (Cambridge: Harvard University Press, 1960).

Sarah Roche-Mahdi

The Cultural and Intellectual Background of German Orientalism

> "Wir sind auf einer Mission: zur Bildung der Erde sind wir berufen". (Novalis, "Blüthenstaub")[1]

German Romanticism has played a particularly important role in the development of an Orientalist perception of the world. Edward Said apologizes for his neglect of the German sources in his study, yet his excuses are couched in terms of what he calls "academic Orientalism" rather than in terms of imaginative knowledge of the Orient. "What German Oriental scholarship did", he says, "was to refine and elaborate techniques whose application was to texts, myths, ideas, and languages almost literally gathered from the Orient by imperial Britain and France".[2] Yet few have demonstrated more persuasively than Said the way in which texts, modes of discourse, can create and perpetuate their own reality. And what better example of the power of texts to create their own reality than a textual reality created exclusively from texts? Inhabiting a mental landscape totally convincing to themselves, the German Romantics were better able than others - regarded as too prosaic to share the Teutonic flights of fantasy - to create an Orientalist discourse unsullied by experience. The roots of Western revisionist ambitions in the East, Said stresses, are Romantic in a specific sense, a reconstituted theology. As such, they are a key expression of the "natural supernaturalism" of the Romantic period.[3] But this reconstituted theology is the product of that higher Biblical criticism[4] which originated in Germany and found its most profound poetic expression and most brilliant and dangerous philological and philosophical formulations in the works of the German Romantics. And if England and France took the major steps in territorial conquest and colonization of the East, German thinkers, in the absence of concrete political power, were engaged in a successful drive for cultural and intellectual domination of the West. It is one of the greatest accidents of cultural history that the British "discovery" of India coincided with the German search for a way to free themselves from the French. The

Romantics dreamt of "enlisting the rediscovered Orient in a vast campaign against the Renaissance, the Reformation, and the French Revolution".[5] Forces which they believed had shattered the political and religious unity of the Holy Roman Empire and plunged the West into materialism and republicanism. France as the land of Louis XIV had been under fire in Germany well before the Revolution and Napoleon. Lessing's "Seventeenth Letter on Literature" (1759), a landmark in the rejection of French theater and German imitations of it in favor of Shakespeare and the Fausttheme, i.e., Nordic cultural roots and native Germanic genius, is representative of the attack of an emerging bourgeois intellectual elite on the French Enlightenment, French Classicism and its German adherents.[6] In opposition to French courtly civilization, which they perceived as godless, superficial, and crassly materialistic, they cultivated a secular religion of *Bildung* - a process of cultural education, felt to be quintessentially German, which aims at the spiritual, intellectual and worldly perfection of the individual personality as an organic whole - which found more or less dogmatic expression in its own literary genre, the *Bildungsroman*, as well as in other writings.

Unfortunately, this emphasis on totality and harmony was a profoundly felt reaction to an accurate diagnosis of ills which are far worse today: the ever-increasing division and fragmentation of the individual and society in an era of technology, the triumph of the profit motive over spiritual values. Schiller's eloquent, sensitive, and highly influential analysis of an alienation in his *Aesthetic Letters* (1975) remains all too valid; his incorporation of ideas from Ferguson, Rousseau and Herder into a dialectic of original harmony, progressive discord, and possibility of renewal of unity on a higher level as paradigm for both individual development and the movement of human history is typically Romantic in its secularized theology. *Felix culpa*, in Abram's formulation, becomes *felix divisio*. Fragmentation is the price humanity has had to pay for progress. But now a new age must dawn, in which the wound inflicted by civilization must be healed by culture. For Schiller, the Golden Age of Ancient Greece replaces the Garden of Eden and shows the way to Elysium; the wound of consciousness will be healed through aesthetic education. Art will replace religion. Most Romantics sought salvation in vaguer combinations of art, imagination, philosophy, and religion. And, with fateful consequences, most of them would look beyond visions of Plotinus' beloved Fatherland to visions of the Orient which culminate in Mother India - and then return home.

In just one paragraph I have mentioned primitive Teutonic inspiration, Ancient Greece, and various Orients. How these disparate elements, consistently used as weapons against the French, can be now equated, now contrasted, now viewed monolithically, now played off against each other, may not be immediately obvious. The answer lies in the different strains of thought - native strains of pre-Enlightenment mysticism, the cult of primitivism, and higher Biblical criticism - which the German Romantics forged into the powerful paradigm of the circuitous journey described above, which occurs as psychological analysis, philosophical system, literary plot, and political ideology.[7]

In Germany, the Enlightenment caused no rupture with earlier irrational movements - Plotinus, Paracelsus, Bruno, Böhme and others continued to be widely read. The idea that the human being is a spark from the divine soul, fragment of an original unity, that each one of us must seek the spiritual path of purification and return was venerable part of the cultural heritage, reinforced by Luther's stress on inwardness, by Pietism, with its emotional probing of the inner life, and by the very important secret fraternities, mainly Freemasonry. Mozart's *Magic Flute* which gives such sublime expression to esoteric (heavily masonic) tendencies within the Enlightenment, offers a positive-negative split in the image of the Orient between the noble ancient Egyptian trapping of Sarasotro, male reason, and the seductive contemporary Arab-Turkish atmosphere of the Queen of the Night and her minions. (A few years ago, I was forcefully reminded of this split while on a tour bus of American scholars tearing through village after village filled with pyramids of glowing oranges and fresh greens, scorning the living inhabitants ["Beautiful? How can you say they are beautiful? They are dirty".] to visit safely dead and decidedly non-Muslim piles of stone - the most ancient pyramids.) Elsewhere, in the *Abduction from the Seraglio*, Mozart's Orient is typically eighteenth century: exotic atmosphere but recognition of a common humanity, the possibility of stereotypes of generosity as well as despotism. Among the Romantics, Novalis most clearly incorporates all the earlier esoteric tendencies, passing effortlessly and without discrimination from Ancient Egypt to Arabia and India, combining Old and New Testaments, medieval contacts with Arabs, current scientific and pseudoscientific theories, the quest for the philosopher's Stone and images of India - brahmins and metempsychosis, but above all the blue flower - into a new mythology.[8]

Primitivist attacks on Enlightenment rationalism first called upon the Semitic East to restore the fallen West to a state of harmony with nature. "How then will we revive the dead language of nature? Through pilgrimages to Arabis Felix, through crusades to the Orient and the restoration of its magic".[9] Men aware of alienation, fearing the effects of the industrial revolution, filled with distrust of science and technology, yearning for harmony with nature, obsessed with the search for primal unity, for the origins of language and culture, glorified the Biblical Orient as the land of primeval revelation. Its purity, simplicity, and spontaneity could be contrasted with and promise redemption of the artificially and depravity of modern Europe. The Biblical Orient as noble savagery and eternal childhood can be seen as original perfection ("zwei Kinder sind, da ist ein goldnes Zeitalter"), infinite potential - or, as an infantile stage which must be overcome. In Lessing's *Erziehung des Menschengeschlechts* (1781), where history is seen as the educational journey of the human race, the Biblical Orient represents the first stage. As divine pedagogue, God adapts his revelations to the limitations of humankind in each period of growth. The Old Testament was a suitable primer for a childish people, but after a while "a better pedagogue was needed to tear the worn-out primer from the child's hand - Christ came" (pars. 51, 53). "We are now on the threshold of a new age which will render the New Testament superfluous (pars. 85-

88)."

Herder, spiritual father of both Sturm-und-Drang and Romanticism, developed Lessing's idea of history as *Bildungsweg* in his *Ideen zur Philosophie der Geschichte der Menschheit* (1784). Changing the movement from linear progression to one of dialectic, he stressed and rephrased Lessing's millenarianism in a typically organic metaphor: "The human race as we know it is only a preliminary phase, the bud of a blossom yet to bloom. . . the current condition of the world is probably the connecting link between two worlds." (Novalis, "Blüthenstaub") His very favorable although not totally uncritical description of Hindu culture, based mainly on the travel account of William Macintosh, did much to awaken enthusiasm for India. He particularly stressed that this paradisiacal land, the cradle of civilization, had suffered much at the hands of Muslims (note already the playing off of Orient against Orient, Islamic against what will later be called Aryan culture) and Europeans - insensitive missionaries and greedy tradesmen. Earlier, Herder had begun his attack on the Enlightenment *Auch eine Philosophie der Geschichte zur Bildung der Menschheit* (1774) with the search for the origin of the human race and praise of the organic, primeval, patriarchal life of the Old Testament as opposed to the cold, sterile "paper culture" of modern Europe. Yet he had portrayed his Semitic way of life as childish. Egypt and Phoenicia shared preadolescence; Greece was youth, the true Golden age; Rome was manhood. This scheme was to prove especially influential. Herder's exaltation of Hebrew poetry a few years later is part of his concern with preserving the very Judeo-Christian tradition which his ideas did so much to undermine. His view of Old Testament literature as expression of a people's primeval energy is shaped by British thinkers as well as by Rousseau, Diderot, and his native mentor Hamann: poetry as the mother-tongue of the human race, Shaftesbury's theories of original genius, Percy's *Reliques of Ancient English Poetry* (1765), Homer and Ossian seen as folk poets. Herder's *Vom Geist der hebräischen Poesie* (1792), in which he argued that the creation story had its origins in primitive folksong, was inspired by Robert Lowth's *De sacra poesi Hebraeorum* (1757), a key text for the development of higher Biblical criticism. Here, primitivism and Biblical criticism intersect and interact in the development of the Romantic view of folklore and mythology.

In reaction to the Enlightenment attack on the factual basis of the Bible, Lessing had already begun to argue for the internal truth of the Christian faith irrespective of historical questions in his debates with the Orthodox establishment; his famous play *Nathan der Weise* (1778) was as much a statement about the unreliability of historical evidence and the inner truth of religions as about religious tolerance and the dangers of emotional unreality inherent in Christianity.

With Herder, Eichhorn, and Heyne's Göttingen seminar, the literary interpretation of the Bible becomes a school of criticism. If the Enlightenment attacks the Bible as just another form of Oriental mythology, the answer developed by higher criticism is, very briefly: yes, the Bible (the New Testament was soon included) is Oriental mythology, is literature which may be freely compared with other ancient texts, particularly Homer. If the books of the Bible were not directly inspired by God in a traditional sense, they were written down by men who had the "capacity to recreate imaginatively the experience of faith" (Shaffer: 85). Inspiration is thus effectively secularized. The implications are staggering. With this secularizing of inspiration, revelation becomes infinitely renewable within the mind of the Romantic sage-seer-poet-philosopher, who thinks in mythical symbols. The Orient landscape as poetic reality, not historical fact, can have multiple perspectives, can be interiorized. There is no open break with Judeo-Christian tradition; instead, the idea of an original revelation and chosen people, the "Oriental scene of the origin of civilization" becomes mobile in time and space, is "gradually released from its Jewish, Christian, and Greek moorings and located in Mohammedan and Hindu settings" (Shaffer: 115).

India, bursting forth upon this intellectual scene in the 1790s, seemed to offer, in contrast to the Semitic Near East and other versions of Asia, not only a living culture (as opposed to Egypt) of greater antiquity than any previously known, but also a perfect harmony of spontaneity (as opposed to China's sterility) and reflection, childhood and adulthood. A return to the womb of this East, the Romantics felt, would bring about a genuine rebirth, a real revolution: the spiritual transformation of Western society. Unfortunately, this passion for India quickly revealed its narcissism: increasingly, the Germans saw themselves as the Brahmins of Europe. The Quest led most of them via the Ganges back to their own version of a Christian-Germanic Middle Ages. And if the Romantics began by seeking the sacred origins of humankind, the primeval sources of poetry, beauty, archaic unity and perfect harmony in an idealized ancient Orient, they soon decided that it was their mission to "educate" the modern Orient, a beautiful but retarded child.

> "Ich lebe jetzt ganz in Indien".
>
> Friedrich Maier [who never left Germany].[10]

India, the answer to a Romantic's prayer,[11] was revealed to Germans in the form of translated texts: George Forster's German version (1791) of Sir William Jones' translation (1789) of Kalidasa's *Shakuntala*; Charles Wilkins' translations of the *Bhagavad-Gita* (1785); Jones' translations of the *Gita Govinda* (1792) and *Laws of Manu* (1794), and Colebrooke's *Vedas* (1802). All were published under the auspices of the Asiatic Society of Bengal (founded in 1784), and all, as well as the Society's journal *Asiatic Researches*, were quickly translated into German (Schwab: 51-53). It is noteworthy that these texts, together with Anquetil's Duperron Persian Upanishads, *Oupnekbat* (1801-1802), were on the whole the only ones available until the 1830s. Thus the German Romantic image of the Orient was based not only solely on texts, but on a very few texts. Of these, Forster's *Sakontala* was the major literary event (Schwab: 57-64; Willson: 69-79). The gentle, placid, plant-and-animal loving heroine Shakuntala seemed the ideal woman; the organic mingling of mundane and supernatural, the harmony of man and nature pleased Romantic sensibilities. Forster's notes (the model for Goethe's notes to his *West-Östlicher Divan*) were as influential as the play itself. He had much to say about Hindu cosmology and about the perfection of Sanskrit and its relationship with Greek and Latin. Certainly, his comments on the blue lotus were crucial for the most famous Romantic symbol, Novalis' *Blue Flower*: the blue lotus plays a leading role in mythology; it is unusually large and beautiful. It is "the flower of night, the timid flower which is alarmed by the light of day and frightened by the stars. It opens and is fragrant only to the moon, and sinks its head under the rays of the sun" (Willson: 77-78).[12] Perhaps most importantly, he specifically offered Indic literature as a means for alienated Western man to get in touch with nature.

Herder's response to *Sakontala* was immediate. In the fourth collection of *Zerstreute Blätter* (1792), he published a review which included a quatrain by Goethe:[13]

> Willst du die Blüthen des frühen, die Früchte des späteren Jahres,
> Willst du, was reizt und entzückt, du, was
> sättigt und nährt,
> Willst du den Himmel, die Erde mit einem Namen
> begreifen,

Needless to say, the review was wildly enthusiastic:

> What a breadth of vision prevails in this work! a view of heaven and earth, What an unusual way of viewing everything! gods and spirits, kings and courtiers, hermits, Brahmans, plants, women, children, all the elements of earth. And how profoundly all is derived from, indeed, interwoven with the philosophy and religion, way of life and customs of the Indians according to their climate, their division of the sexes and other circumstances.[14]

From this single poetic work - which he does not hesitate to compare to Greek tragedy - one had "more true and vivid notions of Indian thought than from all the religious writings put together, with such a manner of representation, infinite metamorphoses are possible while retaining primal forms" (this last from his preface to the second edition of Forster's work in 1803). Like Forster's notes, Herder's own writings on *Sakontala* were tremendously influential; as usual, he was the major force in the development of a Romantic ideal in full flower by 1800: in Edenic contentment on the banks of the sacred Ganges, cradle of humanity, source of all Western science and religion, dwelt a civilized race, beautiful, graceful, eternally smiling vegetarian children of nature who believed in metempsychosis, and whose exceptionally privileged priesthood, which had its origins in remotest antiquity, gave superior moral instruction in a holy language more ancient than Hebrew and far better suited to literature and philosophy.[15] Indeed, interest in the language was soon to prevail. As early as 1786, Sir William Jones had speculated on the relationship between Sanskrit, Greek, and Latin:

> The Sanskrit language, whatever be its antiquity, is of a wonderful structure; more perfect than the Greek, more copious than the Latin, and more exquisitely refined than either, yet bearing to both of them a stronger affinity, both in the roots of the verbs and in the forms of the grammar, than could possibly have been produced by accident; so strong, indeed, that no philologer could examine them all three without believing them to have sprung from some common source, which, perhaps, no longer exists.[16]

Translations were soon not enough - one had to gain direct access to the ancient languages. Many Germans flocked to Paris and several to London to learn Persian, Arabic, and especially the holiest of tongues, Sanskrit.[17] The most notorious of these was Friedrich Schlegel; the most gifted, Franz Bopp. Unfortunately, if Bopp's brilliant philological discoveries, which of course proved Jones right, were of incomparable influence on the development of comparative linguistics, his ideological moderation did not prevail. Friedrich Schlegel's Pan-Germanism, and, for a while, his theory of Sanskrit as mother tongue, did.

From the above comments, it will be clear that of the two most famous German Orientalist works mentioned by Said, F. Schlegel's *Über die Sprache und Weisheit der Indier* will receive more attention in this essay than Goethe's *West-Östlicher Divan*. For, although Goethe was an early discipline of Herder and was introduced to Arabic, Persian, and Sanskrit poetry by Orientalist scholars,[18] his profoundly creative encounter with another culture, with another poet whom he recognizes as mentor and brother, is far too mature in its playfulness and irony to be representative of the age; it is far too subtle, at once far too personal and too universal to lend itself willingly to the nationalistic polemics which prevailed by the time it was published (1819). As usual, Goethe accomplished in literature what the Romantics only talked about and strove for, while never confusing illusion and reality, literature and life. If Marx misuses the *Divan*, it is not Goethe's fault.[19]

Friedrich Schlegel, on the other hand, is a master at confusing poetry and politics. His *Reise nach Frankreich* (1803) bristles with nationalistic rhetoric. In the first two stanzas of a poem - supposedly triggered by his first sight of the Wartburg (Willson: 88) - replete with pre-Wagnerian pseudo-Nordic alliteration, he evokes a Teutonic past with images which anticipate the sets of Fritz Lang's *Nibelungen*, then conjures up a crusade in which the treasures of India are brought to the valleys of the Rhine (he is undoubtedly partially inspired by the Arab cortege of the great Hohenstaufen Frederick II, whom he will praise later):

> Langsam dann im Tal gezogen
> Auf allen, Straßen und Wegen
> Orientes Reichtum in vollem Triumphe,
> Wagen und Männer,
> Elefanten und Mohren,
> Blühende Stein' und farbige Früchte,
> Indiens goldenster Segen.[20]

He laments the loss of the "furor tedesco" (p. 60), the lack of a *Vaterland*. Three great peoples have conquered the known world: Romans, Arabs, and Germans. All have had tragic fates; Rome was suicidal, the Arabs remain as "nur ein totes Schattenbildnis von Enthusiasmus in ewiger Einförmigkeit" (p. 61), but beware - "perhaps the sleeping lion may awake once more, and perhaps, even if we are not to experience it, future world history will be full of the deeds of the Germans" (p. 61). At any rate, Europe can sink no lower than the days of the abortive French revolution (p. 76). Analytical thought has progressively destroyed her unity since the days of ancient Greece, Classical and Romantic elements are artificially separated (p. 74); religion is no longer possible, although Catholicism has maintained a faint sense of unity. Yet in prostrate, degenerate Europe lie the seeds of a higher calling, a real revolution; one that comes from Asia, which has maintained an organic unity (pp. 76-77). The solution is to unite the two forces of good in the world, Nordic iron and Oriental fire - then Europe will arise as it created for the first time: "wir sollen die Eisenkraft des Nordens und die Lichtglut des Orients in mächtigen Strömen überall um uns her verbreiten; moralisch oder physisch, das ist hier einerlei. . ." (p. 78).

As usual, Herder had prepared the way. Already in 1774, in *Auch eine Philosophie der Geschichte*, his stress on the fall of the Roman Empire and his glorification of the Nordic barbarians is extravagant, strident. He delights in the explosion of primitive force, in the destruction of an effete civilization (a thinly veiled France):

> Whoever reflects upon the situation of the Roman territories in their final centuries - and they were the civilized universe at that time - will gaze in astonishment and admiration at the way in which Providence prepared such an extraordinary compensatory renewal of human energy. Everything was exhausted, enervated, in ruins: abandoned by men, inhabited by enervated human beings, sinking deeper and deeper into sensuality, vice, confusion, license, and wild pride in warfare. The fine Roman laws

> and learning could not compensate for vanished energy, restore nerves which felt no breath of life, arouse motivating forces which lay inert - death, then! a worn out corpse lying in its blood - then New Man was born in the North. Under a new and vigorous sky, in the wastes and wilderness, where none foresaw it, new growth ripened, strong, productive, which, transplanted into the lovelier, more southern lands - now dreary, empty fields! - was to takeon new characteristics, yield a rich harvest for world destiny.(514-515)

Herder's own harvest was yielding fruit, although he himself mellowed with the years and gradually adopted a Classical stance. To cite just one other example of the kind of nationalism prevailing around the time Schlegel left for Paris: Hölderlin wrote a cycle of three poems in 1801 called "Die Wanderung", "Der Rhein", and "Germanien". In the first, Teutons meet Hindus on the shores of the Black Sea; in the second, the Rhine longs to flow toward Asia; the third depicts the flight of the Eagle from India to Germany. For all that the eagle is the bird of India and might be a symbol of civilization, the most important literary and political precedent is Dante's "Bird of God", the emblem of Empire, a dead bird which German intellectuals - including Luther - kept trying to resuscitate throughout the centuries, consumed with loathing for the Mediterranean usurpers. If Dante presents Constantine's transfer of the seat of the Roman Empire from West to East as a violation of natural order and sees renewal of the power of the German Emperor (Holy Roman Emperor) as the only possibility of peace, Hölderlin envisions the Eagle finally crossing the Alps, screaming with triumph.

Once Schlegel got to Paris, he began with the study of Persian but soon gave it up as too Muslim. Sanskrit then filled him with enthusiasm - "alles, stammt aus Indien ohne Ausnahme" (Willson: 210) - but, as is clear from his lectures on universal history (1805-6), he was from the beginning most interested in linking the Germanic Middle Ages, Catholicism, and India.

The evils of Mediterranean civilization were for him, materialism and republicanism. Thanks to the Germans, who were untainted by Mediterranean vices, the European Middle ages resembled India. Only the Persians and the Germans retained the essence of the primeval kingship originating in India. Since Persia was corrupted by Islam, Germany remains the only hope for the West. Germany must restore hierarchy and reveal a new Indo-European Christianity severed from its Jewish roots.

No one failed to notice that *Über die Sprache und Weisheit der Indier* appeared a few days after Schlegel's conversion to Roman Catholicism. Goethe considered it a Catholic manifesto. (Of course, Schlegel's brother considered Goethe a "pagan converted to Islam".[21] The preface contains the annunciation of a new, "Oriental [i.e., Indic] Renaissance" (Schwab: 13; the term is Quinet's):

> May Indic studies find only a few of those dedicated scholars and patrons which Germany and Italy saw emerge so suddenly and in such great numbers to undertake the study of Greek in the fifteenth and sixteenth centuries, and may they accomplish such great things in so short a time. The reawakened knowledge of Antiquity quickly transformed and rejuvenated all branches of learning, indeed, we may say it transformed the world. We venture to assert that Indic studies would have the same far-reaching effect on the present age were they undertaken with the same energy and made part of the European sphere of knowledge (VIII: 276).

The entire work ends with the Middle Ages. Indic studies are to serve as corrective to the one-sided study of the Greeks and lead us back to the true medieval spirit which alone can give birth and nurture art and knowledge. He finds alarming strains of materialism in Hindu philosophy, although it is still useful because not separate from religion. Only the language retains its pristine splendor: Sanskrit is the source of Latin, Greek, Persian and Germanic. These languages, which are characterized by internal modifications of root forms, he declares superior to agglutinative languages (e.g. Arabic and Hebrew): their roots are truly organic, living seeds; their creative potential is endless, where as the roots of agglutinative languages are not alive, but rather like a heap of particles which every chance breeze can separate or bring together. Deprived of life, eternally deficient, they are doomed to artificiality if not eccentricity; their apparent wealth is in reality, poverty.

Schlegel had "crystallized the Germanic need for the Orient" (Schwab: 71) and laid the groundwork for Indo-Germanic linguistics - a term not actually used before 1823 and which the upright Bopp explicitly rejected in the preface to the second edition of his *Comparative Grammar*. The essay was of enormous importance, prompting many to follow in his footsteps either in Paris or on the home front. *Über die Sprache und Weisheit der Indier* (1808) is one of the earliest in a series of publications emanating from the Heidelberg group (Schwab: 215), including *Des Knaben Wunderhorn* (1805) a translation of the *Nibelungenlied* (1807), Gorres' *Mythengeschichte der asiatischen Welt* (1810) and Creuzer's *Symbolik und Mythologie der alten Völker, besonders der Griechen* (1810-12).[22] Just the list of titles reveals that the [con]fusion of philosophy, mythology, Germany, Greece and Orient is in full bloom: folksong as primeval expression of ancient heritage, the *Nibelungenlied* as Ingo-Germanic epic; Gorres with India colonizing the world, Abraham and Sarah as exiled Brahmins (Voltaire started this with his etymological game) and Roman Catholicism as Indo-Germanic religion; Creuzer's search for pre-Abrahamic monotheism, which he finds in Egypt, India and Persia.

And then there is Friedrich's brother, the would-be Brahamin, August Wilhelm. Here we have Germany as the India of Europe; if Sanskrit is the purest ancient language, German is the purest living language of Europe. He even thinks that there are still remnants of German-speaking tribes living in India, and is furious when a missionary dares to contradict him (Gerard: 139-40). How infinitely more valid the inspired *Einfühlung* of a great thinker than uninspired eye-witness accounts! He is equally angry with the British, soulless materialists that they are, for constantly advancing the dates of Sanskrit texts. Unlike Friedrich, he renounces Catholicism. His hostility to Semitic literature, particularly Arabic, is increasingly apparent. In his *Zunahme und gegenwärtiger Stand unserer Kenntnisse von Indien* (1829), Muhammad is the greatest ignoramus of all time, the Arabs are fanatical persecutors of Zoroastrians, their poetry is egotistical, it did their poets no good to travel. As for the *Thousand-and-One Nights*, it is high time to expose this supposed Arab creation as a translation from the Indic. To be sure, impurities have crept in, but he confidently separates the various elements. The Arabs have contributed exaggeration. The best thing to do would be to cut out the Indic sections and publish them in their pristine form. It is the same with science. Nowhere did Arabs create. One might mention in passing Wilhelm von Humboldt's pronouncement that only "Sanskrit-speaking" peoples have access to culture, or Carl Ritter's full-fledged Indo-Aryanism, by passing both Greeks and Hebrews, viewing the Jews as enemies who have cut off the West from its real roots (Gerard: 193). One must also remember that Hegel, in his *Lectures on the Philosophy of History* (delivered in various forms between 1822-1831), combines Lessing's and Herder's ages of humankind as *Bildungsweg* with his own history of the evolution of consciousness of self towards freedom into a glorification of German-Christian man and the right of Europe to rule the world:

> And as the germ bears in itself the whole nature of the tree, and the taste and form of its fruits, so do the first traces of Spirit virtually contain the whole of that history. The Orientals have not attained the knowledge that Spirit - Man as such - is free; and because they do not know this, they are not free. They only know that one is free. But on this very account, the freedom of that is only caprice; ferocity - brutal recklessness of passion, or a mildness and tameness of the desires, which is itself only an accident of Nature - mere caprice like the former - that one is therefore only a Despot; not a free man. The consciousness of

> Freedom first among the Greeks, and therefore they were free; but they, and the Romans likewise, knew only that some are free - not man as such. . . The German nations, under the influence of Christianity, were the first to attain - the consciousness that man, as man, is free: that it is the freedom of Spirit which constitutes its essence.[23]

For him, the fantasy of India as a paradise of flower-people is a thing of the past; India is wonderland only in comparison with the prosaic sterility of China. The Arabs do not exist except as a subsection under the Germanic world. "Muhammadanism" is pure, negative subjectivity, abstract enthusiasm; just as in their deserts nothing has form, so all their endeavors ended in formlessness. Here, we have philosophical justification for white supremacy; elsewhere, growing philological and mythological Indo-Germanism culminating in the vilest Anti-Semitism later in the century. Schopenhauer, for example, in the second part of his *World as Will and Representation* (1844), separates Old from New Testament in order to save originally Indic Christianity from the corruption of Judaism (cf. Schwab: 427-431). With Richard Wagner's *Parsifal* (1882), the Romantic ideal of innocently sensuous Indian flower-people, already ridiculed by Hegel as effeminate, has been transformed into a nightmare vision of Oriental decadence and feminine poison, a constant source of danger for the Aryan male. We are treated to the fall and redemption of the Aryan blood line of the Grail Kings, contaminated by intercourse with an impure Semite, restored to racial purity by sexual abstinence, redeemed from the "Gracefulness of vice" so characteristic of the Jews and the French.[24]

Conclusion

German Romantic images of the Orient were tainted from the beginning with nationalism and intellectual and emotional immaturity. The hatred of the French and all who frenchify, the need to hold the French Enlightenment and French Revolution responsible for the psychic as well as political fragmentation of modern Europe, expressed by the small, socially isolated, politically powerless and overly academic German bourgeois intelligentsia, ultimately had their roots in the failure of Germany to achieve national unity in the Middle Ages. Napoleon as "Mahomet d'Occident" dissolving the Holy Roman Empire revived centuries-old fantasies of a Holy Roman Emperor of the Germans who would unite East and West under his rule and bring about the millennium, aroused a fierce urge to compensate for political impotence by cultural dominance. In opposition to French Classicism, they sought the home of poetry in the Orient. Faced with the increasing specialization and resulting alienation of a new age of technology, which they attributed more to metaphysical causes (the triumph of reason) than to Industrial revolution, the Romantics sought refuge in the vision of a precapitalist Orient. In the face of scientific criticism of religion, they could neither preserve the Judeo-Christian tradition nor develop a truly secular humanism. Unable to shake the myth of original unity which dominated the late eighteenth century, they developed a synthetic mythological approach which retained the idea of the chosen people. An already free-floating image of the Orient was revolutionized by the Indo-mania (Gerard's term) of the turn of the century. The Old Testament patriarchs as representatives of an earlier and simpler life yielded to the Hindus as examples of an ancient yet highly complex culture still in existence. Here was a chosen people who, with the help of the developing science of comparative linguistics, could be claimed as racial ancestors. The Germans saw themselves as the Brahmins of Europe. But soon it became clear to them that modern India, like the rest of the East, had degenerated. That left Germany, the land of the new priesthood of poets and thinkers, to combine ancient wisdom and modern energy for the spiritual renewal of the world. Just as the idea of the chosen people became a tool for racism and nationalism (the Semitic peoples could be viewed as aliens, inferior and uncreative invaders who had cut off Aryan Europe from her roots), the semi-secularized, personalized conception of poetic inspiration, the ideal of *Bildung*, the cultivation of personality all too easily degenerated into the cult of personality, the self-sanctification and hero-worship of the great man, whether poet or academic. If the mythic gaze, interchangeability-yet-sameness of Oriental perspectives have been valuable for poetry, they have had baleful effects on scholarship and politics. The entire real world has paid and continues to pay too heavy a price for the dreams of glory of men who, like Canetti's Peter Kien (the world's foremost Sinologist, you will recall - and you will recall his fate), spent too much time in libraries inhabiting the mythical landscapes, both Oriental and Occidental, of their own minds.

Notes

1. "We are here on a mission: it is our sacred duty to civilize the world".
2. Edward Said, *Orientalism.* New York: Pantheon Books, 1978, p. 19. Fortunately, Raymond Schwab's brilliant if eccentric *La Renaissance orientale* (Paris, 1950) has recently appeared in English with a foreword by Said *Oriental Renaissance: Europe's Rediscovery of India and the East*, 1680-1880, trans. Gene Patterson-Black and Victor Reinking (New York: Columbia University Press, 1984). Page references in this article are to the translation.
3. M.H. Abrams, *Natural Supernaturalism*: *Tradition and Revolution in Romantic Literature* (New York: Norton Library, 1973).
4. See E.S. Shaffer, "Kubla Khan" and "The Fall of Jerusalem": *The Mythological School In Biblical Criticism and Secular Literature, 1770-1880* Cambridge: Cambridge University Press, 1975.
5. Rene Gerare, *L'Orient et la Pensée Romantique Allemande* Paris: Marcel Didier, 1963, p.1.
6. For an excellent, succinct formulation of the social and political background and development of the contrast between French "civilization" and German *Bildung*, see Norbert Elias, *The History of Manners*, Vol. 1 of *The Civilizing Process* New York: Pantheon Books, 1978, pp. 1-50.

7. See especially Abrams, *Tradition and Revolution*, Chapter Three: "The Circuitous Journey", for a wonderfully lucid treatment which does not, however, deal with political implications.

8. Novalis, "Blüthenstaub".
9. Hamann, *Aesthetica in nuce*, 1762.
10. Henry E. Allison, *Lessing and the Enlightenment: His Philosophy of Religion and Its Relation to Eighteenth Century Thought*. Ann Arbor: University of Michigan Press,1966, especially pp. 141-2.
11. Majer, one of Herder's disciples, was extremely important in disseminating the Romantic image of India. Cf. Gerard. p. 76, and A. Leslie Willson, *A Mythical Image: The Ideal of India in German Romanticism*. Durham, N.C.: Duke University Press, 1964, pp. 94-104.
12. For the image of India, Willson is very useful if uncritical. It is a pity he did not know Schwab's work (originally published in French in 1950).
13. "Wouldst thou the blossoms of spring and the ripe fruits of autumn/wouldst thou be charmed and delighted, wouldst thou be sated and nurtured/Wouldst thou embrace heaven and earth within one name/I name thee, Sakontala, and there with all is said".

14. *Sämtliche Werke*, ed. Suphan (Hildesheim: Georg Olms Verlagsbuchhandlung, 1967), XVI, p. 88. "Welch ein weiter Gesichtskreis herrscht in diesem Werk! ein Gesichtskreis über Himmel und Erde. Welch eine eigne Art alles anzuschauen! Götter und Geister, Könige und Hofleute, Einsiedler, Bramanen, Pflanzen, Weiber, Kinder, alle Elemente der Erde. Und wie tief ist alles aus der Philosophie und Religion, der Lebensweise und den Sitten der Indier nach ihrem Klima, ihren Geschlechterabteilungen und sonstigen Verhältnissen geschöpft, ja in diese verwebet".
15. See Willson, *passim*, for excellent summaries of the various stages of development in the image of India.
16. Quoted by Said, p. 79; Schwab, p. 41. Note also Shaffer with regard to Jones' "sense of the immediacy, accessibility, and disposability of the whole of Asia" (p. 117).
17. Johann Fück, *Die Arabischen Studien in Europa bis in den Anfang des zwanzigsten Jahrhunderts* (Leipzig: Harrassowitz, 1955), p. 156: "No country, however, sent more students to de Sacy than Germany".
18. See the detailed studies by Katharina Mommsen: "Goethe und die Moallakat" and "Goethe und Diez: Quellenuntersuchungen zu Gedichten der Diwanepoche", *Sitzungsberichte der Deutschen Akademie der Wissenschaften zu Berlin, Klasse*

für Sprachen, Literatur und Kunst, 1960 and 1961; *Goethe und die 1001 Nacht* (Berlin: Akademischer Verlag, 1960).

19. Said's point about Goethe's being the source of Marx's Orientalism (p. 154) needs qualification. Marx has not understood Goethe's irony.
20. *Kritische Friedrich Schlegel -Ausgabe*, Vol. 7 (1966), P. 59: "Moving slowly through the valley on every street and way/Riches of the Orient in full triumphal procession/men and wagons/elephants and Moors/florescent gems and many-hued fruits/India's most precious bounty".
21. For views of the work as Catholic manifesto, see Gerard, p. 111; Goethe as heathen convert to Islam is one of the delightfully malicious bits from Heine's *De l'Allemagen* quoted by Schwab, p. 60.
22. Gerard has excellent summaries of these figures.
23. *The Philosophy of History*, trans. J. Sibree (New York: P.F. Collier & Son, 1900), p. 18.
24. The phrase is Treitschke's, quoted in Robert W. Gutman, *Richard Wagner: The Man, his Mind, and his Music* (New York: Harcourt Brace Jovanovich, Inc., 1968), p. 427.

Norman Daniel

The Image of Islam in the Medieval and the Early Modern Period

This essay surveys a cultural conflict which did not change substantially from its beginnings in Muslim Spain until European colonial expansion. It was based on a distorted image of religious difference. The two revelations, Islam and Christianity, are mutually exclusive in that certain contradictions can be resolved in terms acceptable to only one of them. The two religions might have lived side by side with mutual respect, but this is not quite what happened. Polemic was mostly conducted with disesteem and incomprehension until finally a professed aim of scientific objectivity emerged; whether rightly so called will be for others to determine.

The essential conflict between the religions was from the start exacerbated by conflict in inessentials. If there is no cultural element presumed to exist in any religion in itself, there is obviously one in the way of life, and in many of the religious practices of those who profess it. The traditions of different Christian communities have diverged over the centuries, often over more than a millennium and a half; they have different interpretations of what the same moral system should imply in terms of actual behavior. On the other hand, there are Muslim thinkers today who deny that there is any but one single Islamic civilization. Differences of behavior, quite outside the matters of which the Quran legislates, are imposed by climate, occupation and economic development. We have to trace how far Christians, living in their own changing cultures, included cultural inessentials in their criticism of Islam, itself with its different and changing cultural appearance.

We must be clear from the start about one crucial issue which constantly recurs. Muslims are genuinely and rightly scandalized by the vilification of the Prophet by Christian writers, and they are apt to contrast the respect with which the Quran treats Jesus the Messiah and his mother, and to stress the toleration which in principle, if not always in practice, has been extended to Christians. So far they are quite right, but they should remember that throughout the co-existence of the two religions each has been bound to try to invalidate the text of the revelation of the other. What the Quran says about Jesus, thought respectful, is entirely incompatible with, and totally destructive of, essential Christian belief about him. In attacking the Quran, the polemicists felt that they were doing what the Quran itself had done to the Word of God. This reciprocity does not excuse their virulence against the Prophet; there was nothing quite of that sort in the Quran. But it does help to explain the bitterness which was for so long the chief feature of the Christian tradition about Islam. The advent of Islam had been a shock to the Christians, and, because it was unfamiliar to them, unexpected, different, and because for a long time it dominated them, their cultural resentment magnified their opposition and largely determined the forms it took. Because it is offensive, I shall cut my quotations of scurrilous material to a minimum.

Christians in the East faced Islam at first almost with incredulity, as if it were an ephemeral invasion. The tendentious treatment of the Prophet to which they soon turned also began early in the West, and material derived much later from Syria added little to the substance of what was already known from Spain; we can stick to the West, and we can forget almost all about the Crusades. In the middle of the ninth century in Cordova, Eulogius, later archbishop-elect of Toledo, copied a short polemic life of the Prophet that he had brought back from Pamplona.[1] It attacks the seriousness of the subject matter of the Quran, as that *suras* should be named after animals (unsuitable surely only to the eye of prejudice), and it attacks the Prophet for his marriages, in one case in particular. It would be unnecessary to look any further for sources, it we knew the source of this document, but, although we know nothing about it, we do know that Eulogius and his lay friend, Alvarus of Cordova, were at school with an Abbot Hope-in-God, who himself had written anti-Islamic polemic and had presumably influenced them both. His tone may be inferred from his comment that the Islamic heaven was "not a paradise but a brothel". Christian criticism at all times sought to show that Islam was contrived to appeal to easy converts.

The Christians of Spain bitterly resented their displacement as rulers by Muslims, not only with their different religion, but with a different language and literature and customs. They hated Islam especially in its public aspect. They resented the disappearance of Christian public practices; and on the other hand they particularly resented the call to prayer - "the distended jaw of wild beasts...wide-open gullets", "a young donkey, his jaws open wide", they said of the *muezzin*. Above all, they based a whole movement on their urge to violence against Islam; they could not rebel effectively, but they called down Muslim violence against themselves, and it was no less violence for being provoked in others. The evidence is that the Muslims were reluctant to execute Christians who gave them no alternative when they denounced the Prophet venomously in public places, even in the mosque at the Friday prayer. This public and social resentment in front of all the world is the cultural demonstration of the Christian theme.

Eulogius was rather an innocent person; Alvarus, much more complex, a great rhetorician and a reader of Biblical prophecies that he applied to the Prophet Muhammad in a highly fanciful way. The Quran is hard for foreigners to follow in translation, but so are the Hebrew prophets; readers often do not know their historical context, and so Alvarus could force them to foretell Islam. He used Ezechiel, "she doted upon her paramours", and Jeremiah, "they were well-fed lusty stallions", to condemn the Islamic law of sexual relations.[2] He loved the sound of the prophetic text. He applied the phrase in Job, "pipes of brass" to designate Arabic, because, he says, it is fine-sounding but without sense. Arabs become Chaldeans, also Amelekites; he even attempts to see in the "Maozim" of the Vulgate of Daniel XI - the god of fortresses of Antiochus Epiphanies - a prophecy of the *muezzin*. This is not argument; it is the culture of the Vulgate set up against the culture of Islam as outsiders perceived it.

It was not until much later that Western writers again interested themselves in Islam. When they did so, they added new inventions with no basis in fact at all (a faked revelation on the horns of a bull, or whispered by a dove) or almost none (Muhammad the vindictive Roman cardinal, based ultimately on the Bahira legend) and there was a persistent nasty story of the Prophet's death. None of this was intended seriously to establish fact but just to amuse, although it remained consistent with the main stream of polemic. This developed along the lines of the ninth-century material. The Quran is seen with no effort at sympathetic understanding, as disorderly and confused, contrived to meet the needs of passing, and usually discreditable, circumstances; Islam is seen as war-like and self-indulgent (especially in sexual matters) from its inception (*bellicosus* and *luxuriosus*). This is the all but unchanging pattern of polemic which has even survived into this century among certain groups.

Yet in the twelfth century we come to the first signs of incipient "orientalism". By that I mean serious study of Muslim religion and culture for whatever purpose; in this case, in order to reinforce the polemic by greater verisimilitude. The Jewish convert, Peter of Alfonso, belongs to a different tradition; true Orientalism begins with Peter the Venerable, Abbot of Cluny, whose work is much misquoted. The Cluniac corpus of translations of Arabic religious books is the product of more minds than we can with certainty identify; they cover a range of personal attitudes, the Abbot's own being the most original, but all the product of the Spanish Reconquest. This is of the greatest cultural importance: the renewed study of Islam and the translations of Arab learning were both the consequence of Christian victory; Christians were apparently not interested in Islam, nor even in the Greek and other sources to which Arabic gave them access, nor in Muslim thinkers, until they were masters of the scene by right of conquest. They then translated whatever they judged useful to them. The former cultural resentment of a church and people subject to alien rule no longer governed them, and yet evidently survived.

Peter's summary of the whole heresy of the Saracens, though addressed to St. Bernard, is, as Kritzeck has suggested, doubtless meant for general information and based on wider sources than the body of new translations.[3] It attempts to place Islam among the heresies, though Peter rather doubtfully classifies Muslims as pagans, or, what is more, ethnics; here this can hardly mean "idolaters", but more vaguely "Gentiles", at the time not a familiar usage in this context, or easily expressed in customary language. He is moving beyond the traditional Greek concept of foreigner as "barbarian"; this incipient Orientalism is a stage on the road to the comparative study of cultures, in which even today a sense of superiority survives on the side of the student. Peter sticks to the doctrines of Islam as "heresy". In the "summary" he maintains the traditional abusive language ("execrable books"). He does not suppress aspects of Islam favorable to Christianity, but his intention seems less charitable than in his own longer book *Against the Saracen Sect*, although it, too, faces two ways. There is no evidence of a serious attempt to put it into Arabic, yet it is addressed, earnestly and surely sincerely, to a Saracen audience as a "just and reasonable disputation". The refusal of Muslim societies to permit dispute arouses his indignation to the length of language rivaling that of Alvarus, but he does not find the evidence for it in experience of Islamic practice. He bases it on the Quran "do not dispute with those who have the law" (29:46), an injunction made sinister only by the addition of a misquotation, "killing is better than argument" (which he did not find in his own commissioned paraphrase of the Quran by Ketton, here innocuous; he was misled by another source). He is scholarly in his preference for written sources, which he obtained at great cost for the sake of their authenticity, but, like many scholars, he was carried away by a favorite thesis. Yet there is unmistakably a new note in his approach, conscious of the cultural differences between himself and those he is addressing. "You may well be surprised, and probably you are, that a man in a place so far off, with a different language, divided from you by my occupation, strange to you in ways of life, should write from the further most West to men of the South and East, and address those whom I have never seen and probably never shall see". This is the first conscious expression of cultural difference by an Orientalist.

His advisers chose some very unrepresentative works to inform the West about Islam, and the Quran was a paraphrase because the translator, Ketton, admitted that it did not interest him, and because of his helpers, he understood it very badly. Most damaging to any fair assessment of Islam and the Prophet was the translation of the *Risālah*[4] of the Christian using the pseudonym al-Kindī, which seemingly authenticated with historical fact the distorted picture of the Prophet which was as old as the ninth century and would long dominate the Christian evaluation of Islam. It is an advance in authenticity and a perversion in interpretation. Cultural intolerance is also very apparent in the notes contributed by the Abbot's assistant, Peter of Poitiers, to the preparation of the polemic. He was influenced by Christian folklore current in Islamic Spain; he insists, for example, on the often alleged *res sodomitica* (with the wife), giving, as authority for its being generally practiced, two Christians who had no means of telling. And yet even this implies that he realized that practice is not the same as casuist jurisprudence might suppose. His indignant denunciation reveals the emotional violence which cultural unfamiliarity adds to religious disapproval.

Perhaps most revealing are the anonymous marginal notes to the Quran, which must be the work of at least two people, probably more. The account of the names of God is unusual and well-informed; other comments exhibit the same carelessness or ignorance as the translation itself.[5] This translates *ajamī* as *Latinus*; thus, in *Sūrah* 16, the "Bee", where the text states that those who say that the Prophet is a forger are refuted by its "perspicuous Arabic tongue" (Sale), Ketton's version has "And we know too that now they are going to say that a man teaches you in the Latin tongue, and the Quran is Arabic". The note accepts this loss of the real point and the intrusion of a Latin Teacher: "He says this...because Latins are the purest and truest (sic) Christians, and so he calls them the most untruthful, and abominates them...". All this was flattering to the West, to which the Quran does not refer at all! Another kind of cultural intrusion is the annotator's irritation at every story of an a Biblical figure that does not tally with Christian Scripture: "how very absurd" (*quanta fabulositas*!), or "or a very stupid fable about Moses". Again, this is as much instinctive rejection of the unfamiliar as studious correction by a

Biblical standard. Sometimes the note corrects the text, but not where it is most tendentious; in *Sūrah* 3, "Family of Imrān", where it omits mention of Torah and Gospel, and, very minor, to correct "God" to "in the name of God...". Some notes are general and abusive, *Vana, stulta et impia*. There is the usual emphasis on pugnacity and lubricity, and the Selden MS has a later medieval marginal hand with finger extended to indicate the *res sodomitica* where the note says "a most shameful precept" (it is the translation which makes it so, and, as Bibliander's commentary says, it is "twisted by force by our people as if it allowed something abominable"). The fuss and violence of language marks the cultural shock. That Christians should be thought to believe in three gods is, more understandably, called "an astonishing folly" but similar are only called "the usual follies". There is a certain lack of balance in the degree of outrage expressed at different subjects. The denial of sonship of Christ in *Sūra*h 19, "Maryām", gets a less irritable comment than the *fabula stultissima de Moyse* two leaves earlier in the manuscript, as though bad history were worse than bad doctrine. The Cluniac corpus is marred by abuse, extravagance and irrelevance and by poor and prejudiced selection of material, but there was now more information, even if distorted, in circulation. There was still no understanding how far there was to go, but a scholarly interest in Islam had now been aroused.

The reconquest of Spain progressively uncovered an alien system of life and thought which evoked from some an excessive revulsion but from the contemporary general public, amusement or scandal at a frivolous level. I mentioned absurd legends earlier; they were retailed at the level of gossip or, at best, of journalism. In a different class were the *chansons de geste*,[6] with the imaginary system of Saracen idolatry in which they could extract a good deal of fun. Of course, their joke was in the worst possible taste, but at the opposite pole to that of the theologians, whose opinions are in no way reflected in the poems. The poets showed every sign of liking and admiring the Saracens (by which they probably did not mean only *Arabs*). It was people who disliked Islam who had a genuine interest in it.

In the meantime the twelfth and earlier thirteenth centuries saw the bulk of translations of Arabic philosophy and science.[7] It would be anachronistic to suppose that an interest in such Arabic sources modified the idea of Islam or of the Muslims in the same way as the reception of western technology affected modern Muslim thinkers. The medievals were more obstinate and less sensitive. They hardly seem to have thought of their Arabic sources as the product of Islamic civilization at all, or to have related the Muslim philosophers to the Muslim world with which they fought and traded. Ketton, an enthusiastic admirer of Arabic science, despised religious texts. Ibn Sīnā is found quoted widely and with approval, sometimes specifically against the Quranic paradise, as the Christians understood it. Of course, he was known to be Muslim, but this was acknowledged only on a religious theme that made it unavoidable to do so. On the other hand, one account of doubtful origin dismissed him, incredibly, as a mere translator of Isidore into Arabic. In a history of philosophy, Roger Bacon could happily coordinate the Greek philosophers and the Jewish prophets. But he does not date the Muslim philosophers except as later than Muhammad (also undated), and they seem to float in a cultural vacuum. Aquinas corrects Averroistic philosophy in a *contra gentes* or gentiles, not a *contra Saracenos*. The translators were Orientalists only in the sense that they were Arabists (usually needing Arab help to work); their interest was in scientific subject matter, not language; nor were they Orientalists in the sense that the theologians who cared about Islamic teaching were. The impact of philosophy and science was disassociated entirely from that of Islam.

The first interesting writer on Islam to follow the Cluniacs was over half a century later, Mark of Toledo, discussed and in part published by M. T. d'Alverny. We might imagine that he translated the *laudes* of the unity of God from Ibn Tūmart in order that the Almohad invaders of Spain should be better understood. The greatest of his translations is the Quran, which is much better than Ketton's, but the manuscripts of the latter are still spread widely over Europe while Mark's survives in only a few. Yet his scholarship did not go with sympathy, and his preface to his Quran is as abusive and intolerant as anything in the Cluniac corpus. The anti-Quranic tirade was becoming a convention of its own. Yet improved translation implies better understanding, and Mark had taken a further step towards academic interest in authentic Islam. I want to note what Thomas Aquinas said, not about Islam, but about the methodology of polemic. Speaking of reasoned argument based on authorities acceptable only to Christians, he said that where there is no common authority with an opponent, it is otiose to do more than defend the reasonableness of one's own faith.[8] If this advice had been followed, the course of polemic would have had a very different history without the mainspring of polemic which sustained interest in the field until modern times. Perhaps only one of the thirteenth century writers I am going to mention would have passed this test.

The most like a modern Orientalist is at first glance the author of the *quadruplex reprobatio* (fourfold disproof, a neat order that is sometimes reversed). The writer's Arabic reading, or at least his access to Arabic sources, is wide: he knows two great traditionists (al-Bukhārī and Muslim) and the *Sīrāt Rasūl Allāh* of Ibn Ishāq. This material is made to serve only the usual polemic points, but emphasizing the antisocial legislation of *fiqh*, as the writer puts it (e.g. "against the good of the Commonwealth"). This, as usual, is attributed to the personal proclivities of the Prophet. This author really has gone to the best sources, but he, or someone on his behalf, has gone through them with a fine tooth-comb to find examples of what he intended to reprobate before he began. This meant passing over a mass of material which he did not need, and as he does not refer to it, evidently did not disapprove. This is one of the clearest cases of a painstaking care for authenticity still linked exclusively to the polemic aim. The same may be said of St. Peter Paschasius, who recounted both what he calls the "Christian" version of the life of the Prophet ("ours") and wholly authentic information, from the *Sīra* especially. He draws attention to the remotest similarity to the most absurd and irresponsible legend, so that Christian distortion of Islamic history becomes Muslim distortion of Christian knowledge, another perversion of a scholarly instinct.

Riccoldo da Monte Croce is another knowledgeable polemist.[9] His long *antialcoran* or *Libellus contra sectam serraconorum* is the most ambitious work of its kind of the age and it long influenced other writers who borrowed his material, and many later writers borrowed it from him. His sources are written material from Spain, as in the other cases, but his attributions are less precise. Strangely he claimed in his *Liber peregrinationis*, and the internal evidence confirms, that he journeyed to Baghdad, but it is impossible that he had discussions with the *‹ulamā*', as he also claims. In this account of a journey he also summarizes his polemical position in terms no different from those of his longer work; but he could not have used the material we know him by to a Muslim audience (and gotten away alive), or only by modifying both matter and manner beyond recognition. It would not have stood up to Muslim criticism for a moment. What did he talk about so amicably with the learned? He stresses their courtesy. There is a mystery here still unsolved. One example, not particularly outrageous, but of a niggling attitude, is Riccoldo's treatment of the customary blessing on the Prophet, taken from *Sūrah* 33, "The Confederates", "God...'blesses' the Prophet". Taking the verb in the sense most often used ("prays" for), he makes a theological absurdity out of a minor linguistic puzzle. Where Paschasius tried to show that any Christian authority was better than any Muslim one, Riccoldo seems to think that any written authority is better than an exchange of opinion. They seem blind to their own ill will.

William of Tripoli is most exceptional in his approach to the content of the Quran and to the Prophet, although in his own way he misrepresents both.[10] He wants to show that Muslims are ripe for mass conversion to Christianity, and that the Christian influence on the Prophet was dominant. He quotes almost every praise of Jesus and his mother from the Quran and he stresses the legend of Bahira; of the use of force by the Prophet, he says that it was only when "the brake was released" by the death of his Christian mentor. He is nearly free of the usual abusive style. His sources are vague. He speaks of the *‹ulamā', dicunt Sarracenorum sapientes*. He summarizes Islamic doctrine in sexual practice (polygamy, divorce) and refers to the sensual paradise which had scandalized so many generations of Christians, but adds that Muslims justly despise this teaching of Muhammad "if indeed it is really his (si tantum eius est)". He refers vaguely to the Hadīth that over seventy sects of Islam will fail. To summarize: he retains but plays down the customary polemic lines; his information is good, although his sources are not clear; his purpose is to show how near Muslims are to Christianity. How he could expect the conversion of Muslims when he is writing just before the final collapse of the last vestiges of Latin states in the East we cannot explain; as in Riccoldo's case, the historical circumstances are obscure. There is every possibility that he actually talked to Muslims, all the usual courter-indications are absent. The situation he projects is weird; he is sympathetic, but too sanguine - he has "baptized over a thousand"; unacademic, he seeks a new kind of "objectivity". He had little direct influence (except on Mandevelle), but foreshadows the freer approach of the future.

There is much evidence for a more open attitude to people neither Muslim nor Christian in the thirteenth century, often with a hope of conversion or alliance but still a spontaneous quasi-anthropological interest in the Tatars specially. It is found in travelers like Rubrick, or indeed Riccoldo, it is analyzed by Bacon, and repeated by Vincent de Beauvais in his *Speculum Historiale*.[11] That this happened rarely in the case of the Arabs is a back-handed compliment to the power of Islam as a system of thought, but even here there was some softening, as witness the open-minded approach of Joinville. The theory of crusade was resisted, defended anew and revised: ultimately the papacy developed a business in license to trade *in dispendium Terrae Sanctae* (which included Egypt). Spanish conquerors accepted surrender on terms that in the long run the Church would not accept. Histories among the translations under the patronage of Alfonso the Learned have sound Arabic sources and there is a sensible diminution of virulence. But these were vernacular and the culture of international scholarship long remained Latin. The mercantile city states and Catalonia incurred automatic excommunication if they traded beyond the authorized system, and so of course did individual sailors and ships masters who took service with the Arab rulers. The *romans d'aventur* and the poetic convention surviving from the *chansons de geste*, untouched by theological "orientalism", remained favorable to a noble enemy, but the contrary convention of professional polemic was even more persistent, articulate, and, above all, academic.

It was largely, but not completely, untouched by developments in the world. Raymond Lull, eccentric and individualist, tried to find common ground on which to meet Muslim theology about the Trinity but his philosophy was too idiosyncratic to make a real impact even in Christendom.[12] He was a true Arabist, for the sake of his own kind of polemic. He spent nine years learning Arabic from an Arab slave bought for the purpose: then, as he tells the story, he heard that, while he was out of the house, the Arab had blasphemed Christ; under what provocation, in what circumstances, or what it amount to, we are not told - perhaps it was the denial of the divinity of Christ we should expect from a Muslim; but on this hearsay Lull struck him "on the mouth, and the forehead and face". The Arab attacked him with a knife and was locked up. Lull was frightened to release him, but his perplexity was resolved when he found that his prisoner had cut his own throat. God, he says, had answered his prayers. Lull had more zeal for Muslim souls in the mass; his several attempts at proselytism in North Africa embarrassed the Muslim authorities, and he finally exasperated a crowd who gave him a sort of martyrdom in his eighties as he had long sought. Most medieval polemic was not used in debate, at any rate not in a Muslim country; Lull's was actual proselytism, but he does seem to have used his Arabic to acquire some knowledge of Islamic thought.

Much purely traditional polemic was written in the fifteenth century; for example, by Denis the Carthusian (van Leeuwen) whose work is based entirely on his predecessors, but he was a voluminous author for whom Islamic error was only one subject among many more important to him. The most remarkable man of the century was Nicolas of Cusa, friend of

Pius II (who himself wrote briefly against Islam) and in touch with John of Segovia, a translator and polemicist whose trilingual Quran is lost.[13] I cannot myself see that Cusa's polemic *Cribratio Alchoran* adds seriously to what his predecessors had said; he uses Ketton's Quran, as no serious Arabist would do. Even his quotations are inaccurate, so that often he is paraphrasing a paraphrase. In contrast, his remarkable *De pace fidei* is a short attempt to universalize religion within the framework of Christian belief. It is odd to find him trying to persuade one of his interlocutors, the Arab, that polytheism logically implies the recognition that a single divinity is shared by all the gods. Nicholas' intentions are the best, and he is a real ecumenist, but he is not an Arabist, and he is not interested to find out more about Islam. The concept of a world reconciliation of religions occurs again in the *Heptaplomeres* of Bodin,[14] a much longer dialogue than the *De pace*; Islam is more realistically represented by a European convert. The early attempts to conceive one world are a religious and intellectual exercise not based on linguistic or historical scholarship, and the authors do not understand a number of individual points. From the fourteenth century onwards travelers show a greater practical knowledge, but they rarely increase the sum of theoretical knowledge.

The late Middle Ages, the Reformation and Counter-Reformation and even the seventeenth century saw a spread in the study of Arabic, an increase in the establishment of new schools and the foundation of University Chairs. In the sixteenth century especially, Ottoman pressure was felt continuously, and in the high age of polemic between Catholic and Protestant this was curiously combined with the traditional polemic against Islam; each side accused the other of being Turkish in its religion. This obviously did nothing to favor academic detachment. The extension of travel and trade, of war and diplomacy, made the Ottoman countries relatively familiar. Arabic was linked with Biblical study and with Hebrew. The career of the elder Pococke illustrates the three-way interest. He was chaplain at the English factory at Aleppo in the 1630's, traveled and acquired manuscripts; he was given the Laudian Chair but succeeded with the failure of the King to the Chair of Hebrew. It is an anachronism to see the purchase of manuscripts in the Ottoman Empire as plundering the national treasures of people who had no statehood. A political function in Europe too might be combined with Oriental scholarship, as in the case of the dynasty of Petis de la Croix, *interprètes du roi*, in the later part of the century. There was a new tendency to translate curiosities (such as a brief argument that milk in coffee induces leprosy). There is a frivolity which may be seen as transitional to a later development, but the combination of traditional polemic with sound linguistic scholarship cannot be seen as different in kind from what we have reviewed in the Middle Ages. A case in point, and a very serious one, is the translation of the Quran by Ludovici Marracci,[15] certainly the best ever made into Latin; the commentary omits nothing of the old polemic that was compatible with fact. But by this time few scholars would dare to argue ancient themes without the support of the best contemporary study of language.

The real mutation occurs early in the eighteenth century, and it is with these early moderns that we pass out of the old conventions. This period is also, as it happens, the period when the Ottomans ceased to be a danger to Europe. This certainly favored thc ncw ideas which are not, however, apparently related to the Enlightenment if that is strictly defined. Voltaire, for example, used Islam only as another weapon *pour écraser l'infame*; the old anti-Islamic conventions suited his critique of all religion very well. More representative of the new age are Simon Ockley's *History of the Saracens*[16] and Gibbon's account of the rise of Islam. Ockley attempted to be detached, and certainly thought of himself as free from polemic intent, and yet the sum of a reader's impressions is not so very different from that which already prevailed. He is like Voltaire in that what he says about Islam blends perfectly with his idea of the development of Christianity, but he is of course infinitely more careful to be exact, and he uses all the Arabic sources that then existed in translation. These writers are biased against Islam, but their bias is integral to their general bias. They clearly believe that they have surveyed their sources fully and used them fairly.

They owed everything to the translators of previous generations, including the defects in their sources, which were not always the best choice. They owed even more to the beginnings of true Orientalism in the early years of the century, when writers began to correct errors because they were wrong and without ulterior motive; and to see that they were wrong, unless they used Muslim criteria to interpret Muslim information. The most striking is Adrian Reeland, who *De Religione Mohammedica* (1705, English translation in 1712)[17] is devoted to correcting many of the false notions about Islam which had circulated or still did so. The example I gave of Riccoldo's methods is an example of the corrections made by Reeland. Here is his express view: "If ever any religion was perverted by adversaries, it was this religion". Naturally he dismissed Ketton's Quran as the "worst of translations". Of the polemists in general he says: "These writers seem to me to have employed their wit and parts, not against true enemies, but fictitious ones, where they were sure of victory, since nobody was to defend them". It is difficult not to regard Reeland's book as the real turning point in the European image of Islam.

We have seen that the traditional polemic arose in a subject people in a framework of cultural resentment. We have seen that when the search for authentic information became important, and the treatment of source material more sophisticated, the old resentment of an alien culture appeared to survive almost unaffected. All that was alien in ways of life, language, literature, inherited assumptions, magnified the religious difference between the cultures, and the religious difference was the sole motive for serious study. It was this that changed. It may be that when there was no longer an Ottoman military threat, and European colonial aggression was already beginning, scholars felt detached from the old cultural rivalry. They no longer hated the Islamic world - it interested and amused them. This was a general attitude; the exotic qualities of *The Thousand and One Nights* gave it its attraction at the time. Scholars were not unprejudiced, but their prejudice was centered in a sense of superiority that enjoyed the cultural difference. They would afford to be as scrupulously accurate as the techniques of the day allowed. The new aims and techniques of historiography were in fact an expression of cultural change. The old polemic did survive - Pfander and Muir are nineteenth century examples[18] - but this was now motivated simply by Muslim resistance to conversion (in spite of the increasing political power of Europe).

I want finally to take the examples of two eighteenth-century translators of the Quran to illustrate the change. George Sale (1734),[19] though much indebted to Marracci in linguistic scholarship, made a great advance towards the elusive aim of objectivity. It is fair to say that he made a bit of a parade of it. His work is still valuable, and for the western reader of Arabic in translation, irreplaceable. He renders the long accepted sense of the Quran without reinterpretation, and makes useful extracts from traditional commentators like al-Zamakhsharī easily accessible. This may help the modern reader where some modern Islamic explanations only confuse him. In the historical and analytical *Preliminary Discourse* modern Muslims see anti-Islamic prejudice, but this is in comparison with their understanding of their own religion and cultural achievements. If we compare what he says with what prevailed before, we see how much prejudice he discarded. Whereas Gibbon frankly liked to insinuate mischief to vex the orthodox into his most considered statements, Sale hoped to be seen to be always sober, judicial and detached.

He drops the ancient jeer at the style and arrangement of the Quran; it is "universally allowed to be written with the utmost elegance and purity of language". ("Allowed" by whom? By the Arabic-speaking public, whose opinion it had not been customary to ask!) The old idea that revelations were contrived, however, survives: "Whenever anything happened which perplexed or graveled Muhammad...he had constant recourse to a new revelation". In this the new age shared an essential judgment with preceding ages. It is "beyond dispute" that Muhammad was "really the author", but Muslims "absolutely deny" that it "was composed by their prophet or anyone else...it is of divine original...eternal and uncreated". Sale's account of the Quranic Paradise would in itself satisfy the most outraged medieval critic, who, whoever, would note the absence of an explicit condemnation of it. In the manner of the time, this was left more effectively to the reader. Sale compares "sensible" images used in the Bible, and for sexual images he supposes the influence of the "indecency of the Magians". No Muslim could ever accept Sale's account of the Prophet and could only be scandalized by the discussion of the authorship of the Quran, yet all major misrepresentation of historical events has disappeared. However we judge the achievement, the advance is enormous in that objectivity is now openly the aim.

For a last look at this "mutation" we should briefly consider Savary, a younger contemporary of Sale's who lived to be much older; he published interesting but not always accurate travels in Egypt which were read by Napoleon. His version of the Quran he denominates in the manner of his time the "code des préceptes et des lois de Mahomet"[20] - and yet Ketton's annotator had said, long before, "collectio preceptorum". Intellectuals in Savary's time - and he was an outstanding example - like to praise the Prophet as a great statesman, while unable to do so for his holiness, which was excluded from consideration by the assumptions of the time as much as it had been by the different assumptions of the Middle Ages. "Les Sages d'entre les Orientaux qui, s'élevant au dessus de la faible vue de la vulgaire, lui refusent avec raison le titre de prophète, le regardent comme un des plus grands hommes qui aient existé". These "sages", of course, did not exist, they were invented to speak for the author; but he was an admirer of Sale's *Preliminary Discourse* (in French translation) and he himself was determined to tell the life of the Prophet entirely from Islamic sources. It is significant that he should have invented Muslim authority for his own European opinion. Sale, Gibbon, Savary and their forerunners turned decisively against polemic as their objective, in favor of dispassionate detachment. That their own achievement in the matter was often mediocre, and was much influenced by prevailing intellectual opinion, does not affect their originality in changing the direction of Islamic Studies. Subsequently, these would develop, the new deal of objectivity itself subjectively defined, added to older ones of authenticity.

Perhaps we cannot be objective, but we can achieve something. It is impossible for anyone to assess his own objectivity with confidence, but we approach the objective ideal, in so far as we attempt it. We can establish facts with some probability, although we can judge them only in terms of our day and our own traditions. The presuppositions on which all methods depend are determined by our cultures, and in particular these govern our choice of which facts to study. No one in the periods I have discussed chose to study Islam sympathetically and for its own sake, or wanted to find anything out about the Islamic recognition of holiness in their Prophet. Various barriers made the question impossible to pose. A man must speak Arabic extremely well, he must perhaps be a native speaker, to experience anything like the full force of the Quran. Here the medievals certainly failed, if they can be said to have tried at all; and yet they were serious enough about the need for a translation. The theory of religious war was not the barrier that canonists tried to make it, partly because people evaded it in practice. The experience of war is always a barrier to the sufferers, but there were many who gained from it. The curious notion that Christianity was more peaceable than Islam faded with Christian victory. Sexual moral theory generally arouses strong feelings, and the modern West rejects the theoretical strictness of Islam, where the medievals blamed its theoretic laxity; they were looking at the same object with different eyes. Yet neither can we write of Muslims or of Arabs to their satisfaction, without accepting their assumptions and writing entirely from their point of view; and if we did so, objectivity would again elude us.

And at no time over the centuries that I have so hurriedly reviewed was Islam anything but unfamiliar and alien in ways of life. In fact it is difficult to describe the image formed by the medievals without condemning it on our own cultural principles. Difficult as it is to judge motives, their polemic motive is beyond doubt. They never express a conscious aim to achieve objectivity as distinct from authenticity. Starting from the promise that the Quran was not a true revelation, they dug hard to find evidence to prove it, and this entailed the selection of convenient fragments from the best evidence they could find. Nearly all modern Orientalists start from the same premise, for different reasons, and how far we are blinded in our own cultural limitations only our successors will be able to see. The polemic that gave medieval writers the motivation to look for valid evidence also blinded them in its interpretation. It does give peculiar value to their rare praise of Islam. Every society provides its own motivation, and at the same time limits its own vision. Was the motivation of the eighteenth-century writers a love of objectivity for its own sake, or was it the product of mercantile imperial expansion, or of an incipient revolutionary situation? For us now, it does not matter. When some eighteenth-century writers change the conscious motivation by rejecting polemic, they substituted at best a patronizing and specifically skeptical approach, and neither of these is in fact objective. Nevertheless, these later writers inaugurated modern scholarship just by claiming to establish facts for their own sake, and in making us think that we should be interested only in that, however we measure their actual achievement. We may measure it best by the sympathy and respect they gave their subject; the medievals showed more of the latter, and the early moderns more of the former, but it was when they approached these qualities that both were at their best.

Notes

1. Eulogius, *Liber Apologeticus Martyrum*, Migne, *patrologia Latina 115*, col. 359-60; Alvarus Cordubensis, *patrologia Latina 115*, *5. Eulogii Vita vel passione*, col. 708 and Eulogius, ibid., *Memoriale Sanctorum*, col. 745; Alvarus, *Indiculus Luminosus, patrologia Latina* 121, col. 540 and Eulogius, *Liber Apologeticus* col. 861.
2. Alvarus, *Indiculus*, col. 538, Ezechiel 23.20, Jeremiah 5.8; *Indiculus* 542, cf. 555-6; 539-40, Daniel 11.38. Further bibliography of legends of the Prophet in the West in N. Daniel, *Islam and the West* p.343 and *Arabs and*

Medieval Europe, p. 350.

3. Pedro de Alforso, *patrologia Latina* 157, *Dialogi in quibus impiae Judaeorum confutantur* V col. 597ff. Peter "the Venerable" of Cluny, *Summa Totius Maeresis* and Liber contra Sectam Saracenorum in J. Kritzeck, *Peter the Venerable and Islam*, Princeton, Princeton University Press, 1964, from the master manuscript in the Bibliotheque de l'Arsenal; uncritical editions in Migne, *patrologia Latina* 189 col. 651ff and in Bibliander, *Machumetis Saracenorum principis, eiusque successorum vitae,doctrina ac ipse Alcoran*, Basle, 1150 (*summa* only).
4. *Risālah*, text abbreviated in Bibliander, *loc. cit.*, and in full in manuscripts based on the Arsenal manuscript 1162, e.g., Bodley ccc. d. 184 and Selden Supra 31. *Capitula petri pictaviensis* in *patrologia Latina* 189. col. 663.
5. Ketton, text with annotations in MSS cited above; also in Bibliander, *loc. cit.*, with some annotations from a different manuscript tradition.
6. For a reinterpretation of the attitude to Islam in the *chansons*, see my *Heroes and Saracens*, Edinburgh, 1984; I have repudiated views expressed in some earlier publications.
7. Bacon, *Opus Majus*, ed. J. H. Bridges, Oxford, 1897, pars secunda bol. 3 pp. 54-5, 64, 66; see also *Moralis philsophia*, ed. F. Delorme and E. Massa, Zurich, 1953. Mark of Toledo, parts in M. th. d'Alverny, with G. Vajda, "Marc de Tolede" in *Al-Andalus*,vol. 16 (1&2) and 17 (1), 1951-2. Full text in MS e.g., Vienna, Austrian National Bibliothek cod. 4297.
8. Aquinas, *De Rationibus Fidei ad Cantorem Antiochenum* in *Opuscula Varia, Opera Omnia*, 27, Paris, 1872-88. *Reprobatio*, MSS e.g., Cambridge Dd.1.17 and Bib. nationale lat. 4230; printed as *malensis de origine et progressu...machometis*, by W. Dreschler, Strausburg, 1550; new edition in progress by J. Wernando I Delgado, cf. *Islam et chretiens du Midi* Toulouse and Fanjeaux, 1983, p. 351ff Paschasius, *Obras, sabre el sera mahumetana*, ed. P. Armeugol Valenzuela, Rome, 1903-8.
9. The discovery of MSS corrected by the author himself now demonstrates that the correct form of his name is Riccoldo da Monte di Croce, and that of his works here cited, *libellus contra sectam Sarracenorum* (text in J-M. Merigoux, "L'Ouvrage d'un Frere Precheur" in *Memorie Domenicaneuf*, nuova serie 17, pistoia, 1986) and *liber peregrinationis* (printed from a poor manuscript as Itinerarius by J.C.M. Laurent in *peregrinatores Medii Aevi Quatuor*, Leipzig, 1864; corrected MS in Berlin Staatsbibliothek lat. 4. 446; see *Memorie Domenicane*, *loc. cit.*, E. Panella, presentazione).

10. William of Tripoli: *de Statu Saracenorum*, printed by H. Prutz in *Kultugeschichte der Kreuzzuge*, Berlin, 1883.
11. Beauvais: *Speculum Historiale* in *Biblioteca Mundi*, Douai, 1629, vol. V.
12. Lull: *Vida Coetania* tr. E. A. Peers London 1927; Raymundi Lulli *Opera Omnia*, ed. I. Salzinger, Maniz, 1721ff; *Liber de fine* in A. Gotron, *Ramon Lulls Kreuzzugsideen*, Berlin and Leipzig, 1912; and see B. Kedar, *Crusade and Mission*, Princeton, 1984, pp. 189-99.
13. Cusa, *Cribratio* in Bibliander, op. cit., and *De pace*, ed. R. Klibansky and N. Bascour, London, 1956. Pius II, *Epistola ad Morbisanum*. in Bibliander, op. cit.
14. Jean Bodin: *Colloquium Heptaplomeres*, Schwerin, 1857.
15. L. Marracci (or Maracci) *Alcoran Textus Universus* and *prodromus*, Padua, 1698.
16. Simon Ockley, *History of the Saracens*, London, 1708-9.
17. Adriani Relandi *De Religione Mohammediea*, Utrecht, 1705; 2nd edition, 1717. *Reland on the Mohammedan Religion*, London, 1712.
18. C. G. Pfander, *Remarks on the Nature of Muhammadanism*, Calcutta, 1840. Sir William Muir, *The Mohammedan Controversy*, Edinburgh, 1897, and other works, including a life of the Prophet.
19. George Sale, *The Koran*, London, 1734, and many reprints.
20. M. Savary, *Le Coran, traduit de l'Arabe accompagne de Notes, et precédé d'un Abrege de la Vie de Mahomet*, Paris, 1783. *Moral de Mahomet*, Paris, 1784.

Muhsin Mahdi

The Study of Islam, Orientalism and America

This essay addresses three issues in particular. First, I ask what it means when an institution is established in Great Britain to engage in a new, and in some ways unique, attempt to study and teach things Islamic by Muslims for Muslims, but together and in cooperation with non-Muslims scholars and students. Second, I will recall briefly my own experience of Oriental Studies, dealing with Islamic civilization in general and Islamic philosophy in particular. I shall refer mainly to my experience in the United States, but to some extent in Europe. Readers will, I hope excuse the somewhat autobiographical and anecdotal quality of my account: I have commented on some of the questions raised here on a number of earlier occasions.[1] I would like then to conclude by considering the character of what is nowadays seen as the crisis of Orientalism and of Islamic Studies.

Although contact between Muslim and non-Muslim students of Islam in the West has a long history, the establishment of Muslim institutions of higher learning in the West is a new phenomenon. It is in part related to the migration of relatively large Muslim communities to Europe and the Americas, and the interest of these communities in the religious and secular education of their children. Many European and American institutions of higher learning were established earlier for the same purpose. Like their counterparts in the West in earlier times, these new institutions are meant to be open to the entire scholarly community. The student body and faculty are meant to be mixed, and the Muslim faculty and students will no doubt be eager to learn from and understand what non-Muslims have been saying and writing about Islam on scholarly and popular levels. What kind of intellectual challenge does this kind of institution present both to its Muslim and non-Muslim students and faculty? One can assume that, sooner or later, like other non-Western communities before them, the Muslims established in the West will produce their own intellectual élite who will come to call themselves, and take pride in being, Westerners. What will that mean for the current notion, held by many Muslims and non-Muslims alike, that Islam is an Eastern religion, that a Muslim is not a Westerner, or that there is an unbridgeable barrier between being a Muslim and being a Westerner?

Certainly, the historical-theological problem is not likely to be resolved by the slow process of acculturation or Westernization of many millions of Muslims. To be a Muslim, to be a Christian, to be a Jew, means to develop a sense of identity, a religious and cultural or subcultural identity. Each of the religious communities places its origin at a particular point in history in relation to the others and thereby considers itself not merely different, but in some way superior to them. Each one sees itself as more human, more civilized, more advanced, than the others, and is led sometimes to think that it has the right, or that it is under an obligation, to rule them, civilize them, and improve their lot. The root of this view is the religious community's conception of its place in history and the way it interprets what took place before, after, and outside the moment in history to which it owes its origin. If we think for a moment about what it is to be a Jew, Christian, or Muslim, it is not difficult to see that, if it means anything, it means the belief that one's religious community has reached a stage beyond the others and is closer to the Lord, and that the others are somehow arrested or have remained behind, regardless of their place in secular historical time.

Each of the three religious communities claims the same privilege, and their claims are incompatible. This has been at the root of the theological controversies and religious wars and persecutions in medieval times as well as much of the controversies that assume a secular, scientific or scholarly garb in modern times. You may wish to disagree or wish that this were not the case, but I do not see how one can escape the conclusion that all this is inseparable from being a Jew, Christian, or Muslim. One can engage in a dialogue and continue to discuss what all this means, one needs to have friendly relations, and one can emphasize and develop the tradition of tolerance in one's own religious community. Yet it remains in the main an insoluble problem.

This theological-historical problem was secularized by German Romanticism in the late eighteenth and during the nineteenth century in a manner that sidestepped the original historical and theological controversies. German Romanticism began with the notion that there was something fundamentally wrong with the excesses of scientism or rationalism or philosophy in the modern West and that it was necessary to supplement it with the poetic, religious, and spiritual dimensions of human life, which can be found in the East. The West was incomplete and needed to complete itself with what it has somehow lost during its recent development. It needed to unify the shattered pieces of human experience; and the way to achieve this unity was to learn about it from the East where it continued to exist and where the missing part - the poetic - had survived. This view of the East proved to be paradoxical. On the one hand, one wanted to recover unity from the East. But one soon found that what may have been there in the distant past in a perfect form, was now incomplete too; it lacked the scientific, rational, or philosophic aspect. And when one happened to come across the remnants of the original unity, it turned out to be an arrested or degenerate form of unity: one had to reconstruct the original form and infuse new life into it.

German Romanticism began with the longing for archaic unity which led to a yearning for the Middle Ages and the East. It ushered in a new conception of history that replaced old-fashioned religious beliefs and the faith of the Enlightenment with a desire to unify the shattered pieces of man's experience of nature and human life through a new synthesis that reintegrates the incomplete past into the incomplete present. Medievalism and Orientalism were meant to recover the golden past of humanity, that global counterpart of the present, the West of the Enlightenment as it existed in the late eighteenth century, the West of rationalism and the discovery and the conquest of nature.

If there ever was an idea that was not intentionally political, or at least whose intention was neither massively nor directly political, and was self-centered rather than directed to the domination of others, that was the image of the East in early German Romanticism. In order to integrate the shattered pieces of human experience into a new wholeness in the West itself, one needed to learn about wholeness as it existed initially in the remote past in the West as well as in the East. This explains the interest in past, completed, and closed cultural epochs. Living Easterners and Eastern societies were of interest only to the extent that they exhibited remnants of the Romantics' ideal past; as contemporary men and societies, they came to be seen as at best arrested and at worst degenerate societies. One cannot begin to understand the characteristic features of Oriental Studies throughout the nineteenth and the first half of the twentieth century without an appreciation of the impetus that drove many of the most intelligent and learned men of their time to search for a new human ideal and long for a full understanding of their place in history and their privileged position among the rest of the human race. They were looking for Easterners and Eastern societies that had not been contaminated with rationalism or science or philosophy, but gave free reign to their imagination and thought and lived poetically; Easterners and Eastern societies which, coming into contact with Greek logic and Hellenistic philosophy, remained suspicious of them, rejected and despised them and clutched to their native beliefs in the unseen and in a mysterious, fabulous cosmos, or were searching to recover or yearning to live again their ancient gnostic myths - a task in which the Orientalist was ready to lend a helping hand. When Orientalists expressed views such as these, they were not in fact speaking about what one might call the empirical subject matter of their studies; they were expressing their own hope and disappointment: the hope that such men and societies as they were looking for did in fact exist, and the disappointment in the living members of these societies. For they saw that those whom fate had given the opportunity to possess what the West was now seeking seemed to have lost it and were instead craving for what the West possessed but was not in their nature or mental makeup to possess. One may suspect that this attitude lacked a measure of rationality, but it should be remembered that the Romantics were not devotees of reason.

The counterpart of these views can now be found among modern thinkers and publicists in a number of non-Western societies who have developed what one might designate as a non-Western or Oriental Orientalism. In the Muslim world, for instance, such people have argued that Muslim society have the essentials - the spiritual, the poetic, the religious, and the right way of life - that it needs only to complete its heritage through science, technology, economic development, modernization. Thus the concept is admitted (on both sides, by non-Muslim and Muslim students of Islamic societies) that, on the one hand, there are societies based on science, technology, and rationality, and on the other, societies that have everything else, perhaps, but lack this kind of science and rationality. One can easily begin to think of a number of issues that arise from such views. Many Muslim societies over the past century or so have managed to orientalize their Orient by adopting the view that the perfect condition was in the past, and the further one recedes, the better - for instance, the view that ancient Egypt was the glorious time of Egypt. (Anyone who has been to Egypt knows of the amount of care given to ancient Egyptian antiquities and the relative neglect of Islamic antiquities.) Think of the view that, as the Islamic past was perfect, all Muslims need do now is integrate it somehow into modernity by learning the method and technology of the West, as though method and technology were what the West is all about. Or think about the role romanticization of the past played in the course of the cultural renewal of different Muslim nations, of how it fed into the nascent nationalisms and in some cases gave rise to the type of racism of which Muslims were relatively free until recent times. Finally, think of the views of an influential Muslim revivalist like Sayyid Qutb,[2] who argues that true Islam existed only at the time of the Prophet and his Companions and that all later periods and foreign influences were a reversion to the "Time of Ignorance", and then goes on to say that initially the Islamic community integrated all the foreign elements into a harmonious, dynamic, organic whole.

The Muslim community has had its own versions of romantic attachment to an idealized past and the yearning to re-live such a past. The intense interest in keeping to the form and content of pre-Islamic Arabic poetry and tribal way of life, and the yearning to reinstate the short term unity of religious and secular authority, are just two examples one could cite.[3] These romantic attachments, like German Romanticism, could perhaps be explained on psychological and sociological grounds, and a comparative study of romantic movements in different societies at different times is likely to be instructive. But, unlike German Romanticism, they did not all develop into a discipline that claimed to be a science, a rational discourse about the character and structure of all pre-modern and non-Western societies.

And it is as a subject of a modern scientific discipline that one sees Islam and Islamic civilization being reconstructed to fit the Western image of Islam. This is clear in many of the new academic institutions in the Islamic world. A large number of those now teaching in the new universities came to the West, learned what their Western teachers taught them about Islam and Islamic societies, and went back to teach it to their students, creating or intensifying the cleavage between the way traditional Muslim scholars understood and taught Islam, and what is now considered the new scientific method of studying Islam. It is clear also in the discussions among modern students of Islam in the Muslim world about their own understanding of Islam - whether their primary focus is mysticism or jurisprudence or philosophy - for in many cases these modern Muslim students of Islam argue along the same lines as their Western teachers, who had argued that Islam is essentially a legal religion or that the most important aspect of Islam is its mystical dimension. What are the implications of this intimate relationship that has developed over the past century between Western studies of Islam and studies of Islam in the Muslim world or the rise of a substantial intellectual élite in the Muslim world whose point of view or perspective cannot be distinguished from that of Western Orientalists?

The question is no longer whether one accepts or rejects Orientalist Studies dealing with Islam. They form a significant cultural phenomenon as an aspect of Western history, culture, and politics, even though their perspective is derivative and they tend to confirm rather than evaluate the commonly-received notions which they apply to Eastern societies. And they have become very much an aspect of cultural life in the Islamic world itself. If there is a problem or a difficulty, if there is a crisis or a misunderstanding, it is not one that must be faced in the West and by Western scholars of Islam alone; it is equally present in the Muslim world and must be faced by Muslim scholars of Islam. And if there is any problem with the image of Islam or with the way Islam is being interpreted, it is no longer a problem of some intentional or unintentional misunderstanding by the West alone. It could very well be a more dangerous problem than it may appear to be at first sight: it has led and could continue to lead to errors in self-understanding with serious consequences for Western and Muslim societies alike.

The creation of a Muslim institution of higher learning in the West for the study of Islam confronts Muslim and non-Muslim scholars of Islam with a set of intellectual tasks. It is obviously doing the right thing to be open and friendly, to invite Muslims and non-Muslims to study together, teach together, and learn together. But such an institution will not perform its role if it is just nice to everybody and if those working in it, both Muslims and non-Muslims, are not willing to face the kind of issues I have been referring to, which go beyond narrating the glories of Islam or the glories of Oriental Studies of Islam.

Finally, one may wonder what Islamic Studies will look like when pursued by Muslim scholars in the West over a long stretch of time. What does it mean to be a Muslim in a Western society, and what is the role of Muslim scholars of Islam in a Western society? Will there result a view of Islam that is only satisfying to them as Muslims, or will that be a view that is also convincing to their non-Muslim colleagues? For example, the following question has agitated students of Islam in the West during the past few decades: what is the relation between what Western students of Islam are teaching and writing about Islam and the view of believing Muslims? When the new (second) edition of the *Encyclopaedia of Islam*[4] was being planned, a respected Turkish scholar raised this question and inquired whether Muslim scholars should not play an active role in editing it. The answer was, this was not a "Muslim Encyclopaedia" or an Encyclopaedia for Muslims, but an Encyclopaedia of Islam to be written in the main by Western scholars and those Muslim scholars who are regarded by their Western colleagues as having understood and practiced Islamic studies according to Western criteria. It made no difference what Muslims thought of such an encyclopaedia, whether they liked it or not, whether it agreed with their view of Islam or not, whether they saw themselves reflected in it or not. This question may be raised again as Muslims in large numbers come to the West not just as students but as permanent residents. As this process goes on and many generations of Muslims become part of the West, the idea of publishing an encyclopaedia of Islam that is so bluntly provincial may no longer be viable; just as it is inconceivable today that a major encyclopaedia having to do with Catholicism or Judaism could take the position taken by the original editors of the *Encyclopaedia of Islam*. A new Muslim institution of higher learning established in the West must play a role in finding answers to these questions.

I cannot recall my personal experience with Oriental Studies dealing with Islamic civilization in general and Islamic philosophy in particular, without speaking about a number of acquaintances, friends, teachers - persons I was fortunate to know or be close to, whose scholarly achievements I respected and from whose works I learned a great deal and continue to profit. If I disagreed with them in certain respects, it was because they or their writings encouraged me to do so. I should therefore begin by quoting a line by the famous Egyptian poet Ahmad Shawqī, "Differences of opinion need amity not spoil".[5] I will not be referring to persons and works I found uninteresting or useless, but only to those that were important and played a role in my own thinking about the predicament of Islamic Studies in general and the study of Islamic philosophy in particular.

Poetry and philosophy are pursuits that can easily insinuate themselves into a young man's mind. In the case of poetry, the main question that occupied scholars and publicists at the time had to do with the status of pre-Islamic Arabic poetry - whether it was originally oral and when it was written down, how it was transmitted, how genuine it was.[6] For me, these questions seemed mildly interesting but not crucial for an aesthetic appreciation of that poetic tradition, and I was more occupied with the fate of the fledgling Arabic poetic movements experimenting with new themes and forms. In the case of philosophy, the main question was that of the relation of Islamic philosophy to Greek and Hellenistic philosophy.[7] There were a number of important and intelligent specialized studies of this question at the time: one can think of the works of Gotthelf Bergsträsser[8] and those of Paul Kraus.[9] Then there were those panoramic, apparently opinionated remarks about Islamic philosophy and its relation to Greek philosophy by men like Carl H. Becker "Ich sage der islamischen Philosophie; ich sagte besser der spätantiken",[10] and Hans H. Schaeder,[11] who did not seem to believe that Muslims were capable of genuine, ancient Greek-like philosophic thought or of having anything to do with true philosophy, apparently because Muslims were Semites and therefore created with blinkers - an old story found already in the works of Ernest Renan.[12] A distinguished German scholar who had to leave Germany in the 1930s, once told me that he went to Schaeder, introduced himself, and asked for a letter of recommendation - he was going abroad where people might not know of his writings in German. Schaeder turned to him and said, "Aha, you work on Islamic philosophy! But there were no Muslim philosophers. These were all infidels". This was the general attitude to the study of Islamic philosophy of men who possessed broad cultural interests and had much that was interesting to say about Islamic civilization in general, even though it all turned out to be a "scientific", that is, presumably documented, version of what the German Romantics had imagined an Eastern civilization to be.

Arriving at the University of Chicago in the fall of 1948 to engage in graduate studies, I encountered for the first time Oriental Studies as an institution. The University at large was radiating a particular excitement generated from the confluence of two intellectual traditions - the American and the European, which was represented by the large number of scholars from various European countries, Germany in particular, who had migrated to the United States due to conditions in Europe in the 1930s and during World War II. The European scholars were as fascinated by the American academic system (in which governmental and private funding agencies of all sorts set broad goals and let individual institutions, scholars, and students freely choose the manner of pursuing them) as were the American scholars and students by the presence of renowned foreign scholars whom fate had dropped in their midst and who had brought with them their diverse ways of thinking and teaching. This was the larger institution where one studied the physical sciences, the mathematical sciences, the social sciences, and the humanities, or else enrolled in one of the many professional schools. The social sciences and the humanities I happened to be studying were patterned largely after similar disciplines pursued in German universities in the 1920s and 1930s; and the works of Wilhelm Dilthey, Max Weber, and Martin Heidegger, in cultural history and philosophy were objects of intense curiosity along with the newly developed American social sciences such as anthropology.

Then there was a building that housed the Oriental Institute. As you walked in, you faced massive ancient Egyptian and Mesopotamian figures. The first floor consisted of a museum devoted to Near Eastern - mainly Egyptian, Syrian, and Mesopotamian - antiquities, brought home by the numerous archaeological expeditions (some of which continued year after year for many decades) organized and funded by the Oriental Institute. On the second floor you found a library stacked with all the basic texts, monographs, and dictionaries necessary for research in ancient and medieval Near Eastern languages, history, and culture; offices of the Director and some of the research staff; and the studies of some of the professors. And on the third floor there were more offices for the research staff, studies for the rest of the professors, and the offices of the famous *Assyrian Dictionary* [13] Although I did not spend a great deal of time at the Oriental Institute during the early stages of my studies (there were many exciting things going on at the University at large), as time went on I did quite a bit of work there. The Oriental Institute was founded to make possible research in ancient Near Eastern archaeology, languages, and cultures. "The Institute", wrote its founding father. "is essentially an organized endeavor to *recover the lost story of the rise of man* [emphasis in the original] by salvaging the surviving evidence on a more comprehensive scale than has hitherto been possible, and then by analysis and synthesis building up an account of human development on a broader basis of evidence than has hitherto been available".[14] The teaching of Arabic was relevant because of its importance for the comparative study of ancient Semitic languages. And one needed a historian of Islam because early Islamic civilization preserved evidence useful for the study of the Near East in pre-Islamic times, even though archaeologists at that time were notorious for destroying the Islamic levels of their sites.

The historian of Islam at the time was a woman, Nabia Abbott, an "oriental" from Mardin in southern Turkey or northern Mesopotamia[15] She was one of the few papyrologists anywhere working on early Islamic history.[16] She was interested in Islamic history and philology in a rather strict, old-fashioned way. There was a no-nonsense air about her and the basic research she was engaged in. Her study was like a laboratory. She sat behind a huge desk covered with Arabic papyri, each papyrus fragment carefully pressed between two pieces of glass. If you thought that, because you knew the Arabic language, you could read these papyus fragments just by looking at them, you had a surprise waiting for you. Students walked into her study, sat there, and started with studying the shapes of a single letter. They went to the library and studied the early history of the Arabic script. They found out what the subject matter of the papyrus fragment was and looked up all that was known about the early history of that subject. Then they came back and had to learn, slowly, with her as their guide, to reevaluate the early history of a number of disciplines - the study of the Quran, the *Hadīth*, Arabic literature[17] - but only after a long and painstaking struggle. Nevertheless, this was something they could learn. They could actually walk in there, decipher the material in front of them, and relate it to the supporting texts placed all around them; and at the end of a study period they knew something they had not known before and could do things (figure out the content of a document and its place in a wider historical or cultural context) they could not have done before.

The Professor of Arabic was Gustav E. von Grunebaum.[18] Joachim Wach, the professor of the history of religion at the Divinity School, once introduced him with the following words, "Like so many beautiful things, von Grunebaum hails from Vienna". He should have added that intellectually von Grunebaum hailed from Vienna by way of Berlin, having integrated the aesthetic and scientific traditions of the two great capitals. As Professor of Arabic, he taught a course in elementary Arabic; those students who did not know any Arabic could engage in the formal study of the elements of the language, using a reprint of an old grammar.[19] In addition, he taught a course in elementary Persian; he did not have to do this, but he was interested in Persian literature. Otherwise, he did not have to teach anything in particular - one of the great conveniences of being a Professor of Arabic in a Western research university. He did offer many additional courses, usually on matters he was writing about. The students knew that he had many interesting ideas about Islam and Islamic civilization, and they heard about some of them from occasional public lectures and in conversation with him. But these ideas, such as the ones that had been presented in public lectures in the spring of 1945 and first published in 1946 as *Medieval Islam*[20] were not things he taught his students or that students could learn from him in the course of their studies; there was no systematic way in which a student could make the transition from the course in elementary Arabic or Persian to the conclusions found in a book like *Medieval Islam*.

Von Gruenbaum was knowledgeable and helpful, willing to give the student references to books and articles where he could pursue a particular subject. The "field" was there for you to study, to learn what others had written. But there was no systematic way in which a student could learn from him how to understand or interpret Islamic civilization as he did, which is what he took to be his lifework, except perhaps by reading his books and articles. As a result, there is, as far as I know, no student who can claim to be following in von Gruenbaum's footsteps intellectually, or to have learned from him how to master the comparative cultural method or the rhetoric that characterizes his writings. He had many admirers, and there were many younger scholars whom he helped in many other ways, of course. Many were pleased to be around him and talk to him. When he published a book, students would read it, and they had simply to accept it as his, not knowing how it was related to the extracts of Arab authors that they had been reading with him. And I must add that it was not merely the callow young student who did not understand the transition I have been speaking of. There was a story going about at the time that, at a meeting of a committee sponsored by the American Social Science Research Council of which he and H.A.R. Gibb[21] were members, von Grunebaum read a paper on Islamic civilization after which Gibb looked at him and said something to this effect: "You know, this is like a steel ball, what you said. There is no way to get inside it at all. There is no way to open it and see its internal structure. And if you let it fall on you, it will hurt your feet. So you have to handle it with care". Since then there has been at least one serious attempt to get inside the steel ball, which is well worth your while to ponder on.[22] I have often wondered about his attitude to his American students and why he did not find it possible to train them to follow in his footsteps. This is only an educated guess, but I do think that he realized that the kind of intellectual formation that produced men like Becker or Schaeder could not be transplanted to the United States, at least not in the context of Oriental Studies, and that students who were serious about their intellectual formation had to seek it elsewhere.

Here then were the two models of scholarship in Islamic Studies at the Oriental Institute of the University of Chicago. On the one hand, great distinction in narrowly-based basic research, leading the student step by step, teachable and learnable. On the other, impressive, comprehensive, panoramic studies of Islam in which the relationship between the general ideas and the particular examples, the text and footnotes, was not sufficiently clear to the reader. The overarching idea in the latter case, one that my friend and colleague Marshall Hodgson shared, was that the time had come for a new synthesis; that is, many scholars had already done so many individual and specialized studies - editions, translations, monographic studies, and so on - and the task now was to take what had been done, put it together, and try to see the larger picture. Marshall Hodgson did this in his own fashion in the *Venture of Islam* (1974), a work of immense scope to which the students of Islam in the United States can point with genuine pride.[23] One could of course argue that the individual, specialized studies are not as innocent as they may look and that a synthesis based on them can very well be plagued by the difficulties inherent in each of them. Even when engaged in specialized research, individual scholars have their own opinions and perspectives. The synthesis based on their works adds new perspectives and points of view. And the connection between the specialized studies used in the synthesis and the synthesis itself is not always as clear as it should be.

In order to understand what was happening in this rather narrow field of Islamic Studies at the Oriental Institute, one had to go back to what was being studied and taught elsewhere at the university (in the social sciences and the humanities in general and the recent cultural history of Europe in particular) as it impinged on the understanding and interpretation of non-Western cultures. The question that dominated in the social sciences and the humanities at the time was that of history and the relative weight of the state and the actions of the statesmen in shaping the course of history. In this context, philosophy had become in the main the philosophy of history and science, the science of history, except where the social sciences ignored the question of history and studied social phenomena that lent themselves to direct observation, measurement, and field work. It was in this atmosphere that I had to decide on my own course of action.

There was common agreement that Ibn Khaldūn was a significant figure among pre-modern students of society and history. Numerous social scientists and historians quoted him with approval, both on issues dealing with history and the social sciences in general and on aspects of Islamic civilization about which he was considered a reliable authority. And the leading Islamists at that time, such as von Grunebaum and Gibb, went along, admitting the theoretical or scientific character of his thought, but leaving it at that. Gibb, who was more willing to stick his neck out on such questions that von Grunebaum, had argued in an article[24] reviewing recent studies of Ibn Khaldūn that he must be understood in terms of the Islamic legal tradition. Here I should perhaps add that Gibb's interpretation, which at the time seemed incomplete as far as the foundation of Ibn Khaldūn's new science of culture was concerned, was subsequently developed in a new and more fruitful direction in the context of the economic, social, and political role of Muslim jurists in Andalusia and western North Africa, to whom Ibn Khaldūn belonged. This has provided a better explanation of Ibn Khaldūn's role as state functionary and political activist. But that was not what I was interested in at the time. I meant to look for the foundation on which Ibn Khaldūn constructed the new science of culture and thus understood what terms like "theoretical" and "scientific" meant when applied to him. And it was this question that Gibb addressed as a point that appeared to him "fundamental for any critical study of Ibn Khaldūn's thought". Without further explanation, he stated that "the axioms or principles on which his [Ibn Khaldūn's] study rests are those of practically all the earlier Sunnī jurists and social philosophers"[25] - by "social philosophers" in this context he meant the same as jurists, as the concluding paragraph of the article indicates.[26]

My reading of Ibn Khaldūn led me to the conclusion that the axioms or principles of which Gibb spoke were not those of the jurists but drawn from the sciences that went under the name of rational or philosophic sciences in Islamic civilization; that one cannot understand the principles on which he constructed his science of culture apart from the Islamic philosophic tradition; and that it was this tradition that provided him with the principles of his philosophy of history and science of culture.[27]

As is the case in many investigations, the conclusion may have been arrived at after long and arduous research, but once stated, one begins to wonder why it could not have been seen before, especially in view of the fact that Ibn Khaldūn himself right at the beginning of his work, states the principles of his philosophy of history and science of culture: all one needed to do was look at them and ask to which of the two groups of sciences they belonged, the traditional-religious or the rational-philosophic? Nevertheless, this conclusion ran against the then current view of Islamic civilization, not, it seemed to me, what Islamic civilization was, but what it must or could only have been. According to that view, it made perfect sense to say that a Muslim thinker who became a judge later in life built his new science on legal principles. But that Islamic philosophy, that strange, scarcely legitimate discipline practiced by "infidels", should lead to the construction of the most authoritative, scientific, and comprehensive interpretation of Islamic history and civilization in pre-modern times, that it could help a Muslim thinker develop a new science of culture and receive the (doubtful) praise as the predecessor of Machiavelli, Montesquieu, and Hegel - that could not be accepted because it ran against the view of what Islamic thought should be. There were at least two occasions in which I presented a summary of my findings - which were based on the following proposition: here are the basic notions that Ibn Khaldūn presents as the principles on which he plans to build his science of culture; let us look at them and ascertain their provenance - and Gibb, who was in the audience, felt obliged to defend what I have no doubt he thought was the truth as well as the common view of the profession: the principles of Islamic law and nothing but the principles of Islamic law explain Ibn Khaldūn's new science. Why? Because we all know that the science of the law is the fundamental science in Islam. It was to his credit that, unlike other students of Ibn Khaldūn before and after him, he was weary of interpretations that connected Ibn Khaldūn to Machiavelli or Hegel.

There was also a more general problem that had to be faced: whether the study of Islamic philosophy or of the philosophic sciences that flourished in Islamic civilization is a legitimate subject for Islamic Studies at all. Gibb did not believe it was, not out of ignorance but out of firm conviction. That is, to be a Muslim meant for him not be philosophic or rational in this sense, and to be philosophic or rational in this sense meant for him not to be a Muslim, but something else, perhaps a misguided Muslim or even an "infidel" as Ibn Taymīyya would say.[28] Yet Ibn Khaldūn was not accused of being an infidel. But he seems to have managed to look at his own society with a philosophic eye and interpret it accordingly. He was a "good" Muslim and he learned a great deal from the philosophic sciences of his time.

Therefore the problem of Islamic philosophy became a crucial issue for me: what it is, its relation to the Islamic revelation, its role in Islamic society. And this at a time when a leading authority on Islamic Studies was saying and writing things that discouraged younger scholars from pursuing this issue. Shortly before I arrived at the University of Chicago, the University of Chicago Press had published Gibb's Haskell Lectures (given there in 1945) under the title *Modern Trends in Islam* (1947); and shortly thereafter Gibb published his famous *Mohammedanism*.[29] *Modern Trends in Islam*, an admirably written and informative work that preserves much of its freshness and value to the present time, begins and ends with general remarks on Islamic philosophy and the Muslim mind. "The Foundation of Arabic Thought", is constantly brought up against the striking contrast between the imaginative power displayed for example, in certain branches of Arabic literature and the literalism, the pedantry, displayed in reasoning and exposition, even when it is devoted to these same productions. It is true that there have been great philosophers among the Muslim peoples and that some them were Arabs, but they were rare exceptions. The Arab mind, whether in relation to the outer world, or in relation to the processes of thought, cannot throw off its intense feeling for the separateness and individuality of concrete events. This is, I believe, one of the main factors lying behind that "lack of the sense of law" which Professor MacDonald regarded as the characteristic difference in the oriental". "It is this, too", he adds, "which explains - what is so difficult for the Western student to grasp - the aversion of the Muslims from the thought-processes of rationalism. . . The rejection of rationalist modes of thought and of the utilitarian ethic which is inseparable from them has its roots, therefore, not in the so-called "obscurantism" of the Muslim theologians but in the atomism and discreetness of the Arab imagination".[30] I needed to understand what all this meant, for one could not fail to observe that matters of great import were at issue. There were great philosophers among the Muslim people, and some of them were Arabs, but they were rare exceptions. One did not need to know a great deal about the history of philosophy to realize that great philosophers are always and everywhere the rarest of exceptions - this was true of the Greeks, the Indians, the Chinese, the Latins. Why, then, should Gibb be saying, "It is true. . ., but"? Did he believe in the existence of a time and place in which the Enlightenment view prevailed, wisdom became available to all, everyone who was not mentally deranged was a philosopher, and great philosophers were not rare exceptions? If the "Arab mind" - an expression which doubtless meant something for Gibb -cannot philosophize because of its intense feeling for the separateness and individuality of concrete events, how is one to explain the fact that there were some great philosophers among the Arabs? Was this the exception that confirmed the rule? But great philosophers have always been the exception in all nations and cultures. Or should one take Aquinas' synthesis of Aristotelian philosophy and Christian theology as the model against which to judge the relation between philosophy and theology in Islam? But how is one then to judge Luther's rebellion against the "Aristotelian Church", and how is one to understand Gibb's defense of rationalist modes of thought and utilitarian ethic as inseparable from rationalist modes of thought?

I did not believe that Gibb had made a sustained effort to think through these questions or consider the broader issues of rationalism and its mutation throughout history. To begin with, he did not appear to have had much liking for rationalism. Secondly, he thought that one does not study Islam to learn about rationalism. That there might be, or possibly was, a kind of rationalism different from the one he knew, or thought he knew, and about which one could learn something from the study of Islamic philosophy - such questions do not seem to have occurred to him. If Islam is of any use to us today, it must be to learn about something else, the "imaginative power" or whatever else one might call it. Yet Gibb himself, however much he may have enjoyed the imaginative power displayed in certain branches of Arabic literature, never gave the reader a veritable account of it anywhere in his writings, all of which were models of rational and scientific studies, indeed models of the attempt to transform what is thought to be imaginative or irrational into an object of rational study of sorts.

Due to its conciseness and comprehensiveness, Gibb's *Mohammedanism* continues to withstand the ravages of time. It surveys the place of Islamic philosophy in what is called "Mohammedanism", mentions the names "of that remarkable series of medieval Arabic philosophers"; and speaks of their work as "among the glories of Islamic civilization", without, however, dwelling "upon their services to philosophical thought directly and through the transmission of Greek philosophy to medieval Europe".[31] He pays special attention to the theological school, the Muʿtazila, that showed interest in the Hellenistic philosophic tradition and without whose efforts and impact it would be impossible to understand the rise and development of any school or period of Islamic theology. Its struggle with what is called "orthodoxy", however, is not treated as a historical event with contingent causes; an attempt is made to decide the points at issue on metaphysical grounds: "The points at issue were at bottom metaphysical. Oriental philosophy [Gibb is no longer speaking about Islamic philosophy, but apparently about Islamic philosophy, Indian philosophy, Chinese philosophy, and perhaps others as well] had never appreciated the fundamental idea of justice in Greek philosophy, and it was this which the representatives of the Hellenistic interpretation were attempting to accommodate within Islam".[32] What the Muʿtazila did not and could not know and what Gibb seems to have been certain about, is that they were wasting their time because they lacked his historical insight about the fundamental character of "Oriental philosophy". How one comes to judge historical events through such broad metaphysical convictions is a question that deserves serious reflection. But similar remarks are also made on sociological grounds: "On more sociological grounds, it might be suggested that oriental societies [again without qualification], in contrast to most western societies, have generally devoted much more sustained and successful efforts to building stable social organizations with law as one of their pillars, than to constructing ideal systems of philosophic thought".[33]

It is a pity that Gibb did not elaborate on this important point. I wondered at the time how the statement that Oriental societies in general have lagged behind the Greeks in constructing ideal systems of philosophic thought sounded to a student of Indian philosophy, for example. What the fundamental Greek idea of justice is and why it is that it was never understood by Oriental philosophy - these are questions that Gibb did not care to comment on. But statements like these make sense only within the particular cultural and historical context mentioned earlier: starting with German Romanticism and taking into account the views of men like Renan, Becker, and Schaeder. Gibb did not, of course, claim to possess expert knowledge about all Oriental societies, although he knew more about them than many of his colleagues; he must have learned about their philosophy and general character from the then current lore of Oriental studies. If one decides to study the Orient or Oriental societies, one studies them to learn something other than the Greek idea of justice or ideal systems of philosophy. One goes on using the expression "philosophy", but after emptying it of all its forms and contents and replacing them with feeling, the irrational, the imaginative. Should Oriental societies try to appreciate the Greek idea of justice or construct ideal systems of philosophical thought, as some of them may have done, the function of the historian is to explain their failure on metaphysical and sociological grounds. Gibb tried to spread that net over Islamic thought and society; and commonly-received opinion, which expected something of this sort, could find no fault with what he did.

This general attitude was not shared by the prominent scholars who, unlike Gibb, were interested in the study of Islamic philosophy in particular, especially in Germany where a serious historical and philological tradition in this field was already in place. I have already mentioned Gotthelf Bergsträsser and Paul Kraus, and one would have to add other distinguished scholars such as S. Pines, Franz Rosenthal, and Richard Walzer. We owe them an immense debt of gratitude for their works on Islamic philosophy: the recovery and edition of major historical and biographical works and philosophic texts, as well as numerous studies to which they brought to bear a learning informed by the achievements of classical scholarship. They have provided the basis for what one may call the modern study of Islamic philosophy as against the traditional study of the subject in the Muslim world itself, where it had become dominated by philosophic mysticism and illuminationism. One must say in justification of this modern approach to Islamic philosophy that it is historically and philologically more accurate and that it provides the student with a more a accurate and broader vision of the place of Islamic philosophy in the general history of philosophy, taking into account as it does the history of philosophy in Greek and Hellenistic times, and in medieval and modern times in the West, as recovered and studied by modern scholarship. This does not mean that one must henceforth necessarily restrict one's interest to the role played by Islamic philosophy in the history of philosophy, whether as the continuation of Greek philosophy or as the backdrop of medieval Jewish or Christian Latin philosophy, or centre it on the recovery of presumable lost Greek texts, important as this or that aspect of the study of Islamic philosophy may be for these purposes. Nor does one have to accept uncritically the view that Islamic philosophy is the product of some construct called "Islam" or "Islamic civilization" or any aspect thereof. For here, too, one is likely to be trapped in the old argument: if Islamic philosophy is rational or philosophic in the Greek sense, then it is Greek and not Islamic; if it is irrational, non-philosophic in the Greek sense, then it is the product of Islam or Islamic civilization. And if it is rational and philosophic in the Greek sense, but develops or adds something to the tradition, then that is the product of a certain non-philosophic aspect of Islamic civilization.

Finally, one could not mention recent scholarship in Islamic philosophy without speaking of the work of a revered and greatly regretted teacher and friend, Henry Corbin, who almost single-handedly introduced to Western readers the later period of Islamic philosophy in Iran. I doubt that any Orientalist student of Islam since Louis Massignon possessed the power of his understanding or imagination, to say nothing of his capacity for sustained hard work. Unlike most of the European scholars who worked on Islamic philosophy, Corbin started his career, not as historian, philologist, or archaeologist, but with serious interest in philosophy, both contemporary especially, that of Martin Heideggger and ancient especially, Hellenistic gnosticism. Corbin did not believe in the study of Islamic philosophy as pursued by his contemporaries. In his hermeneutical approach, past and future became signs, and "without *signs*, with hierophanies and theophanies, there is no making history".[34] His main interest was in what he saw as the other, hidden side of the coin; the traces of the creative imagination buried in the early history of the Indo-European peoples. This explains his interest in pre-Islamic Iran, and his interest in Islam as a continuation of pre-Islamic gnostic thought, if it happened to continue it, refer to it, or remind of it. He was not content to present the truth as revealed to him by his vast learning as do many other students of the hidden sciences, but tried to pin it down in space and time. That led to occasional problems.

To take but one example, Corbin published a major work on Avicenna[35] in which he intended to understand Avicenna as the Iranian tradition understood him rather than as he had been interpreted by the rationalist Latin scholastics or the rationalist students of philosophy in modern times. The work deals with Avicenna's visionary recitals and commentaries on them by three representatives of that tradition, two of them Avicenna's immediate students and the third, the great Nāsir al-Dīn al-Tūsī. He goes through the three commentators one by one and reaches the conclusion that they must have understood very little if anything at all, apparently because they were just as rationalistic in their approach to Avicenna's visionary recitals as the Latin and modern rationalists. He develops instead his own framework within which to interpret these recitals, a framework that does not seem to have occurred to the three representatives of the Iranian tradition who were, after all, supposed to have had firsthand knowledge of Avicenna's philosophy and its intention. For Corbin, who was following his own intuition, none of this seemed to matter.

Corbin was in many ways the last of the German Romantics. The living Orient and Orientals, Iranian Muslims in particular, deserve to be reorientalized, reminded of the light that once shone in their minds and the hidden treasures of which they were once the custodians. Because of the power of his thought, he influenced a whole generation of Iranian intellectuals who became convinced of his vision. They thought that to be Iranian Muslim meant to be in some sense a Zoroastrian also, proud of and living imaginatively in the pre-Islamic greatness of Iran; that the early non-Iranian Muslims were rude Arab Semites who came from the desert, gave Iran its new religion, and returned to their tents - everything of importance (the culture, mysticism, spiritual Islam) was contributed by Iranians and their genius, and the rest was legalistic, mundane, political, and therefore not worthy of serious attention. A sort of alliance was formed between them, the earlier proponents of Iranian nationalism, and the political power ruling at the time at whose head stood a monarch who tried to institutionalize the new vision of the Iranian past and become the reincarnation of the great pre-Islamic Iranian kings. The rest of the story is well known. Ignoring the Islamic heritage and institutions of Iran, including Islamic law, as something outmoded or dead was obviously a serious error; the neglect of the mundane, the legal, and the political, instead of making them go away, seems to have made them return with a vengeance.

Corbin distinguished himself from most of his contemporaries by the effort to think both historically and philosophically when dealing with Islamic philosophy. One of the strangest criticisms that continues to be made by some of the representatives of the older, historical and philological tradition of Islamic studies in the West has to do with the validity of attempts to think or rethink the thoughts of a philosopher such as Alfarabi, Avicenna, or Averroës. This means that one can treat their thought historically, biographically, sociologically, and so forth - that is good scholarship. But to think philosophically when dealing with the works of these philosophers, that is said not to be scientific. This view makes no sense, of course. Without thinking theologically, one cannot understand fully the thought of a theologian; without thinking aesthetically, one cannot understand fully the work of a poet or a literary critic, and generally any important work of art; similarly, one can do all the historical or philological or sociological research he wishes, without being able to get to the core of a philosophic work.

On the whole, the Orientalist tradition of Islamic Studies, whether developed by Orientalists with a broad interest in the East as a whole, or by students of Islam in particular, or by Muslim scholars who introduced this tradition in the Muslim world, seemed to me to show a certain neglect or forgetfulness, which made it incapable of recovering and penetrating to the core of certain important aspects of its subject matter. For reasons to which I have alluded already, this was particularly true in the study of Islamic philosophy. I missed the kind of concentrated analytical and interpretive ethos that characterized the great philosophic works themselves and the efforts of their commentators and interpreters throughout the history of philosophy. This seemed to me to be the task of the new generation of students who occupy themselves with Islamic philosophy: they must start by understanding the predicament in which they find themselves and figure a way out.

It is not surprising, therefore, that attempts were made during the last decade or two to look critically at that tradition and evaluate its shortcomings as an academic discipline. There were, it is true, numerous efforts to criticize and refine the tradition all along. But the more recent critique, which has originated largely among French literary critics and students of Islam,[36] tended to be more radical. It revealed that scholars who were disciplined and rigorous when investigating specialized questions could not withstand the temptation of speaking, and showed a certain lack of discipline when they spoke, about the Orient, the Oriental (Islamic, Arab) mind, and Orientals (Muslims, Arabs), as though these were distinct human categories that can be identified and spoken of in a general sort of way. It pointed out that for reasons not always explicit, conscious, or easy to explain, these scholars seemed to be under some sort of inner compulsion or outer pressure - social, political, cultural, or academic--to pontificate as Orientalists concerning things about which they in fact knew nothing or very little: things that were not the legitimate findings of their own specialized investigations, but derived from commonly-received opinions.

This critique culminated in Edward Said's *Orientalism* (1978), which, analyzing the writings of certain Orientalists in a deconstructionist manner, emphasized the political intention and use of much of the Orientalist literature as well as of the scholars producing it.

It is not my intention to comment on the controversies generated by Edward Said's *Orientalism*: most of these are somewhat puzzling and needlessly defensive, especially in the United States where criticism of European Orientalism on grounds not very different from those suggested by Edward Said was common among social scientists, although perhaps not so outspoken or centered on a particular political theme. Nevertheless, it is the kind of book that Orientalists or Islamists or Arabists can ignore at their own peril. Among themselves, Orientalists have tended to be too timid to engage in the kind of self-criticism that is necessary if they were to cope with the rapid changes in the intellectual climate, and the political and human relationships, that characterize the contemporary world. It is not enough to speak and write with pride but only occasional criticism (frequently relative to side issues) of the history and achievements of their special field or discipline. They ought to have welcomed the few attempts to look at the study of the East as a whole and disengage the guiding notions, human intentions, and general view of the course of human history that led to the distinction between the West and the East, supported a massive interest in the study of the East, determined its course, and shaped the peculiar relationship between a group of highly specialized scholarly enterprises and popular beliefs about the peoples and cultures of the East on the one hand, and such practical movements and policies that developed into imperialism, colonialism, and economic exploitation, on the other. It is true that such attempts can be disturbing at first; and they may even raise questions about the validity and practical use of the discipline which its practitioners may wish to avoid. But Oriental Studies have for long suffered from a stodgy self-satisfaction and the belief that hard work and rhetorical flourish are sufficient to make one a celebrity in a field where it is not common for others to have access to one's sources and therefore be in a position to judge one's work apart from the impression it makes.

Edward Said presented the impressions this body of literature made on him, and that was fair enough.

But he went beyond this and imputed to Orientalism[37] a vision of reality that it could never have created itself. For throughout modern history, Orientalism has been a by-product of influential currents in Western thought and attitudes, both sublime and vulgar. The "political vision of reality" imputed to Orientalism, for instance, was not created but merely confirmed by Orientalism. And as far as the practical use of Orientalism is concerned, it was used for practical or political ends just as any other type of knowledge that is thought to be practically useful is promoted and used by any society and its leaders.

It is sometimes said that this critique applies to the older tradition of Orientalist studies but not to more recent, specialized studies. True, one observes a rapid fragmentation of the other tradition; yet fragmentation and specialization by themselves do not necessarily mean freedom from commonly-received unexamined opinions. A scholar could say to himself, I will no longer talk about the Orient, but only about the economic foundation of the labour movement in Egypt in the twentieth century. However, this does not by itself mean freedom from the older intellectual baggage. That is why I believe that there is a question that overrides everything else in this matter. One could say that, at their best, Oriental Studies are meant to be a scientific, rational discipline, and in this sense they are part and parcel of what one may call modern Western rationalism. As such, they share its view of what can be called pre-modern rationalism, whether Greek, Islamic, or medieval European, and try to show that pre-modern rationalism, which is characteristic of pre-modern philosophy, did not exist (some of the quotations given earlier say or imply as much), was not important, was irrational, or was not based on a rational but mythological, poetic, or religious foundation - it was a superstructure and hence a surface phenomenon in those cultures. But the modern scientific study of the East also claims that it appreciates and understands and can give a scientific, rational account of the irrational foundations that determined the characteristic features of Eastern societies, Eastern philosophy, and the Eastern mind.

The recent critical literature on Orientalism has shown that this claim is untenable; that, in fact, Oriental studies of Islam and Islamic civilization have been founded on a mixed bag of religious, cultural, ideological, ethnic (in some cases even racist), and scientific prejudgments and practical political interests. But if true, this seems to come down to saying that these studies are guided by irrational motives and by political interests, with the result that "Islam", in Edward Said's words, "*has* been fundamentally misrepresented in the West". What, then, is the answer? The recent critical studies of Orientalism seem to agree that there is no escape from this predicament - that we are impotent, condemned to remain constantly torn by the conflict between the rational and the irrational, and that our rational thought is ultimately embedded in the irrational, which comes down to saying that we are simply dealing with a conflict of irrationalities. That is to say, if what claims to be rational, scientific thought in the modern West is guided by irrational motives, and if it in turn, studies irrational phenomena in the East (say Islamic Philosophy) that also claim to be rational or scientific, a claim which the Orientalist knows not be true, then one should describe our predicament as one of irrational motives misrepresenting other irrational motives.

To show you that this is in fact the case, I refer you to Edward's Said's concluding remarks. "The real issue", he says, "is whether indeed there can be a true representation of anything, or whether any and all representations, because they are representations, are embedded first in the language and then in the culture, institutions, and political ambience of the representor. If the latter alternative is the correct one (as I believe it is [he adds in parenthesis]), then we must be prepared to accept the fact that a representation is *eo ipso* implicated, intertwined, embedded, interwoven with a great many other things besides the "truth" [a word placed between quotation marks], which is itself a representation".[38] This seems to be the conclusion of the current critical account of Orientalism. It joins other strands in contemporary Western thought that have abandoned the hope for the pursuit of the truth as a rational, scientific enterprise.

But not quite. Edward Said adds that he and those who agree with him are able to free themselves from old ideological straight-jackets through "methodological self-consciousness".[39] Yet it all depends on what is meant by methodological self-consciousness. It can mean that one is conscious of the fact that the human predicament is a permanent state of war among irrational motives, which does not go beyond a restatement of the position advocated by the ancient Greek sophists. Or it may mean self-knowledge - "know thyself" was the original injunction that led to the kind of human thought identified with the rise and development of philosophy and science since Socrates questioned the motives behind, as well as the adequacy and coherence of, the sophistic position.

If there is a crisis of Orientalism, it cannot be separated from the more general crisis of modern rationalism and the recognition that in many ways it is dogmatic and irrational. Methodological self-consciousness is of course a start. But if it is to provide a solution to the crisis of Oriental Studies and, within it, of the study of Islam and Islamic civilisation, it must lead to a search for a genuine form of rationalism. And it is here that I believe the study of pre-modern rationalism - represented in Greek, Islamic, and medieval Western philosophy - and its understanding of irrational and imaginative phenomena (indeed the very question of "representation") can be of some use.

It was the need for a genuine form of rationalism that gave rise to and explains the enormous success of German Romanticism. Understanding the reasons for the limited scope and humanly unsatisfying character of modern rationalism, and the search for a more wholesome unity that satisfies both the rational and imaginative or poetic aspects of man's life, are tasks that are still before us. Whether and on what level such a unity is possible as a stable condition in a higher culture, or whether the rational and poetic are two poles that remain in creative tension and societies are characterized by the degree of equilibrium they achieve and preserve between the two poles - these, too, are questions one can learn something about from the old conflict between philosophy and poetry. Only a genuine rationalism can understand and appreciate the role of the poetic in human life, not a rationalism that ignores the poetic, abdicates its own role, or allows irrational motives to determine the course and results of its inquiry.

One may retort that this is a tall order, especially given the tradition of Oriental Studies, their constant effort to apply and validate commonly-received notions rather than engage in a critical inquiry into them, and the dominant skepticism about the possibility of replacing commonly-received notions by true knowledge about man and society. But the debate must remain open. If Orientalism is derivative in respect of its beliefs and motives, one needs to go back to the sources from which they were derived. And if recent and contemporary currents of philosophic thought do not seem to be helpful in providing a defensible direction for the study of man and society, then the debate must be enlarged to include pre-modern currents of philosophic thought. If the study of Islamic philosophy is to make a contribution to this debate, it must first free itself from the commonly-received notions that have transformed it into a ghost of its true self.

Notes

1. Review of *Das Problem der islamischen Kulturgeschichte* by Jörge Kraemer, *Journal of Near Eastern Studies* xxi, (1962), 230-2. Review of *Islam and the Integration of Society* by W. Montgomery Watt, *Journal of Near Eastern Studies* xxiii, (1964), 285-9. "Islamic Philosophy in Contemporary Islamic Thought" in *God and Man in Contemporary Islamic Thought*, ed. Charles Malik (American University of Beirut Centennial Publications, A.U.B., Beirut, 1972), 99-111.
2. Sayyid Qutb, *Maʿālim fī al-Tarīq* (Cairo, n.p., n.d. (196?). Trans. As *Milestones* (Kazi Publications, Chicago, 1981).
3. Abdallah Laroui, *L'idéologie arabe contemporaine: essai critique* (Préface de Maxime Rodinson. Les textes à l'appui. F. Maspéro, Paris, 1967), 81 ff.

4. H. A. R. Gibb *et al.*, eds., *Encyclopaedia of Islam* (New edn., prepared by a number of leading orientalists under the patronage of the International Union of Academies; E. J. Brill, Leiden/Luzac, London, 1960-).
5. Ahmad Shawqī, *Majnūn Layla* (Matbaʿat Misr, Cairo, 1916), 4.
6. Tāha Husain, *Fī al-Shiʿr al-Jāhilī* (Matbaʿat Dār al-Kutub al-Misriyya, Cairo, 1926), and *Fī al-Adab al-Jāhilī* (Lajnat al-Ta'līf wa'l-Tarjama wa'l-Nashr, Cairo, 1927).
7. ʿAbdurrahmān Badawī, *al-Turāth al-Yūnānī fi al-Hadāara al-islāmiyya: Dirāsāt li-Kibār al-Mustashriqīn* (Maktabat al-Nahda al-Misriyya, Cairo, 1946). This work contains an Arabic translation of Becker 1931 (see no. 11), 3-33, and other important essays by European Orientalists on the relation between Islam and the Greek heritage. ʿAbdurrahmān Badawī, *Rūh al-Hadāra al-ʿArabiyya* (Dār al-ʿIlm li'l-Malāyīn, Beirut, 1949). This contains the Arabic translation of Schaeder 1928 (see no. 12).
8. Gotthelf Bergsträsser, *Hunain ibn Ishāq über die syrischen und arabischen Galenübersetzungen* (Abhandlungen für die Kunde des Morgenlandes, Deutsche morgenländische Gesellschaft, 17/2, F.A. Brockhaus, Leipzig, 1925). And *Neue Materialen zu Hunain ibn Ishāq's Galen-bibliographie* (Abhandlungen für die Kunde des Morgenlandes, 19/2, Duetsche morgenländische Gesellschaft, Leipzig, 1932).
9. Paul Kraus, *Jābir Ibn Hayyān: Contribution à l'histoire des idées scientifiques dans l'Islam* (Mémoires de l'Institut d'Egypte, 44-45. Institut Français d'Archéologie Orientale, Cairo, 1942-3).
10. Carl H. Becker, *Vom Werden und Wesen der islamischen Welt: Islamstudien* (2 vols.; Verlag Quelle & Meyer, Leipzig, 1924-32), i, 427. Also *Das Erbe der Antike im Orient und Okzident* (Verlag Quelle & Meyer, Leipzig, 1931).
11. Hans Heinrich Schaeder, "Der Orient und das griechische Erbe", *Die Antike* iv (1928), 262-64. (The piece was dedicated to Werner Jaeger, editor of *Die Antike*.)
12. Ernest Renan, *Averroès et l'averroïsme: essai historique* (2nd edn. Michel Lévy Frères, Paris, 1852). See also Muhsin Mahdi, "Averroës on Divine Science and Human Wisdom" in *Ancients and Moderns: Essays on the Tradition of Political Philosophy in Honor of Leo Strauss*, ed. Joseph Cropsey (Basic Books, New York, 1964), 114-31. And Muhsin Mahdi, "Islamic Philosophy in Contemporary Islamic Thought" (n. 2).
13. Ignace J. Gelb *et al.*, eds. *The Assyrian Dictionary of the Oriental Institute of the University of Chicago* (Oriental Institute, Chicago, 1956-?).
14. James H. Breasted, *The Oriental Institute* (University of Chicago Press, Chicago. University of Chicago Survey, 12, 1933) ix, see also 2ff.
15. Muhsin Mahdi, "Foreword", *Journal of Near Eastern Studies*, xl (1981), (in honour of Nabia Abbott), 163-64.
16. In addition, Nabia Abbott pioneered the study of the history of Muslim women, not a subject that drew much attention at the time: *Aisha: the Beloved of Mohammed*

(University of Chicago Press, Chicago, 1942) and *Two Queens of Baghdad* (University of Chicago Press, Chicago, 1946).

17. Nabia Abbott, *Studies in Arabic Literary Papyri* (Oriental Institute Publications, University of Chicago Press, Chicago, vols. 75-7, 1957-72).
18. Muhsin Mahdi, "The Book and the Master as Poles of Cultural Change in Islam" in *Islam and Cultural Change in the Middle Ages*, in honour of Gustav E. Von Grunebaum, ed. Speros Vryonis Jr. (Giorgio Levi della Vida Biennial Conference Publications, no. 4. Otto Harrassowitz, Wiesbaden, 1975), 3-15.
19. G. W. Thatcher, *Arabic Grammar of the Written Language* (F. Ungar, New York [1911] repr. 1943).
20. Gustav E. Von Grunebaum, *Medieval Islam: A Study in Cultural Orientation* (An Oriental Institute Essay. University of Chicago Press, Chicago [1946] 1947).
21. Muhsin Mahdi, "In Memoriam", *Middle East Studies Association of North America Bulletin*, vi.1, (1972), (in honour of H. A. R. Gibb), 88.
22. Abdallah Laroui, *La crise des intellectuels arabes* (F. Maspéro, Paris, 1974), trans. Diarmid Cammell as *The Crisis of the Arab Intellectual: Traditionalism or Historicism?* (University of California Press, Berkeley, 1976), ch. 3.
23. Marshall G.S. Hodgson, *The Venture of Islam: Conscience and History in a World Civilisation* (3 vols.; University of Chicago Press, Chicago, 1974).
24. H.A.R. Gibb, "The Islamic Background of Ibn Khaldūn's Political Theory" in *Studies on the Civilisation of Islam,* ed. Stanford J. Shaw and William R.Polk, Beacon Press, Boston [1933] 1962), ch. 10.
25. *Ibid.*, 167.
26. *Ibid.*, 173.
27. Muhsin Mahdi, *Ibn Khaldūn's Philosophy of History: A Study in the Philosophic Foundation of the Sciences of Culture* (University of Chicago Press, Phoenix Books, Chicago [1957] 1971).
28. Personally, I have never been able to figure out why so many Western students of Islam feel most comfortable with so-called Muslim fundamentalists and so uncomfortable with men like Avicenna, for example; or why they are so willing to take sides in what were, after all, internal differences of opinion and conflicts within the Muslim community.
29. H. A. R. Gibb, *Modern Trends in Islam* (University of Chicago Press, Chicago, 1947). *Mohammedanism: An Historical Survey* (Home University Library of Modern Knowledge, no. 197. Oxford University Press, London [1949] 1953).
30. Gibb, *Modern Trends in Islam*, 7. See also 109, 116. And cf. Edward Said, *Orientalism* (Pantheon Books, New York, 1978), 106ff.
31. Gibb, *Mohammedanism* 118-9. See also 164, 185, 188 for references to Islamic philosophy in Iran and India.
32. *Ibid.*, 111.

33. *Ibid.*, 88.
34. Henry Corbin, "The Time of Eranos" in *Man and Time: Papers from the Eranos Yearbooks* (Bollingen Series, no. 30-3. Princeton University Press, Princeton, 1954), xiii-xx. See xvii.
35. Henry Corbin, *Avicenne et le récit visionnaire*. (Bibliothèque Iranienne, vol. 4. Département d'Iranologie de l'Institut Franco-Iranien. Librairie d'Amérique et d'Orient, Adrien-Maisonneuve, Paris [1954] 1960).
36. For example, Maxime Rodinson, "The Western Image and Western Studies of Islam" in *The Legacy of Islam*, ed. Joseph Schacht and C. E. Bosworth (2nd edn., Clarendon Press, Oxford, 1974), 9-62. And *La fascination de l'Islam* (Petite Collection Maspéro. F. Maspéro, Paris [1968, 1976] 1980).
37. Said, *Orientalism*, (n. 30), 43.
38. *Ibid.*, 272.
39. *Ibid.*, 326.

Jacques Waardenburg

Islamic Studies and the History of Religions: An Evaluation*

The scholarly study of religious data aims at knowledge that can, by means of a rational inquiry into facts, be demonstrated to have general validity. For each statement evidence should be adduced on the basis of empirical data and rational argumentation, and although either the first or the second may be stressed, both elements should always be present. As a consequence, the conclusions of such research must be acknowledged by scholars of different specializations and persuasions, provided that they are aware of the assumptions and presuppositions that occur in this area of study, and that they do not dogmatically hold to a particular set of assumptions and presuppositions as exclusively true at the expense of other theoretical starting points. When, as students of religious data, we strive after scholarly impartiality and even objectivity, we try to know, explain, and understand data - facts and meanings - as they are, and not as we or others would like them to be.[1]

In this field of research we have to do with data which have certain religious meanings for particular societies or communities, or for certain groups or individuals within them. So, for Islamic Studies it is a primary requirement of method from the point of view of *Religionswissenschaft* that one must take into full account what is understood by "religious" and "religion" in different Muslim societies and by particular Muslim religious scholars. Research itself concerns the precise linguistic expression, the literary dependence and ramifications, the historical causes and effects, the social functions and implications, and the other aspects of the data under investigation. A second requirement of method, from the point of view of the study of religion, is to give full weight to what has been or is at present the particular "religious" meaning of the data for the Muslim people concerned, and then to determine how such data, when organized into a

---

*Reprinted (with some slight changes) with permission of the Publishers from *Scholarly Approaches to Religion, Interreligious Perceptions and Islam* (*Studia Religiosa Helvetica*, Jahrbuch, Jg. 1). Bern: Peter Lang, Europäischer Verlag der Wissenschaften, 1995, pp. 413-51.

set, constitute a religious pattern as well, which then also has a religious meaning for these people. A third requirement of method in any study of religious data is to recognize that all religious meanings have their specific empirical vehicles and that, whatever the religious meaning of particular phenomena, these data have at the same time historical, social, cultural, and often also political aspects. Consequently, in their empirical forms, religions are always part of given total historical and social settings of particular communities.

There is a growing awareness of the variety of scholarly *approaches* in the field of Islamic Studies and a concern about the problems resulting from this variety.[2] One can distinguish, for instance, philological, historical, anthropological, and sociological approaches that may or may not be directed toward the same data. In some cases several approaches may be combined by one scholar. Within each approach, however, different *methods* are again possible, some more critical than others, and certain methods can be applied within more than one approach. An historian analyzing al-Shahrastānī's description of the religions of India has to investigate the literary sources used in this description,[3] but if he wants to trace, for instance, the medieval Muslim trade routes via Eastern Europe to Scandinavia he would do well to analyze the Arab coin hoards left on the way.[4] Once formulated, and to a great extent depending on what sources are available, a specific problem will require a specific method in order to be solved, and a specific method will lead to a specific use of available sources. Sociologists working on present-day Muslim societies use different methods and research techniques largely depending on what they want to know, and on the kinds of data to which they have access; consequently, their formulations of particular problems will vary accordingly. In Islamic Studies there is a *multiplicity of approaches and of methods within these approaches*, which sometimes cross and bypass each other, or which may occur within more than one approach.

Until recently Islamic Studies were part of what was called

"Orientalism", and attention has been drawn to the fact that this implied certain views on non-Western societies, including Muslim societies.[5] The history of non-Western civilizations has often been seen and appreciated from the point of view of European history.[6] Generally speaking, the unequal political relationships between Western states and Muslim countries have influenced the way in which Muslim societies and "Islam" have been viewed and judged in the West. In this regard many would argue that prevailing ethnocentric attitudes in the West have distorted perceptions and interpretations of "other" societies and cultures. Analysis has shown that certain theories held in the West about Islam and other non-Western cultures were not so much detached scholarly theories, but rather were explainable by political and other material factors with great social and psychological consequences.[7] Nonetheless, among the Orientalists of the past century were scholars who were motivated by the ideal to dispel Western ignorance and prejudice against the Muslim Orient.

Even apart from the cultural and religious differences that often separate scholars from the societies they study, scholars personally have always had different views on humankind and the world at large, and they personally have lived by different philosophical or moral, aesthetic, and religious convictions. Such presuppositions sometimes affect directly, but often indirectly, the precise inferences drawn from given facts. In the study of religious data in particular, such as the Quran, religious poetry, or certain mystical texts, and specifically in the interpretation of their religious meanings, even if the same approaches and methods are used, scholarly conclusions tend to differ because there are different presuppositions and sensibilities at play. A similar situation prevails in the study of religions and cultures other than Islam, and the present generation of scholars of religion has become perhaps more conscious of this state of affairs than previous generations.

Islamic Studies in any case have become the subject of scrutiny and soul-searching. A growing interest has arisen not only in the history of this kind of study but also in the intrinsic relationship between our concept of Islamic Studies and our conceptualization of Islam.[8] This also holds true for specialists who are not particularly interested in the history of religions but who are working in the broad field of Islamic Studies.[9] In recent years, a reassessment of Islamic studies from the point of view of the history of religions has begun.[10]

In the following pages, I will examine three meanings for the term "history of religions". First is the precise meaning for the term, as the *historical* study of religions and religious data; second is the broader sense in which the term is used as the *comparative* study of such data and religions; and finally I shall examine history of religions in the concentrated sense of *Religionswissenschaft*, as the methodical study of religious data, especially in view of their meanings. These meanings for "history of religions" will be discussed in relation to Islamic Studies.

Islamic Studies and the Historical Study of Religions

1. The historical study of religions stands in contrast to the mostly ahistorical self-view held by adherents - in the sense that they often disregard historical sources and explanations, preferring a different notion of historical truth. Strictly speaking, historical study could only establish itself academically after texts, archaeological remains and other types of evidence had become available to be studied. In the second half of the nineteenth century the history of religions became a recognized discipline at several universities. One of the major figures working in Islamic Studies largely within the context of the history of religions - itself part of the general study of the history of culture(s) - was Ignaz Goldziher (1850-1921).[11] It is significant that he first applied the historical approach and historical criticism to his own religious tradition, that of Judaism, before applying it much more elaborately to that of Islam. He also did thorough work in the field of Arabic language and literature in the broad sense of the word. For instance, because he was aware of developments in the general history of religions, he could place Muslim saint veneration and the cult of the dead within a much broader context than that of Islam. Similarly, an

anthropologist like E.A. Westermarck (1862-1939) could place data on Moroccan Islam within the wider context of similar ways and forms of religious behavior elsewhere.[12]

Such a breadth of view, however, was held by only a few Islamicists. Most professional scholars working on Islamic data had only a limited interest in the general history of religions. Various reasons could be given to explain this. Like Judaism, Islam was very different from the religions of Antiquity and of non-literate people, which were at the centre of interest of historians of religions at the time. So, although several Islamicists paid attention to the historical relations between Islam and Judaism, or between Islam and Christianity, they could not find much profit for their work in the history of ancient Mediterranean, Indian, or Far-Eastern religions. Secondly, the demands of linguistic specialization in Islamic Studies became ever more severe, given the abundance of texts available in Arabic, Persian, and other "Islamic" languages which had to be collected, catalogued, and edited before they could be studied properly. Thirdly, scholars of Islam often had to teach the so-called "Islamic" languages in university programmes as well. This left little time for interests beyond the Islamic orbit, with the exception of the Semitic languages in some cases. A fourth reason for the relatively scanty interest of Islamicists in the general history of religions is that on the whole their interest in religion at large - and consequently in the religious aspects of Islamic materials - was less than that among general historians of religion. The latter often focused on the Greek or Roman religion, or on religions to be found in the *Umwelt* of the Israelite religion and of early Christianity. In the latter case they worked mostly within theological faculties, usually with commitments to some kind of general philosophical or theological concept of religion. Nevertheless, some Islamicists kept track of the general history of religions and the development of this discipline. Some of them actively carried out research on religions other than Islam: for instance several Jewish scholars of Islam with regard to Judaism and Jewish influences on Islam,[13] Louis Massignon (1883-1962) with regard to Christianity and Indian religions in his study of Islamic mysticism,[14] Tor Andrae (1885-1947) with regard to the Syriac and Manichaean context of early Islam[15] and Henry Corbin (1903-1978) with regard to the Zoroastrian background of Persian Islam.[16] Yet, there have been only a few professional general historians of religion who have shown an active interest in Islamic religion. An exception is Geo Widengren who, thoroughly familiar with ancient Near Eastern, including Iranian religions, did much original research on Islamic materials and showed the continuation of certain motifs of ancient Near Eastern religious traditions persisting in the area after its Islamization.[17] For most other historians of religions, who were less familiar with prophetic, book, and law-based religions, Islam was either uninteresting, profoundly foreign, or technically inaccessible because of the subtleties of the Arabic language. Perhaps, also, it was somewhat morally despised.

With regard to their materials, however, Islamic historians followed the same methods and research procedures as those applied in the study of religions other than Islam, so that among historians of religions there was not only a common historical approach but also a substantial unity in method. One may think of the internal and external textual criticism applied to Quran, *hadīth* and early texts, or of the historical explanations by means of outside influences which were given to numerous Islamic textual and other data. One may also recall in this regard the debates on the historical origins of mysticism in Islam and of the discussions on the influence - often through polemics - of Christian theology and Greek philosophy on the development of *kalām* and *falsafa*. Looking back, one is struck by the hypercritical tendencies of some scholars who endeavored to explain Muhammad's ideas and actions completely in terms of Christian or Jewish influences to the neglect of Muhammad's own originality or the socio-political context within which he lived. Such historical criticism, however, can also be observed in research on religions other than Islam, where historical truth is put in opposition to what people believed and where, if the historical reality of something cannot be proved, it is simply denied.

On the whole, it is fair to say that in contrast with some other branches of the history of religions, Islamicists - to the extent to which they were not the victims of ethnocentricity - largely studied Islamic religion within the context of Islamic civilization and culture. They thereby kept aloof from hasty comparisons, stressed the logic of internal religious developments once the foundations of Islam had been established, and defended the uniqueness of Islam within the religious history of humankind. It is because of the meticulous investigations of the precise historical study of Islam that we now know so much more about Islam than we did a century and half ago. But we may remind ourselves that Islamic studies are now at the stage classical studies reached around the turn of the sixteenth century, when only the most important texts had been published and when only the most obvious archaeological remains had become known. Only a minute part is now known of what potentially can be known of Islamic history.

History of religions in its precise "historical" sense, then, can make a major contribution to Islamic Studies. It can delineate the life of the Prophet and his message, the growth of the prophetic movement into a religious community with its own tradition, and then institutionalized into a universal religion. The history of Islam, like the history of Judaism, is basically the religious history of a community that defines itself explicitly as earthbound, and of the numerous communities constituting it, each with its particular cultural and religious traditions. Consequently, such religions as Islam and Judaism by and large fell outside the interest of historians of religions who were keen on the supernatural, the religious, and the holy as subjects in themselves.

The historical study of Islamic religious data should proceed, then, on at least two levels. On one level, the historical contexts and the network of conditions, causes, and effects of what has happened should be analyzed and described as well as explained as much as possible. On another level, the problems with which specific Muslim communities and their leaders have been confronted in particular periods should be analyzed, and the different solutions which were proposed should be studied. It will be of particular interest to know whether and in what ways the different Muslim leaders with their proposed solutions referred to Islam, or what they considered to be specifically Islamic values. A closer analysis should then seek to determine whether such references really provide a clue to the chosen solution or whether they were simply used as a religious legitimation for a solution that could be fully explained without necessarily taking into consideration the religion at the time. And always, when particular Muslim groups and their leaders appeal to Islam, the question has to be put: What kind of Islam do they have in mind?

This historical approach also opens the door to cross-cultural comparisons with non-Muslim communities. If we may assume that similar biological and psychological, technological and economic, social and political laws and rules are at work in all human societies, then the interesting question is this: What specific solutions may be associated with the fact that the community concerned was Muslim and with the kind of Muslim community it was?

Islamic Studies and the Comparative Study of Religious Data

The name "history of religions" has also been used in the wider sense of comparative religion, including also phenomenology of religion. Broadly speaking, this means that besides the historical approach to data in their uniqueness, a comparative approach should be used in the study of religious data insofar as they are comparable. Until now this *comparative* study of religious data, as distinct from the *historical* study of influences and developments, seems to have yielded its best fruits for Islamic Studies in the realm of Semitic languages. Biblical scholars such as Julius Wellhausen (1844-1918) and W. Robertson Smith (1846-1894), famous for their historical-critical studies of the Old Testament, were not only aware of the affinities between Hebrew and Arabic, but they also looked at present-day Bedouin practices with the hope that some clues could be found to solve particular problems of ancient Israelite religion.[18] A.J. Wensinck (1882-

1939) threw light on certain parallels and structural elements held in common by West-Semitic religions and Islam, certain comparable developments in Israelite and early Islamic religion, a number of historical and literary connections between early Islam and its Syriac *Umwelt*, and the ascetic climate within which Eastern Christian and early Muslim spirituality developed from the fourth to the eighth centuries C.E.[19] This scholarly tradition has been maintained by some Old Testament scholars who are perfectly familiar with Arabic, among whom, for example, the name of H. Ringgren in Uppsala may be mentioned. The attention of these scholars is directed not only to historical influences but also to parallel phenomena, developments, and structures.

Comparisons between religious data can be made, of course, in different ways and also with different aims. If, for instance, the significance of certain data in one religion is not well known but analogous data in another religion (preferably belonging to the same culture area) are well established, then a comparison between these data may elucidate the significance of the lesser known, at least by approximation. On a larger scale one can make structural comparisons between religions, for instance, in order to understand the distinctive character of each of them, or to demonstrate the existence of a common underlying pattern. Attempts have also been made to describe larger patterns of meaning that encompass individual phenomena classified by means of comparison under such larger patterns. Comparisons of the first sort are more precise and verifiable, and such comparisons have led to a better understanding of the details of Islamic religious texts, rituals, and forms of piety that might otherwise have remained obscure. Structural comparisons between Islam and Christianity can clarify distinctive differences in a better way than by pursuing polemical confrontations of theological doctrines.[20] As a prophetic religion, Islam can be considered as one variation within the larger pattern of prophetic religions having many traits in common with other prophetic religions that developed scripture and law.[21]

It has been rightly observed by Charles Adams that phenomenology of religion, with its descriptive classificatory surveys of a broad range of religious phenomena, has thus far been of little use to Islamic Studies. Among the reasons for this is, first of all, the fact that religions such as Islam and Judaism in their normative forms cannot be analyzed according to the scheme: "conceptions of the Divine, conceptions of humankind, and interaction between the Divine and humankind" (see note 10 above). It is striking to see how relatively lacking these two religions, at least in their official normative forms, appear to be in concrete and visible phenomena compared with the rich stock of symbols, myths, rituals, and other religious expressions of, for instance, the religions of Antiquity, India, or peoples with an oral culture. In fact, Islam seems to be one of the marginal religions for phenomenologists, who have traditionally studied religious fields that included pantheons of divinities, multitudes of souls, and complicated communications between the natural and supernatural.

Secondly, with the exception of Widengren's *Religionsphänomenologie*,[22] largely based on the author's own sourcework, no previous phenomenology of religion has done justice to Islamic religious phenomena; in order to do that, another approach should be taken so that not just visible phenomena are treated. The fervent quest for general religious phenomena, themes, and structures such as myth and ritual, sacred kingship, or even monotheism has been significant for the understanding of a number of religions; but strikingly enough, never fruitfully applied to the study of the Islam. Consequently, Islam does not seem to fit the general idea of what religions are, and Islamic data do not seem to correspond well to what are held to be religious phenomena at large, with the exception of forms of popular religion which, of course, do not have a normative character that is officially recognized.

Thirdly, until now Islamic data have not been made readily available by Arabists and Islamicists at large to general historians of religions who do not know the languages in question. Also, attempts to explain religion with the help of theories developed from comparative studies of non-literate religions have been of little relevance to Islamic Studies, whether these attempts relied on theories of animism, dynamism, magic, or even primal monotheism. Is Islam the great exception to the religious life of humankind, or is it rather that Islam (as well as Judaism) demonstrates some inherent limitations of the phenomenology of religion which developed in the period between the two World Wars?

Islam, like other prophetic religions, seems to have a "revolutionary" aspect, or at least an aspect of protest. It rejects a number of religious phenomena that are usually studied, such as gods, spirits, demons, souls, myths, rituals, and most visible symbols. It replaces them, however, with new ones, such as the appearance of prophets, scriptures and traditions, ethical-juridical and ritual prescriptions, certain forms of mystical expressions and organizations, a great number of social and political concepts as to the ideal society, and a smaller number of theological doctrines. Consequently, phenomenology of religion should be readapted so as to do justice to the Islamic phenomena, and to the phenomena Islam shares with other religions of protest, rejection of idolatry, prophetic reform, or puritan iconoclasm. In addition, the kinds of comparative research mentioned earlier, besides offering surveys of religious phenomena in the way of classical phenomenology of religion, can offer new insights. Such comparative studies, as distinct from the study of historical developments and derivations, can make a contribution to Islamic Studies by investigating how certain movements have arisen and developments have taken place in Muslim and in other societies.[23] Some examples may suffice to indicate what is meant here.

(1) Comparative studies of prophetic figures including Muhammad, and of the rise of religions of a prophetic type including Islam, should take into account the conditions under which prophets arose in the Middle East and beyond, and the significance they had for their societies.

(2) The development from prophetic word into canonized scripture, from oral to written tradition, and the concurrent processes of sacralization in Islam should be compared with similar developments from prophetic preaching, to a prophetic movement, to a religion which claims universality and which consolidates itself with scripture and law as forms of institution-

alization.

(3) Attention should be given to the rise and further development of religious movements of a puritanical, mystical, gnostic, or philosophical type within Islam analogous to similar movements in other religious traditions. Such studies might include the social and political context in which they arise and the ways in which they appeal to the given tradition and legitimatize themselves by it. Consider, for example, those trends in the monotheistic religions that want to bypass established tradition in order to nourish themselves again with the original revelation or Divine Word brought into Holy Scripture, such as the Karaites, Kharijites, and first Lutherans, in Judaism, Islam, and Christianity respectively.

(4) Specific elements of the Islamic religious structure, as they function within particular Muslim societies, can usefully be compared with elements that perform an analogous function in other religious structures than the Islamic one, and within varying types of societies. The *Sunna* in Islam, for instance, might be compared with other kinds of normative tradition in other religions.

(5) There is also a need for comparative studies of the treatment of particular problems in the ethics, jurisprudence, and theology of Islam, Judaism, and Christianity in their historical development. This may lead to a better insight into such matters as the specific ways in which such problems have been formulated in each religion or have not been seen at all, which solutions have been envisaged, and the extent to which such solutions have had a universal tendency or direction.

(6) In the course of history different thinkers and groups have given various interpretations of Islam, just as the historical development of Muslim societies has brought changes to Islamic religious practices, and such changes of interpretation and of practice have, of course, been linked to each other. The resulting self-interpretative process of Islam up to the present time lends itself to comparison with similar self-interpretative processes of other religions and ideologies, in particular when people who belong to different religions and ideologies experience similar developments or events and when they respond to these in terms of their specific

religion or ideology. Of particular interest here are processes of rediscovery and rejection, and of sacralization and desacralization of specific elements of the traditions involved.[24]

(7) To be more specific, movements arising within or in reaction to the Islamic religious tradition and practice in the nineteenth and twentieth centuries can be validly compared with similar movements in other religious traditions in the same period. Such comparisons will not only lead to a better understanding of the different positive and negative kinds of responses to "modernization" processes as they arise within the religious communities, across religious boundaries; they may also show different kinds of secularization processes,[25] or the occurrence of new developments of older religious traditions, or even the rise of "new" religions out of older ones. If one could carry out comparative studies of the rise and fall of certain elements in different religious traditions over a particular period of time, taking into account the historical and social context, one might be able to discover why particular data in the Islamic and other religious traditions undergo a reinforcement or a weakening of their religious meaning. Sacralizing tendencies within different religious and cultural traditions at the present time, for instance with regard to state and national interests, deserve the utmost attention and should be compared with each other.

Islamic Studies and the Discussion of Method in the Study of Religion

Within the history of religions in the broad sense there have been from the start undercurrents of a sometimes very sharp questioning of methods between the extremes of, for instance, critical historical research and philosophical phenomenology. In most disciplines there is a quest for the right method to explore particular sources or to select data for a particular inquiry, and it includes not only questions of research techniques but also larger problems of definition, the elaboration of a hypothesis, or the development of a theory or conceptual framework. In the case of the history of religions this quest has been more complicated than in most other disciplines, since the meaning and the evaluation of "religion" itself have been determined for a long time by Western religion, though refined by theological and philosophical interpretations. It has taken a long time for the concept of "nature", for instance, to be deprived of its ancient metaphysical and theological connotations, and similar observations can be made about concepts such as "culture" and "society", which have been determined for a long time by western ways of thinking. Classical phenomenology of religion has rendered a primary service to the study of religion by insisting that religion should be described without immediate philosophical or theological evaluations. Although religious and ideological impulses have continued to play a role in the study of religion, this century has already witnessed the establishment of a science of religion (*Religionswissenschaft*) as a specific discipline - or rather an area of studies - with its own autonomy and integrity.[26]

On the whole there do not seem to have been such intense epistemological in Islamic studies until the last few decades. The main effort in Islamic Studies has been devoted to textual research: philology in the best sense of the word and historical inquiry into written and archaeological sources were the disciplines to be mastered. Islamic Studies, like Indology and Sinology, had developed more or less on the pattern of Classical Studies, though with a broader notion of culture and a greater awareness of the plurality of civilizations. Yet there have been other currents in Islamic Studies too, mostly incorporating textual research within a larger perspective. As far as religion is concerned, Louis Massignon's personal involvement in the Sufi spirituality he studied, indicates that his scholarly aims went beyond philology and history for their own sake.[27] Wilfred Cantwell Smith analyzed modern Islam in India by looking at the class interests involved, and later came to a personalistic interpretation of Islamic thought, with a clear personal involvement as well.[28] W. Montgomery Watt arrived at new interpretations not only of the origins of Islam but also of early history and theology by analyzing religious phenomena within their socio-political structure and by using the finding of the sociology of knowledge in his interpretation of Islamic thought.[29] C.A.O. van Nieuwenhijze asked in 1961 whether sociology might not be the next phase in Islamic Studies,[30] while at the same time Gustav E. von Grunebaum envisaged Islamic studies within the broad concerns of cultural anthropology as the study of man and his different cultural (including religious) orientations.[31] Clifford Geertz, starting from living symbols in specific Muslim societies, initiated a study of patterns of symbolic meaning according to particular Muslim groups and communities in his studies on Islam.[32] All of these scholars (and they are not the only ones) have showed considerable methodological concern.[33] These epistemological concerns in Islamic Studies seem to have been related only indirectly to the questions of method that have been raised in the history of religions and the study of religion in general, to which we have already referred. It seems reasonable to infer that these concerns have been due to a considerable extent to a growing awareness of and interest in Islam as a *living* religion and faith. As the second largest world religion in population, Islam makes an impact on the present-day world scene, most obviously in its political aspects, in different ways: the role of Islam first in the independence movements in Muslim regions and later in the independent states; the conflicts in the Middle East and in the Indian Subcontinent; and last but not least the "Islamic" revolutions and movements which have occurred in some Muslim countries. Islam is also indirectly connected with certain political solidarities and with certain economic issues such as Third World development and the control of oil prices. Classical Islamic studies was obviously not equipped to explain the role of Islam in all of these aspects; new approaches have to be developed and used.

A second impulse to recognize the importance of Islam as a living religion and faith has come, paradoxically, from missionary circles. The fact that considerable efforts over the past century notwithstanding, no significant number of Muslims have converted to Christianity has simply forced the recognition of Islam as a separate religious identity with its own distinctive life and continuity. When both Christian and Muslim leaders became increasingly aware of common problems confronting all believers with regard to the very future of humankind, new ways of communication on a more spiritual level were sought, more or less aptly symbolized by a call for dialogue. The growing interest in Islam as a living religion with a very significant cultural record, in addition to being stimulated by the media, has also been enhanced by teaching programmes in world religions and civilizations at colleges and universities. Courses on Islam as a world religion have forced general historians of religions and Islamicists to present Islam not only as a story whose greatest moments were its formative and classical periods, but also as a history which is still being made. Present-day Muslim interpretations of the Quran and Sunna,[34] of religious and social movements, and of legal and political issues[35] have become further subjects of interest. Consequently, the *nature of Islamic studies* has become a focus for scholarly discussion in which Muslim scholars are actively participating, especially the question of its distinctive features and whether such studies constitute a whole, and what different scholarly and unscholarly concerns play a role in these studies. Most interestingly, perhaps, the question of the *nature of Islam* has arisen: In what sense is it a subject for scholarly research? Is it a law, an ideology, a system of symbols, a tradition, a faith, or something quite different?[36]

The epistemological concerns of immediate interest to us here surround the problem of how the *religious aspects of Islam* ought to be studied and interpreted. This has led to a renewed and revived interest in the function and meaning of religious data, movements, values, and so on in the context of Muslim societies. Such inquiries had already been made in the period of colonial rule under the pressures and limitations of that time, but these studies have benefitted tremendously from the swift development of the social sciences over the last decades, in particular cultural anthropology and sociology. So it has become possible to study the meaning of events and processes in Muslim countries in the context of the cultural-religious Islamic framework that is alive there. Three problems are paramount in these studies:

1) Which kinds of groups support and transmit various particular interpretations of Islam, and who are the religious leaders (*ʿulamā*ʾ, *shaykhs*, the "lay" leaders) and the adherents?

2) How do particular changes occurring in the religious institutions (or in institutions that are legitimatized by religion) relate to changes in society at large, and what are the consequences of the changes of these institutions for the societies concerned, and vice versa?

3) What general political or social role or function do different Islamic ideas and practices perform within particular Muslim societies, apart from the specifically Islamic religious meaning they are meant to have for the believers?

Such questions can also be asked about Muslim societies of the past, provided that there are enough historical data available to answer them. In any case, it is a mark of epistemological progress that a number of subjects can be examined in Islamic Studies now, which some fifty years ago were excluded, not because the phenomena did not exist, but because the methodological tools to handle them were not yet developed. Several publications give evidence of the recent expansion of approaches to the study of such data as we find in Islam.

Just as we are now more aware of the general political, social, and economic processes that play a role in Muslim societies as they do in other developing countries, and just as more attention is now paid to different forms of the cultural-religious Islamic framework within which particular practices and ideas are significant for Muslims, so also the notion of tradition, whether great or little, has attracted new attention in Islamic Studies both in history and in anthropology. In Islam this religious tradition in the widest sense of the word is now some fourteen centuries old. Claiming as it does to go back ultimately to divine revelation contained in the Quran, it contains a great number of tributaries that have nourished many successive generations of Muslims who have transmitted this tradition with several local variations. One difficulty is how to study the different elements not only separately but also as an integral part of the larger tradition, with its branches that have moved on through history in Muslim societies.

The normative character of certain elements of the Islamic tradition has been recognized throughout the history of Islam by Muslims who have wanted in principle to believe and act accordingly. One thinks of the Quran and *Sunna*, certain parts of the *Sharīʿa* in particular, (e.g., the religious duties (*ʿibādāt*), the regulations on personal status, elements of dialectical theology (*kalām*), such as the "unity" of God (*tawhīd*), prophethood (*nubuwwa*), the Quranic miracle (*iʿjāz al-Quran*), and the creeds (*aqāʾid*), certain practices of piety (with reference to *hadīth*) which may be elaborated in *tasawwuf* or Sufism, certain paradigmatic figures and episodes in Islamic history: the life of Muhammad and for the Sunnis the period of *al-khulafāʾ al-rāshidūn*, the "rightly guided caliphs"; for the Shia the life of ʿAlī, the events round Karbala and the history of the Imams. The idea of Islam itself is also such a basic normative element: as a spiritual reality, it is regarded by its adherents as the true law and order of things, the supreme value on earth, the absolute religion.

To the study of such elements of the normative "great tradition" should be added, for each region, numerous elements of the local "little tradition",[37] including legendary events in the history of the region, deeds and blessings of particular saints, the meritorious character of particular practices, and so on. All official doctrine notwithstanding, when particular men or women have served a mediating function in local "popular" religion because of their sanctity or insight, their authority has often become part of that religious tradition as well. This aspect of the "little tradition" is one of the prisms through which life's meanings are refracted. It is an epistemological advance in Islamic Studies to take cognizance of the fact that successive generations of Muslims have interpreted their lives, world, and history through the spectrum of the religious tradition in which they stood and of the religio-cultural framework of the society into which they were born. This religious tradition and this religio-cultural framework require attention beyond the professional historical and anthropological work, and it would be precisely the task of the history of religions to show the religious aspects of the historical continuity and human solidarity that can be found in Muslim societies.

Some Basic Distinctions

We may look, then, at Islam as the religious tradition and the religio-cultural framework of a living community - consisting of a number of concrete Muslim communities with all kinds of variations of both this tradition and this framework.[38] Before proposing a way in which to study the religious aspects of Islam in particular, we should first make some distinctions that may be self-evident.

First, we should recognize that the word "Islam" itself is used in very different senses: by scholars (Islamicists with different approaches) as a subject of study, or a "symbol" for their concrete subject of inquiry; by Muslims who, as Fazlur Rahman points out, may have different orientations as to what they consider to be religiously normative, to them; and in ordinary language in the West (with different evaluations and appreciations of what is felt to be "foreign" to the West).[39]

Second, a sharp distinction should be made between "normative" Islam and "actual" Islam. Normative Islam consists of the prescriptions, norms, and values that are recognized as divine guidance by the whole community. These are taken from the basic normative texts, mostly with what is held to be their normative interpretation. Actual Islam comprises all those forms and movements, practices and ideas that in fact have existed in the many Muslim communities in different times and places, and that have been considered to be "Islamic" and consequently legitimate and valid.[40]

Third, an equally sharp distinction should be made between Islamic *data* as presented to someone who is interested in and seeks to become conversant with them for the sake of scholarly truth, and the *ideals* that

Muslims as Muslims attach to them, the meaning they derive from them or the truth they recognize in them.[41] This old distinction between practice and ideal, fact and (subjective) meaning of a religious datum is necessary not only for the purpose of analysis, but also in order to make valid comparisons. One should distinguish, for instance, the practice of the *hajj* as it actually takes place from the norms, values, and ideals attached to it by the participating pilgrims: both can be studied.[42] In any comparison between the *hajj* and other pilgrimages, one will have to juxtapose either the practice of the *hajj* with the practice of pilgrimages elsewhere, or the ideals Muslims have of their *hajj* with the ideals existing in other religious communities about their pilgrimages. In any case, in scholarly work one should avoid comparing the practice of one kind of pilgrimage with the ideal of another pilgrimage and this holds true for all comparisons between religious data.

Fourth, a similar distinction should be made in comparisons between different Muslim societies or groups. We can very well compare the factual data and actual practices of one society with those of another one, or particular values, norms, and ideals of one society with those of another society. But in Islamic Studies, from a scholarly point of view, we have no reason *a priori* to say that one specific society represents Islam as a norm and ideal better than another. Unless all Muslims agree that one particular group or society is the best Islamic one - and one still has to know what is understood by "best" - we must proceed by reporting that in one group certain ideas and practices of Islam prevail, while in another other ideas and practices can be found, and by trying to explain this difference and to look for its implications.

The Study of Religion in Islamic Studies

The major epistemological problem in Islamic Studies still seems to be the correlation between the scholarly categories of description, analysis, and interpretation, and the adequate translation and conceptualization of Islamic realities on the basis of the raw data themselves. Several studies of the image of Islam presented in scholarly work have shown the tremendous role the "subjective" values and norms of a scholar play in his study of any foreign culture and religion, including Islam.[43] Such "subjective" values and norms can in part be traced back to the cultural and ideological factors that determine the relationship under study, and in part to quite personal preferences and evaluations made by the scholar himself and which are sometimes difficult to explain or even to understand. We have written about these values and factors elsewhere as "assumptions" and "presuppositions" in Islamic Studies.[44] Since "Islam" is not an empirical datum in the same way as concrete texts, practices, and even ideals, what is held to be the "reality" of Islam largely depends on the concepts and categories with which a particular scholar is working. It is logical that certain sets of concepts and categories will lead to the denial of any "reality" of Islam, or at least the denial that any such "reality" can be known in a scholarly way. This does not mean, by the way, that on the basis of this position one could not do important work in Islamic Studies, but rather that the concept of "Islam" in this case makes no scholarly sense. Given these problems, I would like to present some proposals for obtaining a better grasp and understanding of what may be called "religion" in Islamic Studies, or still better, the religious aspects of Islam. It seems to me that these proposals find a particular application in the case of Islam but that they are in principle valid for the study of all religions and ideologies. They will have to be developed, then, according to the specific data of each religion or ideology in particular. Until now, as far as I know, Islamic religion has not yet been studied systematically from this angle.

To the extent that Islam is a religious tradition and a religio-cultural framework, it is linked to people, societies, and communities at large identifying themselves as "Muslim". Whereas texts, social practices, monuments, and so on, sacred or profane, somehow exist in themselves, this is not the case for "Islam" which, first of all, seems to exist as a meaning for people, not only for Muslims but also for "outsiders" including non-Muslim Islamicists.[45] If a particular scholar works, for instance, on texts and discovers what he may call "essentials" of Islam as a religion, this is always a construction by scholarly methods, containing both subjective and objective elements. The work of scholars such as Louis Massignon, Henry Corbin, and to a certain extent also Wilfred C. Smith, has opened up dimensions of mystical experience, gnostic spirituality, and personalistic faith in Islam; but it would be untenable to pretend that anyone of these dimensions "is" Islam. They are rather aspects of Islamic religion.

Perhaps I may draw some conclusions from this state of affairs for the study of religion in Islamic Studies. I would like to explain them in the form of an argument kept as simple and reasonable as possible in the hope that this may lead to further discussion.

The starting point is this: what is a religious fact for one person is not necessarily a religious fact for another person unless both happen to belong to the same religious community; even then the "subjective" meaning of this fact may be different for each person. Or, put in more abstract terms: religious meanings are not inherent in particular facts.[46] We are concerned, rather, with data which convey religious and other meanings to particular people and which tend to become sacralized in particular communities. These communities then acquire a "religious" character.

As a consequence, on the level of the empirical analysis of Islamic data, one should avoid as much as possible using such general terms derived from Western parlance as "religion", "world view", "ideology", "faith", and so on. The accurate scholarly study of the religious aspects of Islam starts with looking at those data possessing significance for a certain number of Muslims, and it continues by paying special attention to those data to which they attach a religious significance, largely in their own terms. Such religious data have a sign or symbol value for the people concerned.[47]

It is fair to say that the primary and intrinsic religious datum for Muslims is the Quran, since only the words of the Quran and their meaning are considered to have an immediate divine origin. Because of the sheer fact that in the West most scholars of Islam are non-Muslims, and that empirical research methods are used, this religious or even "divine" dimension of the

Quran as Muslims perceive it, is bound to be underestimated in Islamic Studies. The same observation applies to the understanding of Christ by non-Christian scholars who, equally, cannot but underestimate the "divine" dimension of Christ as Christians perceive it. In fact, the persistence of Islam as a religion may very well be ascribed to the continued recognition by the Muslim community of the Quran as divine revelation (apart from the shared rituals and other duties), just as the persistence of Christianity may be ascribed to the continued recognition by the Christian community of divine revelation in Christ (apart from the organization, rules, and authority of the church).[48]

Of considerable though not equal authority as the Quran are those data which for the Muslim community are religious and normative in a derived sense: the Sunna and the prescriptions it contains, traced back to the Prophet but not transmitting an immediate divine communication as does the Quran. Several scholars have shown the importance of Muhammad as an Islamic paradigm. Put in more abstract terms, the life of the Prophet is for Muslims a "sign" although not on the same level as an *āya*. All the rest of the Islamic religious data seem to be of tertiary importance as far as the community as a whole is concerned; even if this religious meaning is vividly felt and experienced by particular groups, it has nevertheless a derived character. These data not only vary according to different places, but also may be superseded by later practices and formulations based on new insights.

In the strict sense of the word, Islam, according to the way it is presented in the Quran, can probably best be called a collection or network of signs or even a sign system.[49] Islam constitutes the right human responses in acting and thinking to the *ayāt*, "signs" which have been provided to humankind in the Quran and elsewhere, and from which a Muslim has to draw the right conclusions by the full use of reason, for life on earth, for the life and order of society, and for eternal bliss. A Muslim is called upon to abandon him- or herself to the God who sent the *ayāt* and to obey His will as communicated through them, appealing to others to follow and understand the signs as well; and, in the first place, to understand the

Quran itself as a "sign" revealed to humankind. The *ayāt*, indeed, are nexus points of divine revelation and human reflection.[50]

There is no reason not to call Islam a religion so long as we constantly keep in mind that it is not a religion like others but that it has its own particular notion of what "religion" is. Calling Islam a "sign system", however, has definite advantages for research purposes. In the first place, it avoids stamping Islamic data and materials with Western-coined concepts which are part of the ideals and view, ideologies and faiths that are fundamentally foreign to Islam itself, as Muslims see it. Second, it leads positively to a kind of investigation that runs parallel to the Muslim's focus of interest. It looks for the sense of the universe, humanity and society, and of being brought to right action, by means of the study of the *ayāt* which are recognized as "signs" in the Quran and elsewhere. Seen in this perspective, the history of Islam is essentially the history of what has been done in the Muslim community with the signs revealed and confided to it, not only theoretically in its religious sciences but also practically in its social life, its political organization and action. In the course of history it is with reference to these signs that the religious sciences were developed and that social values, norms, and ideals were formulated for the praxis of the community as a response to the many problems with which Muslim communities have been confronted. Both theoretically and practically there have been a number of readings of these signs in the Muslim community, and these various readings are subject to study.[51]

A third advantage of approaching Islam as a network of signs is that this can lead to a better insight into certain basic and recurring patterns of meaning in thought and action within the Muslim community. For instance, certain Quranic texts are often quoted in support of particular solutions to certain problems. The most significant and original elaboration by Muslims of the "sign system" was probably the attempt to establish a normative pattern of the Islamic social order, i.e., the *Sharīʿa*. This seems to include laws, not only to be applied as they are in our Western legal systems, but that also serve as "signposts" for how life should be lived, though in juridical disguise. Is the religious meaning of the prescriptions of the *Sharīʿa* not also to be found (at least in part) in their character of signs as to how people and society should be but are not yet? From a methodological point of view, such a study should begin with certain permanent vehicles of Islamic religious meanings as "signs" which are recognizable by Muslims and which constitute some kind of communicative sign system - even if circumstances of place and time vary.[52]

The role of religion in Muslim societies

There is no justifiable sense, from a scholarly point of view, to maintain a cause-and-effect relationship between Islam and a particular society. Apart from some common religious prescriptions (e.g., the religious duties [*ʿibādāt*] and some basic rules of family law), different societies have different social rules and structures and consequently different empirical forms of Islam. In some cases, one can measure the varying ways the same legal prescriptions have been implemented in different countries; but there are other and more important differences than only juridical ones between different regions. It is, for example, misleading to say that in Iran or Saudi Arabia Islam is applied, but that it is not applied in Turkey or Indonesia; or that Islam is the cause of the underdevelopment of certain so-called "backward areas," or responsible for undemocratic political behavior. The truth is that networks of signs such as those that constitute Islam can be read, interpreted, and practiced in many different ways in Muslim societies, depending not only on the different intentions of the interpreters, but also on contingent "infrastructural" and political factors obtaining in these societies. It can legitimate or contradict a particular state of affairs or policy; it can bridge or exacerbate conflicts of interests; and it can refrain or encourage absolutist tendencies. The number of ways in which such sign systems can be interpreted, applied, and used are probably infinite, although a certain number of patterns of interpretations, applications, and uses of Islam can be distinguished when more data have become available and our insight has increased. All that can be said in general (and with the necessary caution) is that this particular religion tends to regulate social relations in such a way that explosions are avoided, that it tends to take the golden mean between extreme alternative solutions, and that it provides hopes and ideals for masses living under the greatest hardships, often being able to move them. In any case it is never something called "Islam" that is the immediate cause of attitudes and actions taken by people and groups, which may consider these norms to be "Islamic" but whose referent in fact is an Islamic text or a *hadīth* that is taken to be authoritative. It is not Islam as substance[53] that is implemented but a cluster of norms, values, and ideals formulated by the leaders and understood by Muslims with reference to Quranic verses and *hadīth*.

The role of religion in constituting Muslim identity

It is significant that hardly anyone who identifies him- or herself as a Muslim ever exchanges Muslim identity for another one. Although this is a social fact, there is something elusive about it, since it means different things at the same time. It implies basically a confession of faith and, though often indirectly, membership of a Muslim community and of the Muslim *umma* at large. Consequently, however "social" a Muslim may be, an appeal can always be made by fellow Muslims to the fideistic aspect of Muslim identity. Apparently a Muslim receives his or her identity less by merely adhering to the "religion" of Islam than by actually becoming aware of - and arriving at a reasonable insight into - the "signs" of God, reading and understanding them as such, taking an attitude of *Islam* towards God, and participating in communal life with other Muslims, with an adherence to its basic values and with great mutual solidarity.

The role of religion in inspiring Muslim spirituality

Muslim spirituality in the broad sense clearly expresses itself in very different ways and forms, from more traditional piety to forms of personal mystical experience, and in its different expressions, from the use of *ḥadīth* to poetic hints at the absolute. Although there are always references to the "signs" of God, they play very different roles in different ways. Consequently, it would be superficial to say that Islam, as such, leads to one particular form or type of spirituality. In fact, quite the reverse seems to be the case: in different forms of Muslim spiritual life different elements of the total network of signs are used, or people use the same signs in different ways according to different intentions. This does not preclude the possibility of distinguishing a certain number of patterns of Muslim spirituality when more data are available and our insight actually increases; but, again, in principle there is an almost infinite number of possible variations. Even those forms of spiritual life which go back to the immediate reading and application of the Quran already show considerable variations.

To summarize, just as certain religions within a particular smaller cultural context have aptly been described as "symbol system,"[54] so Islam as a world religion can be approached fruitfully as a broad and rather loosely structured sign system overarching local symbol systems that are linked to particular cultures and societies.[55] In the strict sense of the word, the āyā*t* of the Quran are the only immediate signs,[56] but somewhat more loosely, ancient *Sunna*, the practice of the *ʿibādāt*, and the main rules of the *Sharīʿa* can be considered as signs as well - just as we should not overlook a number of signs of nature and history to which the Quran refers as signs of God. In the course of the history of the Muslim community and communities different world views and ideologies, juridical and theological schools, and forms of piety and spirituality have developed which all made an appeal to Islam and referred to particular signs which may have inspired them or which were quoted as a kind of legitimation. In particular, the ideal of an Islamic social order and the longing for an Islamic state have had great practical consequences in the field of social and political action throughout the history of Islam.

Consequently, the religious data of Islam in different times and places are facts which are first of all subject to investigation in themselves and in their connections with the concrete social and historical context at a given time and place. These data are also to be studied, secondly, in their context as signs referring to Islam or interpreted and read as signs referring to transcendent realities. Thirdly, when the main readings which Muslim practitioners and theoreticians have given of their "signs" have been decoded, it may eventually be possible to establish certain patterns of meaning that have evolved in the course of the Islamic religious and cultural tradition in reference to the Islamic sign system.[57] This more or less discrete view of Islam as a sign system avoiding any "imperialistic" approach from outside is not foreign to Muslims in principle since it corresponds to the self-view given in the Quran. It allows for reconsideration of certain basic problems in Islamic Studies, in particular where religious issues are concerned.[58]

To what extent religious meanings intensify, change, or disappear in contemporary history is a subject of concern to students of any living religion. It may even turn out to be one of the leading problems of the contemporary history of religions as a whole. For the treatment of problems like this, Islamic Studies undoubtedly can make a positive contribution,[59] since, in the world where Muslims live, so many different orientations have taken place and still are taking place with an appeal both to Islam and to the "divine signs" of the Quran. The nature of this appeal has still to be explored.[60]

Notes

1. On the study of religions and religious data, and some relevant literature, see for instance Jacques Waardenburg, "Religionswissenschaft New Style: Some Thoughts and Afterthoughts," *Annual Review of the Social Sciences of Religion* (The Hague: Mouton), vol. 2 (1978): 189-220.
2. See for instance Charles J. Adams, "Islamic Religious Tradition," in *The Study of the Middle East: Research and Scholarship in the Humanities and the Social Sciences*, ed. Leonard Binder (New York: John Wiley, 1976), pp. 29-95. On pages 34-35 a survey is given of the different approaches in Islamic studies. See also the same author's contribution "Islam" in *A Reader's Guide to the Great Religions*, ed. Charles J. Adams, 2nd edn. (New York: The Free Press, and London: Collier-Macmillan, 1977), pp. 407-466 (cf. 1st ed. 1965, pp. 287-337). These two volumes also give a good survey of the progress of Islamic studies. Cf. J. Waardenburg, "Changes of Perspective in Islamic Studies over the Last Decades," *Humaniora Islamica*, (The Hague: Mouton, 1973), I, 247-260.
3. Bruce L. Lawrence. *Shahrastānī on the Indian Religions*. Series Religion and Society no. 4. (The Hague and Paris: Mouton, 1976).
4. Papers on this topic were read and relevant coin collections were shown at the Congress of Arabists and Islamicists held at Visby and Stockholm, in August 1972.
5. See for instance the comprehensive account by Edward W. Said, *Orientalism* (New York, 1978). We do not discuss here the issues involved.
6. Important is the account given by Maxime Rodinson, "The Western image and Western studies of Islam," in *The Legacy of Islam*, 2nd ed., ed. Joseph Schacht with C.E. Bosworth (Oxford: Clarendon Press, 1974), pp. 9-62. See by the same author *Europe and the Mystique of Islam*, Seattle and London: University of Washington Press, 1987.
7. C.H. Becker, "Der Islam in Rahmen einer allgemeinen Kulturgeschichte," in the author's *Islamstudien: Vom Werden und Wesen der islamischen Welt*, vol. I (Leipzig: Quelle & Meyer, 1924; Hildesheim: Georg Olms, 1967), pp. 24-39; H.H. Schaeder, "Die Orientforschung und das abendlandische Geschichtsbild," *Welt als Geschichte*, II (1936): pp. 377-396; J.W. Fück, "Islam as an Historical Problem in European Historiography since 1800," in *Historians of the Middle East*, ed. Bernard Lewis and P.M. Holt (London: Oxford University Press), pp. 303-314; Jörg Kraemer, *Das Problem der islamischen Kulturgeschichte* (Tübingen: Max Niemeyer, 1959). Alessandro Bausani approached Islam's

relationship to Western culture in a new way. See A. Bausani, “Islam as an Essential Part of Western Culture”, in *Studies on Islam* (Amsterdam and London: North-Holland Publishing Company, 1974), pp. 19-36.

8. See, besides M. Rodinson's publications mentioned in note 6, for instance Jean-Paul Charnay, “Jeux de miroirs et crises de civilisations: Réorientation du rapport Islam/Islamologie”, *Archives de Sociologie des Religions*, 33 (1972), pp. 135-174. Compare Bryan S. Turner, *Marx and the End of Orientalism* (London and Boston: Allen and Unwin, 1978); and the same author's "Orientalism, Islam and Capitalism", *Social Compass*, 25 (1978), pp. 371-394.

9. Jean-Jacques Waardenburg, *L'Islam dans le miroir de l'Occident* (The Hague and Paris: Mouton, 1973 [hereafter abbreviated as *L'Islam*]); F. Meier, "Methods of Approach," in *Unity and Diversity in Muslim Civilization*, ed. G.E. von Grunebaum (Chicago: University of Chicago Press, 1955), pp. 38-46; Robert Brunschvig, "Situation de l'Islamologie," in *Actes du Colloque sur la sociologie musulmane* (Brussels, 1962), pp. 75-83 (reprinted in the author's *Etudes d'islamologie*, I, Paris: G.D. Maisonneuve et Larose: Paris, 1976, pp. 39-47; C. Cahen and C. Pellat, "Les études arabes et islamiques," *Journal Asiatique* CCLXI (1973), 89-107.

10. Cf. W.A. Bijlefeld, "Islamic Studies Within the Perspective of the History of Religions," *The Muslim World*, LXII (2972), 1-11; Charles J. Adams, "The History of Religions and the Study of Islam," in *The History of Religions: Essays on the Problem of Understanding*, ed. J.H. Kitagawa with the collaboration of M. Eliade and C.H. Long (Chicago and London: University of Chicago Press, 1967), pp. 177-193; Richard Martin, ed. *Approaches to Islam in Religious Studies*, Tucson: University of Arizona Press, 1985.

11. Ignaz Goldziher, "Le culte des saints chez les musulmans," *Gesammelte Schriften - Collected Works* (Hildesheim: Georg Olms, 1973), VI, pp. 62-156; and *idem*, "Le culte des ancêtres et le culte des saints chez les Arabes," pp. 157-184. For bibliographical data on Goldziher's work, see J. Waardenburg, *L'Islam*, pp. 332-338. A unique document is Goldziher's diary which was published recently: *Ignaz Goldziher, Tagebuch*, ed. Alexander Scheiber, Leiden: E.J. Brill, 1978.

12. For bibliographical data on E.A. Westermarck's work, see J. Waardenburg, *Classical Approaches to the Study of Religion*, II, Bibliography (The Hague and Paris: Mouton, 1974), pp. 312-313. (Hereafter abbreviated as *Classical Approaches*, II).

13. For instance, Erwin I.J. Rosenthal, *Political Thought in Medieval Islam: An Introductory Outline* (Cambridge: The University Press, 1958); idem, *Islam in the Modern National State* (Cambridge: The University Press, 1965); and other

publications by the same author. Cf. Bernard Lewis, "The Pro-Islamic Jews," *Judaica*, XVII (1968): pp. 391-404, and his subsequent study, *The Jews of Islam*, Princeton: Princeton University Press, 1984.

14. For bibliographical data on L. Massignon;s work, see J. Waardenburg, *L'Islam*, pp. 351-358; idem, *Classical Approaches*, II, pp. 176-177. See also, Herbert Mason, *Memoir of a Friend, Louis Massignon*, Notre Dame, Ind., University of Notre Dame Press, 1988.

15. For bibliographical data on Tor Andrae's work, see J. Waardenburg, *Classical Approaches*, II, p. 16.

16. For the bibliography of Henry Corbin up to 1976, see "Liste des travaux et publications d'Henry Corbin," in *Melanges offerts à Henry Corbin*, ed. Seyyed Hossein Nasr (Tehran: Institute of Islamic Studies, McGill University, Tehran Branch, 1977), pp. iii-xxxii. Also, Henry Corbin/cahier dirigé par Christian Jambet, Paris: Herne, 1981.

17. For the bibliography of Geo Widengren up to 1972, see *Ex Orbe Religionum: Studia Geo Widengren* (Leiden: E.J. Brill, 1972), pp. 451-464 (prepared by Kaarina Drynjeff).

18. For bibliographical data on the works of J. Wellhausen and W. Robertson Smith, see J. Waardenburg, *Classical Approaches*, II, pp. 308-311 and 265-266 respectively. See also T.O. Beidelman, *W. Robertson Smith and the Sociological Study of Religion* (Chicago: University of Chicago Press, 1974).

19. For bibliographical data on A.J. Wensinck's work, see J. Waardenburg, *Classical Approaches*, II, pp. 311-312. See also W.C. van Unnik, "Prof. Dr. A.J. Wensinck en de studie van de Oosterse mystiek," in *Woorden gaan leven: Opstellen van en over Willem Cornelis van Unnik* (1910-1978) (Kampen: J.H. Kok, 1979) pp. 238-263.

20. Wilfred Cantwell Smith, "Some Similarities and Differences Between Christianity and Islam: An Essay in Comparative Religion," in *The World of Islam: Studies in Honour of Philip K. Hitti*, ed. James Kritzeck and R. Baily Winder (London: Macmillan, 1959), pp. 47-59 and *On Understanding Islam: Selected Studies*, The Hague and New York: Mouton, 1981. M.G.S. Hodgson, "A Comparison of Islam and Christianity As a Framework for Religious Life," *Diogenes* XXXII (1960)", pp. 49-74 and William Montgomery Watt, *Muslim-Christian Encounters: Perceptions and Misperceptions*, London and New York: Routledge, 1991.

21. See, for instance, Jacques Waardenburg, "`Leben verlieren' oder `Leben gewinnen' als Alternative in prophetischen Religionen," in *Leben und Tod in den Religionen: Symbol und Wirklichkeit*, Darmstadt: Wissenschaftliche Buchgesellschaft, 1980, pp. 36-60.

22. This German edition is a translation of the second Swedish edition, with considerable revisions, Berlin: Walter de Gruyter, 1960.
23. Comparative studies of religious data, movements, etc., which occur in different religions should take into account the historical and social context within which these data and movements have occurred.
24. For the historical process of self-interpretation in religions, see *The Cardinal Meaning. Essays in Comparative Hermeneutics: Buddhism and Christianity*, ed. Michael Pye and Robert Morgan, Series Religion and Reason, (no. The Hague and Paris: Mouton, 1973).
25. Trends in secularization in modernizing societies should be compared against the background of the corresponding religious traditions. Comparative studies of secularization in different societies should take into account the technological and economic as well as the religious and ideological conditions in the societies concerned. Cf. Robert N. Bellah, "Islamic Tradition and the Problem of Modernization" in his *Beyond Belief: Essays on Religion in a Post-Traditional World* (New York: Harper & Row, 1970), pp. 146-166. See also *Religion and Progress in Modern Asia*, ed. Robert N. Bellah (Glencoe, Ill.: Free Press, 1965).
26. See for instance Kurt Rudolph, "Das Problem der Autonomie und Integrität der Religionswissenschaft," *Nederlands Theologisch Tijdschrift*, XXVII (1971): pp. 105-131. On method in history of religions, see especially *Science of Religion: Studies in Methodology*, ed. L. Honko, Proceedings of the I.A.H.R. Conference at Turku, 1973, Religion and Reason no. 13 (The Hague: Mouton, 1979). See also *On Method in the History of Religions*, ed. James S. Helfer, History and Theory no. 8 (Middletown, Conn.: Wesleyan University Press, 1968); and *Methodological Issues in Religious Studies*, ed. Robert D. Baird (Chico, Calif.: New Horizons Press, 1975). For an overview see, Ugo Bianchi, "History of Religions" in *The Encyclopaedia of Religion*, Vol. 6, pp. 399-408.
27. See J. Waardenburg, *L'Islam*, pp. 257-263, 283-289, 300-303, 306-308, and Mason, *Memoir*, *op. cit*.
28. Wilfred Cantwell Smith, *Modern Islam in India: A Social Analysis* (Lahore: Minerva, 1943; rev. edn. London: V. Gollancz, 1947). See also idem, *The Meaning and End of Religion: A New Approach to the Religious Traditions of Mankind* (New York: Macmillan, 1963), idem, *Faith and Belief* (Princeton: Princeton University Press, 1979), idem, *On Understanding Islam*, *op. cit*.
29. For the bibliography of W. Montgomery Watt, see *Islam: Past Influence and Present Challenge*, ed. Alfred T. Welch and Pierre Cachia, Edinburgh: Edinburgh University Press, 1979, pp. 331-347, and *Early Islam: Collected Articles*, Edinburgh: Edinburgh University Press, 1990.

30. C.A.O. van Nieuwenhuijze, "The Next Phase in Islamic Studies: Sociology?", *Actes du collogue sur la sociologie musulmane* (Brussels, 1962), pp. 393-429. Cf. idem, "The Trend in Middle East Studies - As Illustrated by the Dutch Case," in *Middle East Studies - Whence and Whither*, M.O.I. Publication no. 1 (Nijmegen, Netherlands, 1978), pp. 11-37.
31. See, for instance, G.E. von Grunebaum, "An Analysis of Islamic Civilization and Cultural Anthropology," in *Modern Islam: The Search for Cultural Identity*, New York: Vintage Books, 1964, pp. 40-97. This essay appeared in a shorter form in *Actes du colloque sur la sociologie musulmane* (Brussels, 1962), pp. 27-71. Cf. idem "Islamic Studies and Culture Research," in *Studies in Islamic Cultural History*, ed. G.E. von Grunebaum, *The American Anthropologist*, LVI, no. 2, part 2, Memoir no. 76, April 1954: pp. 1-22. For the bibliography of G.E. von Grunebaum up to 1968, see G.E. von Grunebaum, *Studien zum Kulturbild und Selbstverständnis des Islams* (Zurich and Stuttgart: Artemis Verlag, 1969), pp. 427-443. A critical evaluation of von Grunebaum's approach is given, for example, by A. Laroui, "For a Methodology of Islamic Studies: Islam seen by G. von Grunebaum," *Diogenes*, LXXXIII (1973), 12-39. This article was reprinted in the same author's *The Crisis of the Arab Intellectuals: Traditionalism or Historicism?* Berkeley, Calif.: University of California Press, 1976. Cf. David Waines, "Cultural Anthropology and Islam": The Contribution of G.E. von Grunebaum," *Review of Middle East Studies*, II (1976), 113-123.
32. See, for instance, his *Islam Observed: Religious Development in Morocco and Indonesia*, New Haven and London: Yale University Press, 1968. See also idem, *The Religion of Java*, New York: The Free Press of Glencoe, 1960, and idem, *The Interpretation of Cultures: Selected Essays*, New York: Basic Books, 1973.
33. We may refer here to the work of the late Marshall G.S. Hodgson, in particular *The Venture of Islam: Conscience and History in a World Civilization*, 3 vols (Chicago and London: University of Chicago Press, 1974). See also, for instance, the papers of a methodological panel discussion on Islamic studies, published in *Humaniora Islamics*, II (The Hague: Mouton, 1974), 207-299, under the title of "Methodology: On History and Anthropology in the Study of Islam." For more recent studies, see the bibliographical references at the end of the volume.
34. J.M.S. Baljon, *Modern Muslim Koran Interpretation, 1880-1960* (Leiden: E.J. Brill, 1961); J.J.G. Jansen, *The Interpretation of the Qur'an in Modern Egypt* (Leiden: E.J. Brill, 1974); J. Jomier, *Le Commentaire coranique du Manar: Tendances modernes de l'exégèse coranique en Egypte* (Paris: G.P.

Maisonneuve, 1954); G.H.A. Juynboll, *The Authenticity of the Tradition Literature: Discussions in Modern Egypt* (Leiden: E.J. Brill, 1969), and his *Muslim Tradition: Studies in Chronology, Provenance and Authorship in Early Hadith* (Cambridge and New York: Cambridge University Press, 1983).

35. See, for instance, Malcolm H. Kerr, *Islamic Reform: The Political and Legal Theories of Muhammad Abduh and Rashīd Riḍā* (Berkeley and Los Angeles: University of California Press, 1966). On law, see James Norman Dalrymple Anderson, *Islamic Law in the Modern World* (New York: New York University Press, 1959), and Noel J. Coulson, *A History of Islamic Law*, Islamic Surveys no. 2 (Edinburgh: Edinburgh University Press, 1964), pp. 149 ff. ("Islamic Law in Modern Times"). For law reforms in the Maghrib, see the excellent study by Maurice Borrmans, *Statut personnel et famille au Maghreb de 1940 à nos jours* (Paris and The Hague: Mouton, 1977). Most studies of present-day movements in Islam and interpretations of the *Sharīʿa* concentrate, of course, on particular countries.

36. Such questions present themselves in a particularly acute way in debates and discussions between Muslim and non-Muslim Islamicists. This was sensed already by C.A.O. van Nieuwenhuijze, "Frictions between Presuppositions in Cross-Cultural Communication," written in 1957 and republished in the author's *Cross-Cultural Studies* (The Hague: Mouton, 1963), pp. 192-221. There is now an extensive literature on the subject. See for instance A.L. Tibawi, *English-Speaking Orientalists* and *idem*, *A Second Critique of English-Speaking Orientalists* (London; Luzac, 1979). A present-day interest in the history of Islamic studies in the period of colonialism is linked to this discussion on the nature of Islamic studies. The volume *Islamic Studies: A Tradition and Its Problems*, ed. Malcolm H. Kerr, Malibu, Calif.: Undena, 1980, contains the papers read at the seventh Giorgio Levi Della Vida Conference held in Los Angeles, April 22, 1979. Although no paper is devoted to the study of the religious aspects of Islam, the volume as such is relevant to the discussion on the nature of Islamic Studies.

37. There has been a discussion of the relationship between the "great" and the "little" traditions in Muslim societies, but this discussion has largely remained restricted to anthropologists; cf. J. Waardenburg, "Official and Popular Religion in Islam," *Social Compass*, XXV (1978), 31; pp. 5-341. This paper was also published under the title "Official and Popular Religion As a Problem in Islamic studies" in *Official and Popular Religion: Analysis of a Theme for Religious Studies*, ed. Pieter H. Vrijhof and Jacques Waardenburg, Religion and Society, no. 19, The Hague, Berlin and New York: Walter de Gruyter, 1979, pp. 340-386.

38. Empirical research, of course, is carried out on such communities separately. From the point of view of Islamic studies, all these communities, however different they may be, have Islam in common and identify themselves as "Muslim." They can therefore be seen as being part of the Muslim *umma*, though with immense factual variations and differences.
39. A precise terminology is needed. See M.S.G. Hodgson's proposal to distinguish "Islam" and "Islamdom" as substantives, and "Islamic" and "Islamicate" as adjectives in *The Venture of Islam*, vol. 1, pp. 57-60. Cf. "A Note on Terminology in the Study of Religion" as Appendix 1 of J. Waardenburg, "Official and Popular Religion in Islam," *Social Compass*, XXV, (1978), 333-334 or "Some Further Terminological Considerations" as Appendix A of this paper in the book edition, pp. 369-371 (see full reference in 37 above). Fazlur Rahman, *Islam and Modernity: Transformation of an Intellectual Tradition*, Chicago: University of Chicago Press, 1982, attempts to address the problem.
40. Both normative and actual Islam are valid subjects of scholarly study, although in the past Islamicists tended to concentrate on the first and anthropologists on the second.
41. This seems to be a crucial point in the discussion between Muslim and non-Muslim Islamicists. Since no believer will admit that he "attaches ideals to facts," a better starting point for this discussion would be to say that the same fact may have different meanings for different scholars as persons, depending on their sympathy or antipathy, degree of participation and commitment, in view of the kind of truth of the data under consideration.
42. See William R. Roff, *The Wandering Thoughts of a Man, the Life and Times of Haji Abdul Majid bin Zainuddin*. Kuala Lumpur: Oxford University Press, 1978: see also J. Vredenbregt, "The *Haddj:* Some of its Features and Functions in Indonesia," in *Bijdragen tot de Taal-,Land- en Volkenkunde*, CXVIII (1962) 91-154; J.M.S. Baljon, *De motivatie van de Moslimse pelgrim*, inaugural address (Leiden: E.J. Brill, 1972).
43. This holds true not only for historians of religions and Islamicists but also for social scientists. See, for instance, Bryan Turner, *Weber and Islam: A Critical Study* (London and Boston: Routledge & Kegan Paul, 1974), and more recently, *Orientalism, Postmodernism and Globalism*, London and New York: Routledge, 1994.
44. Jacques Waardenburg, "Assumptions and Presuppositions in Islamic Studies," in *Rocznik Orientalistyczny* (Warsaw), XLIII (1985) (Festschrift Jozef Bielawski).
45. The way in which we view Islam determines largely the way in which we establish the foundation for Islamic studies as well, and vice versa. Whereas

Islamwissenschaft has often been founded in terms of cultural history, and later also in terms of cultural anthropology, in what follows we shall make an attempt to found the study of Islam rather in terms of religious studies, with attention paid to problems of religious and other kinds of meanings. As far as Islamicists are concerned, their interest in Islam is articulated in terms of scholarly research on Islamic data. Whether or not an Islamicist happens to be a Muslim is secondary to the question whether he or she is a good scholar.

46. The point actually seems to be that such religious data as rituals, myths and sacred texts are studied by us as "facts" but that they are much more than sheer facts for the people concerned. They are rather signs and symbols for them, and they are read and associated with each other in such a way (partly consciously, partly unconsciously) that people perceive a coherence in them, orient themselves to and through them and acquire an identity in terms of the signs and symbols they use and understand. In our studies of religious data we should acknowledge the semiotic or symbolic character of these data for the people concerned.

47. Whereas a sign in principle has one main meaning, a symbol by definition has more than one meaning: the *referee of a sign* is situated "outside" the sign itself, whereas the *referee of a symbol* is in principle part of the symbol. Whereas a sign is much less ambivalent than a symbol, there are of course borderline cases where a sign functions in fact as a symbol; symbols also can become signs. In what follows, the concept of "sign" then also implies the meaning of "potential symbol". Whereas over the last thirty years considerable attention has been given to religious symbolism, the role and use of "signs" in religions such as Islam, Judaism, and Christianity has hardly been studied and research is needed on religious signs as well as religious symbols. On symbolism, including religious symbolism, see Dan Sperber, *Rethinking Symbolism*, trans. Alice L. Morton (Cambridge: Cambridge University Press, 1975). Frederick M. Denny shows the importance of Islamic symbolism and he indicates ways to arrive at a better understanding of it, for instance through the study of ritual activity. Signs, as symbols, are bound to recognizable facts. They not only convey meanings and provide communication, but they also play a primordial role in the constitution of identity. Recognition of a sign or symbol gives to the person or group concerned further identity. This needs more research, in particular as far as religious signs and symbols are concerned. Suffice it to remind ourselves here that in actual experience religious signs and symbols impel both a cultural, this-worldly identification and a religious timeless identification.

48. If the fundamental problem for Christians has been to respond to the words and deeds of Jesus recognized as Messiah or Christ, that for Muslims seems to have

been to respond to verses or "signs" (*āyāt*) of the Quran and to the Quran itself recognized as Divine Word. Is the Quran in Islam the "sign" par excellence? Apparently this is the case, though some Hanbalite theologians seem to hold that the Quran is not referential but it just "is" God's Word being spoken. Is *āya* in the Quran then to be understood as "sign" or "symbol or even "sacrament"? Apparently it is to be interpreted by "sign", with the understanding that any sign may be used as a symbol, obtain a symbolic content and may finally end up becoming a symbol itself, as may happen in Muslim Quranic meditation. It is interesting that M.S.G. Hodgson views the Quran as a symbol on pages 222 and 241 of his article "Islam and Image," *History of Religions*, III (1964), 220-260; cf. idem, *The Venture of Islam*, II (1974), p. 504. According to its own testimony, the Quran is a collection of signs and a sign itself, pointing at spiritual truths, but it can function as a symbol both socially and more personally through a kind of spiritual assimilation.

49. Fundamentally, any religion functions as a sign or symbol system for its adherents and these adherents have their own particular ways of reading the signs of their system. We stressed this state of affairs first in a paper entitled "The Language of Religion, and the Study of Religions as Sign Systems" presented at the I.A.H.R. Conference in Turku in 1973 and published in its Proceedings in 1979 (Lauri Honko, ed., *Science of Religion: Studies in Methodology*, Religion and Reason no. 13, The Hague: Mouton, 1974, pp. 267-285. Most important perhaps is that this view of Islam, first of all based on theoretical considerations, was then supported by the fact that the Quran itself constantly preaches God's *āyāt* to man. Our notion of "sign" in scholarly research, consequently, corresponds to a basic notion in Islam itself. For some consequences of this particular view of Islam for the scholarly study of Islam, see Note 51 below.

50. To put it succinctly: Islam provides signs, primarily through the Quran, but then also in many other ways. It makes people sensitive to such signs, gives instruction as to their meaning, and tries to make people behave according to what they read as the meaning of these signs in ethics and law.

51. If this view of Islam as a sign system or as a collection or network of signs is justified, at least for the study of Islam as a religion, the consequences for scholarly research are clear, whether we have to do with Quranic *āyāt*, with particular rites, religious prescriptions or other religious data. A careful philological study in the best sense of the word must be made of the factual aspects of the data, including origin, context, etc. Yet attention has to be given to the various readings which particular Muslim authors or communities have given of the meaning of these data as signs. The result will be an assessment of

the factual aspects of a religious datum, and of the full range of its actual interpretations. As in the study of linguistic signs, one cannot hope to find out, within the boundaries of scholarship, what the essential reality and the ultimate true meaning of the religious data themselves would be. Therefore, precisely, they are to be named "signs"!

52. By definition, each religious datum has a semiotic or symbolic character, since it is apparently only by recognizing its character as a sign or symbol that the "religious" meaning of such a datum can be grasped. It should be stressed that the study of religious signs and symbols as such has nothing mysterious about it. It implies, first, a careful study of their "literal" meanings; secondly, an analysis of their "subjective" meanings for particular Muslim people (including scholars) or communities with their own ways of reading them; and finally a grasping of what may be called their "spiritual" meanings. We understand this to be the reference made by such signs and symbols to spiritual truths and realities which are supposed to exist objectively with a universal validity. Fundamentally, this kind of study is looking for the internal logic of religious data and clusters of such data considered as signs and symbols. See also Jacques Waardenburg, *Reflections On The Study of Religion*, series Religion and Reason no. 15 (The Hague etc.: Morton, 1979). The author's theoretical stand in Islamic Studies is summarized in his paper "Islamforschung aus religionswissenschaftlicher Sicht", republished in his book *Perspektiven der Religionswissenschaft* (Würzburg & Altenberge, 1993), Ch. 9, pp. 181-195.

53. The idea of Islam as a substance or "thing" seems to have been one of the great burdens on the progress of Islamic studies. Wilfred C. Smith, in *The Meaning and End of Religion*, traced the origins of this idea. Without going so far as to say that an outsider "as such" is forced to rectify Islam, it is safe to say that those who considered Islam to be a thing (in one of the many ways possible!) apparently had little or no idea of what Muslims have understood by religion, or that Muslims have been reading "religious signs". We seem to have become aware now of the West's many ethnocentric views of the non-Western world in general and of Muslim countries in particular, and thus we may be at the point of an epistemological break-through within Islamic studies. Needless to say, Muslims too can be tempted to see Islam as a substance or "thing".

54. One thinks here of the work of Clifford Geertz. See for instance his paper "Religion as a Cultural System," in *The Interpretation of Cultures: Selected Essays* (New York: Basic Books, 1973), pp. 87-125.

55. Although on theoretical grounds and on a certain level of abstraction we would prefer to speak of Islam as a "world religion" with its own sign system, it is implied that in practice in many societies it functions in the sense of the "local

religion" of a particular culture and as a symbol system. The universal sign system of Islam, consequently, is a potential symbol system on the local level (cf. n. 47). Perhaps we may add here that it only makes sense to call Islam a religious sign system at all if one wants indeed to grasp Islam in terms of religious meaning. In terms of history, Islam is rather to be called a religious tradition moving through the succession of generations of Muslims. In terms of social reality, Islam could be called, rather, the religious cultural framework of Muslim societies.

56. This is held by normative Sunnī Islam, with the exception of some theologians (see n. 48). In actual or living Islam there are, of course, many more "immediate" religious signs, not only among mystics and gnostics but also in the many shades and varieties of popular Islam. Still we could contend that all Muslims agree that the Quranic *āyāt* and the Quran itself are unique in the sense that they are an immediate sign *from God* and that they are of *universal* validity.

57. The search for such basic patterns of meaning should be done in Muslim terms. No western ideological reading - whether structuralist, Marxist, theological or "religious" - should be imposed upon what Muslims have accepted as their "Islamic" readings. But we are interested in the internal logic of these readings!

58. In the study of each religious issue from Muhammad up to the present day, the basic question should always be: how did the people involved read these signs, given their particular situations and intentions?

59. In the first part of this paper we mentioned some ways in which Islamic Studies have benefitted from the History of Religions. It should be stressed that Islamicists and Islamic Studies have started to contribute in several respects to the further development of the History of Religions and *Religionswissenschaft* as a distinct area of studies.

60. In view of this appeal, the polyvalence and fundamental polyinterpretability of religious data as signs and symbols should in their study be methodologically secured.

Mohammed Arkoun

Rethinking Islam Today

> Shall I seek other than Allah for Judge, when He is who hath revealed unto you the Book, fully explained? Those unto whom we gave the Book know that it is revealed from thy Lord in truth. So be not O Muhammad, of the waverers. Perfected is the word of thy Lord in truth and justice. There is naught that can change His word. He is the Hearer, the Knower.
>
> Quran 6: 114-15.

Islam holds historical significance for all of us, but at the same time, our understanding of this phenomenon is sadly inadequate. There is a need to encourage and initiate audacious, free, productive thinking on Islam today. The so-called Islamic revivalism has monopolized the discourse on Islam; the social scientists, moreover, do not pay attention to what I call the "silent Islam" - the Islam of true believers who attach more importance to the religious relationship with the absolute God than to the vehement demonstrations of political movements. I refer to the Islam of thinkers and intellectuals who are having great difficulties inserting their critical approach into a social and cultural space that is, at present, totally dominated by militant ideologies.

My own ambition as a Muslim intellectual is not the result of my academic training; rather, it is rooted in my existential experience. I entered high school in Oran and then the University in Algiers. It was the colonial time in Algeria, and like all Algerians, I was continually shocked by the sharp, hard confrontation between the conquering French culture and language and my own Algerian culture. (I speak Berber and Arabic.) When I heard lectures on Islam at the University of Algiers I was, like others, deeply disappointed by the intellectual poverty of the presentation, especially when burning issues were being raised in Algerian society between 1950 and 1954. The national movement for liberation was countering the colonial claim to represent modern civilization by emphasizing the Arab-Muslim personality of Algier. As a result of this brutal confrontation I resolved: (1) to understand the Arab-Muslim personality claimed by the nationalist movement, and (2) to determine the extent to which the modern civilization, represented by the colonial power, should be considered a universal civilization.

These are the roots of my psychological concerns. As a scholar and a teacher at the Sorbonne since 1961, I have never stopped this *ijtihād*, my intellectual effort to find adequate answers to my two initial questions. At the same time, this explains my method and my epistemology. For me, as an historian of Islamic thought, there is one cultural space stretching from the Indian to the Atlantic Oceans. This space is, of course, extremely rich in its languages and ethno-cultural variety. It also has been influenced by two axial traditions of thinking: the ancient Middle Eastern culture, which has a special place for Greek thought, and the monotheism taught by the prophets. I learned to discover Islam in this wide, rich, intricate space, which is why I am not comfortable with the English title imposed on me for this lecture. I could not find a relevant translation of the French *Penser l'Islam* or the Arabic *Kayfa naqilu al-islām*. *Penser l'Islam* suggests the free use of reason aimed at elaborating a new and coherent vision which integrates the new situations faced by societies and the living elements of Muslim tradition. Here I emphasize freedom. *Rethinking* Islam could suggest that I am repeating the well-known position of the *isāhī* - the reformist thinking represented since the nineteenth century by the *salafī* school. I want to avoid any parallel between the modern perspective of radical critical thought applied to any subject and the *islāhī* thinking which, in the Islamic tradition, is a mythical attitude more or less mixed with the historical approach to the problems related to religious vision.

I favor the historical approach, with its modern enlarged curiosities, because it includes the study of mythical knowledge as being not limited to the primitive archaic mentality, according to the definitions imposed by the positivist historical school since the nineteenth century. On the contrary, the main intellectual endeavor represented by *thinking* Islam or any religion today is to evaluate, with a new epistemological perspective, the characteristics and intricacy of systems of knowledge - both the historical and the mythical. I would even say that both are still interacting and interrelated in our modern thought after at least three hundred years of rationalism and historicism. There is no need to insist on the idea that *thinking* Islam today is a task much more urgent and significant than all the scholastic discussions of Orientalism; the ultimate goal of the project is to develop - through the example set by Islam as religion and a social-historical space - a new epistemological strategy for the comparative study of cultures. All the polemics recently directed against Orientalism show clearly that so-called modern scholarship remains far from any epistemological project that would free Islam from the essentialist, substantialist postulates of classical metaphysics. Islam, in these discussions, is assumed to be a specific, essential, unchangeable system. It is time to stop this irrelevant confrontation between two dogmatic attitudes - the theological claims of believers and the ideological postulates of positivist rationalism. The study of religions, in particular, is handicapped by the rigid definitions and methods inherited from theology and classical metaphysis. The history of religion has collected facts and descriptions of various religions, but religion as a universal dimension of human existence is not approached from the relevant epistemological perspective. This weakness in modern thought is even more clearly illustrated by the poor, conformist, and sometimes polemical literature on the religions of the Book, as we shall see.

For all these reasons, it is necessary to clear away the obstacles found in Islamic as well as Orientalist literature on Islam and to devote more attention in our universities to teaching and studying history as an anthropology of the past and not only as narrative account of facts. I insist on a historical, sociological, anthropological approach not to deny the importance of the theological and philosophical, but to enrich them by the inclusion of the concrete historical and social conditions in which Islam always has been practiced. My method is one of deconstruction. For centuries religions have dominated the construction of different, intricate *Weltanschauung* through which all realities were perceived, judged, classified, accepted, and rejected without the possibility of looking back at the mental-historical process which led to each *Weltanschauung*. The strategy of deconstruction is possible only with modern critical epistemology. Reason needs to be free from the ontology, transcendentalism, and substantialism in which it has made itself a prisoner, especially in the various theologies elaborated through Greek logic and metaphysics.

Thus presented, the enterprise of *thinking* Islam today can only be achieved - if ever - by dynamic teams of thinkers, writers, artists, scholars, politicians, and economic producers. I am aware that long and deeply-rooted traditions of thinking cannot be changed or even revised through a few essays or suggestions made by individuals. But I believe that thoughts have their own force and life. Some, at least, could survive and break through the wall of uncontrolled beliefs and dominating ideologies.

Where can we start under these conditions? Where is the authorized voice or the accepted theory which could give expression to an Islam integrated into our modern, scientific mentality and at the same time into the religious experience of Muslims? In other words, is it possible to articulate a modern vision of Islam which could have the same impact on the community as the *Risāla* of al-*Shāfiʿī* or the *Ihyā*' *ʿulūm al-dīn* of al-Ghazālī? I refer to these two major books because they illustrate the same intellectual initiative as the one I propose, namely, to integrate, as al-Shafiʿī and al-Ghazālī did, new disciplines, new knowledge, and new historical insights into Islam as a spiritual and historical vision of human existence.

Actually, I started this project with an article written in 1969 in which I asked "How to read the Quran"? One necessarily has to start with the Quran because, historically, everything started with what I called the "Experience of Medina", including the communication of the Quran received as revelation and the historical process through which a social group, named believers (*mu'minūn*), emerged and dominated other groups - named unbelievers, infidels, hypocrites, polytheists (*kāfirūn*, *munāfiqūn*, *mushrikūn*). For the first time in the history of Quranic exegesis, I raised the crucial issue of reading texts according to the new epistemology introduced by modern linguistics and semiotics. When I applied this epistemology to the reading of the *Fātiha*, I received the usual response that there is nothing new in this essay; everything already has been well explained through classical exegesis. Other essays collected in my book, *Lectures du Coran* (Maisonneuve-Larose, 1982), did not evoke more than a passing interest among Orientalists or Muslims who read French. I mention this fact because it illustrates clearly the concept of epistemological space.

It is true that I use grammatical and lexicographic material collected by classical exegeses. However, the epistemological perspective of linguistic analysis is totally different from the theological postulates accepted without discussion in the Islamic, Christian, and Jewish traditions of thought. This will appear in the following analyses.

I shall not insist any longer here on the decisive importance of linguistics and semiotics in rethinking the cognitive status of religious discourse. Rather, I would like to stress various views already developed in several essays which I collected in my *Critique de la raison Islamique* (Maisonneuve-Larose, 1984). I shall tackle the following points:

1. Tools for new thinking.
2. Modes of thinking.
3. From the unthinkable to the thinkable.
4. Societies of the Book.
5. Strategy for deconstruction.
6. Revelation and history.

Many other problems must be raised and solved because Islam has regulated every aspect of individual and collective life; but my wish here is to indicate a general direction of thinking and the main conditions necessary to practice an *ijtihād* recognized equally by Muslims and modern scholars.

Tools for New Thinking

Periodization of the history of thought and literature has been dictated by political events. We speak currently of the Umayyad, ʿAbbāsid, and Ottoman periods. However, there are more enlightening criteria that we can use to distinguish periods of change in the history of thought. We must consider the discontinuities affecting the conceptual framework used in a given cultural space. The concepts of reason and science (*ʿilm*) used in the Quran, for example, are not the same as those developed later by the *falāsifa*, according to the Platonic and Aristotelian schools. However, the concepts elaborated in Quranic discourse are still used more or less accurately today because the *épisteme* introduced by the Quran has not been intellectually reconsidered.

Episteme is a better criterion for the study of thought because it concerns the structure of the discourse - the implicit postulates which command the syntactic construction of the discourse. To control the epistemological validity of any discourse, it is necessary to discover and analyze the implicit postulates. This work has never been done for any discourse in Islamic thought (I refer to my essay "Logocentrisme et vérité religieuse selon Abu al-Hasan al-Amiri", in *Essais sur la pensée islamique*, Maisonneuve-Larose, third edition, 1984). This is why I must insist here on the new *épisteme* implicit in the web of concepts used in human and social sciences since the late sixties.

It is not possible, for example, to use in Arabic the expression "problem of God", associating Allah and *mushkil* (problem); Allah cannot be considered as problematic. He is well-known, well-presented in the Quran; man has only to meditate, internalize, and worship what Allah revealed of Himself in His own words. The classical discussion of the attributes has not been accepted by all schools; and finally the attributes are recited as the most beautiful names of Allah (*asmā' Allah al-husnā*) but are neglected as subjects of intellectual inquiry.

This means that all the cultures and systems of thought related to pagan, polytheistic, *jāhilī* (pre-Islamic), or modern secularized societies are maintained in the domain of the *unthinkable* and, consequently, remain *unthought* in the domain of "orthodox" Islamic thought or the *thinkable*. In European societies since the sixteenth century, the historical role that the study of classical antiquity played in initiating the modern ideas of free thinking and free examination of reality is significant; based on this link we can understand the intellectual gap between Muslim orthodoxy and Western secularized thought (cf. Marc Auge, *Le Genie du paganisme*, Paris: Gallimard, 1982).

Tradition, orthodoxy, myth, authority, and historicity do not yet have relevant conceptualizations in Arabic. Myth is translated as *ustūra*, which is totally misleading because the Quran uses the word for the false tales and images related in "the fables of the ancient people", and these *asāṭīr* are opposed to the truthful stories (*qasas haqq* or *ahsān al-qasas*) told by God in the Quran. The concept of myth as it is used in contemporary anthropology is related more to *qasas* than to *ustūra*, but even anthropology has not yet clarified the difference between myth and mythology, mystification and mythologization, as well as the semantic relationship between myth and symbol and the role of the metaphor in mythical and symbolic discourse.

We still approach these concepts and use them with a rationalist positivist system of definitions, as the Quran did with *asāṭīr al-awwālīn* (pre-Islamic mythology of the ancient people). However, the Quran created a symbolic alternative to the competing mythical and symbolic constructions of the ancient cultures in the Middle East. Our positivist rationalism criticizes symbols and myths and proposes, as an alternative, scientific conceptualism. We have neither a theory of symbol nor a clear conception of the metaphor to read, with a totalizing perspective, the religious texts. Religious tradition is one of the major problems we should *rethink* today. First, religions are mythical, symbolic, ritualistic ways of being, thinking, and knowing. They were conceived in and addressed to societies still dominated by *oral* and not written cultures. Scriptural religions based on a revealed Book contributed to a decisive change with far-reaching effects on the nature and functions of religion itself. Christianity and Islam (more than Judaism, until the creation of the Israeli state) became official ideologies used by a centralizing state which created written historiography and archives.

There is no possibility today of *rethinking* any religious tradition without making a careful distinction between the mythical dimension linked to oral cultures and the official ideological functions of the religion. We shall come back to this point because it is a permanent way of thinking that religion revealed and that social, cultural, and political activity maintained.

Tradition and *orthodoxy* are also unthought, unelaborated concepts in Islamic traditional thought. Tradition is reduced to a collection of "authentic" texts recognized in each community: Shīʿī, Sunnī, and Khārijī. If we add to the Quran and Hadīth, the methodology used to derive the *Sharīʿa* and the *Corpus juris* in the various schools, we have other subdivisions of the three axis of Islamic tradition. I tried to introduce the concept of an *exhaustive tradition* worked up by a critical, modern confrontation of all the collections used by the communities, regardless of the "orthodox" limits traced by the classical authorities (Bukhārī and Muslim for the Sunnīs; Kulaynī, Ibn Bābūye, Abū Jaʿfar al-Tūsī for the Imāmīs; Ibn Ibād and others for the Khārijīs). This concept is used by the Islamic revolution in Iran, but more as an ideological tool to accomplish the political unity of the *umma*. The historical confrontation of the corpuses, and the theoretical elaboration of a new, coherent science of *Usūl al-fiqh* and *Usūl al-dīn*, are still unexplored and necessary tasks.

Beyond the concept of an *exhaustive tradition* based on a new definition of the *Usūl*, there is the concept of tradition as it is used in anthropology today - the sum of customs, laws, institutions, beliefs, rituals, and cultural values which constitute the identity of each ethno-linguistic group. This level of tradition has been partially integrated by the *Sharīʿa* under the name of *ʿurf* or *ʿamāl* (like *al-ʿamāl al-fāsī* in Fas), but is covered and legitimized by the *usūlī* methodology of the jurists. This aspect of tradition can be expressed in Arabic by *taqālid*, but the concept of exhaustive tradition can be expressed by the word *sunna* only if it is re-elaborated in the perspective I mentioned.

Likewise, *orthodoxy* refers to two values. For the believers, it is the authentic expression of the religion as it has been taught by the pious ancestors (*al-salaf al-sālih*); the "orthodox" literature describes opposing groups as "sects" (*firāq*). For the historian, orthodoxy refers to the ideological use of religion by the competing groups in the same political space, like the Sunnīs who supported the Caliphate (legitimized afterwards by the jurists) and who called themselves "the followers of the tradition and the united community" (*ahl al-sunna wa-al-jamāʿa*). All the other groups were given polemical, disqualifying names like *rawāfid*, *khawārij*, and *bātinīyya*. The Imāmīs called themselves "the followers of infallibility and justice" (*ahl al-ʿisma wa-al-ʿadāla*), referring to an orthodoxy opposed to that of the Sunnīs.

There has been no effort (*ijtihād*) to separated orthodoxy as a militant ideological endeavor, a tool of legitimation for the state and the "values" enforced by this state, from religion as a way proposed to man to discover the Absolute. This is another task for our modern project of *rethinking* Islam, and other religions.

Modes of Thinking

I would like to clarify and differentiate between the two modes of thinking that Muslim thinkers adopted at the inception of intellectual modernity in their societies that is, since the beginning of the *Nahda, the renaissance,* in the nineteenth century. I do not need to emphasize the well-known trend of *salafī* reformist thought initiated by Jamāl al-Dīn al-Afghānī and Muhammad ʿAbduh. It is what I call the *islāhī* way of thinking which has characterized Islamic thought since the death of the Prophet. The principle common to all Muslim thinkers, the *ʿulamā' mujtahidūn*, as well as to historians who adopted the theological framework imposed by the division of time into two parts - before/after the Hijra (like before/after Christ) - is that all the transcendent divine Truth has been delivered to mankind by the Revelation and concretely realized by the Prophet through historical initiatives in Medina. There is, then, a definite model of perfect historical action for mankind, not only for Muslims. All groups *go back* to this model in order to achieve the spirit and the perfection shown by the Prophet, his companions, and the first generation of Muslims called the pious ancestors (al-salaf al-sālih).

This vision has been faithfully adopted and assumed by the program of the International Institute of Islamic Thought (founded in 1981 in Washington, D.C., "for the reform and progress of Islamic thought"). The publication of the Institute's International Conference in the "Islamization of Knowledge" notes that the "human mind by itself with its limitations cannot comprehend the totality of the matter". This means that there is an "Islamic framework" constantly valid, transcendent, authentic, and universal in which all human activities and initiatives ought to be controlled and correctly integrated. Since the Islamic framework is part of the "Islamic legacy," one must always *look back* to the time when the Truth was formulated and implemented either in the model set in Medina by the Prophet and the Revelation or by recognized *ʿulamā' mujtahidūn* who correctly derive the *Sharīʿa* using the rules of valid *ijtihād*.

This is at the same time a methodology, an epistemology, and a theory of history. It is certainly an operative intellectual framework used and perpetuated by generations of Muslims since the debate on authority and power started inside the community according to patterns of thinking and representing the world specific to the *islāhī* movement. I do not want to engage in a discussion of the intellectual and scientific relevance of this mental attitude which is now generalized on a worldwide scale by the so-called Islamic revivalism.

In order to *rethink* Islam one must comprehend the socio-cultural genesis of *islāhī* thinking and its impact on the historical destiny of the societies where this thinking has been or is actually dominant. To assess the epistemological validity of *islāhī* thinking, one has to start from the radical and initial problems concerning the generative process, the structure and the ideological use of knowledge. By this, I mean any kind and level of knowledge produced by man living, acting, and thinking in a given social-historical situation. Radical thinking refers to the biological, historical, linguistic, semiotic condition shared by people as natural beings. From this perspective, the Revelation of Islam is only one attempt, among many others, to emancipate human beings from the natural limitations of their biological, historical, and linguistic conditions. That is why, today, "Islamicizing knowledge" must be preceded by a radical epistemological critique of knowledge at the deepest level of its construction as an operative system used by a group in a given social-historical space. We need to differentiate *ideological* discourses produced by groups for assessing their own identity, power, and protection, from *ideational* discourses, which are controlled along the socio-historical process of their elaboration in terms of the new critical epistemology.

Given the sociological diffusion today of *islāhī* thinking, I must insist on the characteristics of this critical epistemology applied not only for *thinking* Islam, but also, beyond the rich example of Islamic tradition, for a rationality based on a *comparative* theory of all cultural traditions and historical experiences.

Any attempt to *think* an object of knowledge relies on epistemic postulates, as I have said. The difference between the emerging rationality and all inherited rationalities - including Islamic reason - is that the implicit postulates are made explicit and used not as undemonstrated certitudes revealed by God or formed by a transcendental intellect, but as modest, heuristic trends for research. In this spirit, here are six fundamental heuristic lines of thinking to recapitulate Islamic knowledge and to confront it with contemporary knowledge in the process of elaboration.

1. Human beings emerge as such *in* societies through various changing uses. Each use in the society is converted into a *sign* of this use, which means that realities are expressed through languages as systems of *signs*. Signs are the radical issue for a critical, controlled knowledge. This issue occurs *prior* to any attempt to interpret revelation. Holy scripture itself is communicated through natural languages used as systems of signs, and we know that each *sign* is a locus of convergent operations (perception, expression, interpretation, translation, communication) engaging all of the relations between language and thought.

Remark **1.1**: This line of research is directly opposed to a set of postulates developed and shared by Islamic thought on the privilege of the Arabic language elected by God to "teach Adam all the names (Quran, 2:31)". The ultimate teaching is the Quran as revealed in the Arabic language. These postulates command the whole construction of *Usūl al-dīn* and *Usūl al-fiqh* as a correct methodology with which to derive from the holy texts the divine laws. The core of Islamic thought is thus represented as a linguistic and semantic issue. (This is true for all religious traditions based on written texts.)

Remark **1.2**: This same line is equally opposed to the philological, historicist, positivist postulates imposed by Western thinking since the sixteenth century. That is why we have made a clear distinction between the modernity (or rationality) of the Classical Age and the heuristic trends of the present rationality (Prefigurative Age). (I refer to my book, *L'Islam hier, demain*, Paris: Buchet-Chastel, second edition, 1982).

2. All semiotic productions of a human being in the process of his social and cultural emergence are subject to historical change which I call *historicity*. As a semiotic articulation of meaning for social and cultural uses, the Quran is subject to historicity. This means that *there is no access to the absolute* outside the phenomenal world of our terrestrial, historical existence. The various expressions given to the ontology, the first being the truth and the transcendence by theological and metaphysical reason, have neglected historicity as a dimension of the truth. Changing tools, concepts, definitions, and postulates are used to shape the truth.

Remark **2.1**: This line is opposed to all medieval thinking based on stable essences and substances. The concept of Revelation should be reworked in the light of semiotic systems subjected to historicity. The Muʿtazilī theory of God's created speech deserves special consideration along this new line.

Remark **2.2**: The Aristotelian definition of formal logic and abstract categories also needs to be revised in the context of the semiotic theory of meaning of theory and the historicity of reason.

3. There are many levels and forms of reason interacting with levels and forms of imagination as is shown in the tension between *logos* and *mythos*, or symbol and concept, metaphor and reality, or proper meaning, *zāhir* and *bātin* in Islam.

Recent anthropology has opened up the field of collective social *imaginaire* not considered by traditional historiography and classical theology.[1] Imagination and social *imaginaire* are reconsidered as dynamic faculties of knowledge and action. All the mobilizing ideologies, expressed in a religious or a secular framework, are produced, received, and used by social *imaginaire*, which also is related to imagination. The concept of social *imaginaire* needs more elaboration through many societies and historical examples. In Muslim societies, its role today is as decisive as in the Middle Ages because rationalist culture has less impact and presence there than in Western societies, which, nevertheless, also have their own *imaginaire* competing with various levels and forms of rationality.

4. Discourse as an ideological articulation of realities as they are perceived and used by different competing groups occurs *prior* to the faith. Faith is shaped, expressed, and actualized in and through discourse. Conversely, faith, after it has taken shape and roots through religious, political, or scientific discourse, imposes its own direction and postulates to subsequent discourses and behaviors (individual and collective).

Remark **4.1**: The concept or notion of faith given by God and the classical theories of free will, grace, and predestination need to be re-elaborated within the concrete context of discourses through which any system of beliefs is expressed and assimilated. Faith is the crystallization of images, representations, and ideas commonly shared by each group engaged in the same historical experience. It is more than the personal relation to religious beliefs; but it claims a spiritual or a metaphysical dimension to give a transcendental significance to the political, social, ethical and aesthetic values to which refers each individual inside each unified social group, or community.

5. The traditional system of legitimization, represented by *Usūl al-dīn* and *Usūl al-fiqh*, no longer has epistemological relevance. The new system is not yet established in a unanimously approved form inside the *umma*. But is it possible today, given the principles of critical epistemology, to propose a system of knowledge or science *particular* to Islamic thought? What are the theoretical conditions of a modern theology not only for political institutions, but also for universal knowledge, in the three revealed religions? We are in a crisis of legitimacy; that is why we can speak only of heuristic ways of thinking.

Remark **5.1**: This line is opposed to the dogmatic assurance of theology based on the *unquestionable* legitimacy of the *Sharīʿa* derived from Revelation or the classical ontology of the first Being, the neo-Platonic One, the Origin from which the Intellect derives and to which it desires to return. That is why the problem of the state and civil society is crucial today. Why should an individual obey the state? How is the legitimacy of power monopolized by a group over all other established groups?

6. The search for ultimate meaning depends on the radical question concerning the relevance and existence of an ultimate meaning. We have no right to reject the possibility of its existence. What is questionable is how to base all our thoughts on the postulate of its existence. Again, we encounter the true responsibility of the critical reason: To reach a better understanding of the relationship between meaning and reality, we must, first, improve our intellectual equipment - vocabulary, methods, strategies, procedures, definitions, and horizons of inquiry.

To illustrate all these theoretical perspectives, let us give an example from classical Islamic thought. Al-Ghazālī (d. 505/1111) and Ibn Rushd (d. 595/1198) developed an interesting attempt to *think* Islam in their historical context. We do not need an exhaustive analysis of their discussion. The most relevant to our project is to be found in *Fasl al-tafrīqa bayn al-islām wa-al-zandaqa* by al-Ghazālī and *Faṣl al-maqāl* written as an answer by Ibn Rushd. Al-Ghazālī declared the *falāsifa* infidels on three basis: They deny the resurrection of the body; they deny the knowledge of particulars (*juz'īyāt*) by God; and they claim that God is anterior ontologically, not chronologically, to the world. These three theses are matters of belief, not demonstrative knowledge. The *falāsifa* have been wrong in trying to transfer to demonstrative knowledge matters which, in fact, depend on belief. Ibn Rushd used the methodology of *Usūl al-fiqh* to solve a philosophical question; even the formulation of the problem, at the beginning of the *Faṣl*, is typically juridical.

This does not mean that al-Ghazālī chose the right way to tackle the question. Actually, the most significant teaching for us is to identify, through the discussion, the epistemic limits and the epistemological obstacles of Islamic thought as it has been used by its two illustrious representatives. The new task here is not to describe the arguments, but to *think* through the consequences of the epistemic and epistemological discontinuities between classical Islamic thought (all included in medieval thought) and modern thought (the Classical Age, from the fifteenth to the twentieth century, up to the 1950s; the Prefigurative Age of a new thought, since the 1950s). Before we move ahead in the search for an unfettered way of *thinking* Islam today, it is worth noting some theories on the medieval system of intelligibility as it is shown in al-Ghazālī and Ibn Rushd's discussion.

1. Both thinkers accept the cognitive priority of revealed truth in the Quran. Reason has to be submitted totally to this clearly formulated truth (Ghazālī) or to be elaborated as a coherent articulation of the truth established through demonstrative knowledge (in the conceptual and logical framework of Aristotelian methodology and philosophy) and the revealed truth. This last contention is served by intermingling or interweaving juridical and philosophical methodologies.

2. Both mix at different degrees but with a common psychology commanded by beliefs between religious convictions and legal norms on one side (*ahkām*, explicated by the science of *Usūl al-dīn* and *Usūl al-fiqh*) and philosophical methodology and representatives on the other side. Left to themselves, the milk-sisters (*Sharʿ* and *Hikma*) are "companions by nature and friends by essence and instinct" (*Fasl* 26).

3. Both ignore the decisive dimension of historicity to which even the revealed message is subjected. Historicity is the unthinkable and the unthought in medieval thought. It will be the conquest - not yet everywhere complete - of intellectual modernity.[2]

4. Historiography (*ta'rīkh*) has been practiced in Islamic thought as a collection of information, events, biographies (*tarājim*, *siyār*), genealogies (*nasab*), knowledge on countries (*buldān*), and various other subjects. This collection of facts is related to a chronology representing time as *stable*, without a dynamic movement of change and progress. No link is established between time and historical dynamic process (historicity) and the elements of knowledge collected by historiography. Ibn Khaldūn can be cited as the exception who introduced the concept of society as an object of knowledge and thought,[3] but even he could not think of religion, society, history, or philosophy as related levels and ways to achieve an improved intelligibility. On the contrary, he contributed to eliminating philosophy and to isolating the *Ashʿarī* vision of Islam from history as a global evolution of societies influenced by various theological expressions of Islam.

5. In the case of Islamic thought, the triumph of two major official orthodoxies with the Sunnīs (since the fifth century Hijra) and the Shīʿa (first with the Fāṭimid Ismāʿīlī and second with the Twelver Safavids in Iran) imposed a mode of thinking narrower than those illustrated in the classical period (first to fifth century Hijra). Contemporary Islamic thought is under the influence of categories, themes, beliefs, and procedures of reasoning developed during the scholastic age (seventh to eighth century Hijra) more than it is open to the pluralism which characterized classical thought.

6. The historical evolution and intellectual structure of Islamic thought create the necessity of starting with a critique of Islamic reason (theological, legal, historiographical) as well as of philosophical reason as it has been understood and used through Aristotelian, Platonic, and Plotinist traditions (or legacies).

We shall not do this here.[4] We have to think more clearly about new conditions and ways to *think* Islam today.

Intellectual modernity started with Renaissance and Reform movements in sixteenth century Europe. The study of pagan antiquity and the demand for freedom to read the Bible without the mediation of priests (or "managers of the sacred," as they are sometimes called) changed the conditions of intellectual activities. Later, scientific discoveries, political revolutions, secularized knowledge, and historically criticized knowledge (historicism practiced as philosophies of history) changed more radically the whole intellectual structure of thought for the generations involved in the Industrial Revolution with its continuous consequences.

This evolution was achieved in Europe without any participation of Islamic thought or Muslim societies dominated, on the contrary, by a rigid, narrow conservatism. This is why Muslims do not feel concerned by the secularized culture and thought produced since the sixteenth century. It is legitimate, in this historical process leading to intellectual modernity, to differentiate between the ideological aspects limited to the conjunctural situations of Western societies and the anthropological structures of knowledge discovered through scientific research. Islamic thought has to reject or criticize the former and to apply the latter in its own contexts.

We cannot, for example, accept the concept of secularization or laicité as it has been historically elaborated and used in Western societies. There is a political and social dimension of this concept represented by the struggle for power and the tools of legitimization between the church and the bourgeoisie. The intellectual implications of the issue concern the possibility - political and cultural - of separating education, learning, and research from any control by the state as well as by the church. This possibility remains problematical everywhere.

Similarly, we cannot interpret religion merely as positivist historicism and secularism did in the nineteenth century. Religion is addressed not only to miserable, uncultivated, primitive people who have not yet received the light of rational knowledge; human and social sciences, since 1950-1960, have changed the ways of thinking and knowing by introducing a pluralist changing concept of rationality, according to which religion is interpreted in a wider perspective of knowledge and existence.

The project of *thinking* Islam is basically a response to two major needs: 1) the particular need of Muslim societies to think, for the first time, about their own problems which had been made unthinkable by the triumph of orthodox scholastic thought; and 2) the need of contemporary thought in general to open new fields and discover new horizons of knowledge, through a systematic cross-cultural approach to the fundamental problems of human existence. These problems are raised and answered in their own ways by the traditional religions.

From the Unthinkable to the Thinkable

Islam is presented and lived as a definite system of beliefs and non-beliefs which cannot be submitted to any critical inquiry. Thus, it divides the space of thinking into two parts: the unthinkable and the thinkable. Both concepts are historical and not, at first, philosophical. The respective domain of each of them changes through history and varies from one social group to another. Before the systemization by Shāfiʿī of the concept of *sunna* and the *usūlī* use of it, many aspects of Islamic thought were still thinkable. They became unthinkable after the triumph of Shāfiʿī's theory and also the elaboration of authentic "collections," as mentioned earlier. Similarly, the problems related to the historical process of collecting the Quran in an official *mushaf* became more and more unthinkable under the official pressure of the caliphate because the Quran has been used since the beginning of the Islamic state to legitimize political power and to unify the *umma*. The last official decision closing any discussion of the readings of the received orthodox *mushaf* was made by the *qādī* Ibn Mujāhid after the trial of Ibn Shunbudh (fourth/tenth century).

We can add a third significant example to show how a thinkable is transformed into an unthinkable by the ideological decision of the leading politico-religious group. The Muʿtazila endeavored by their *ijtihād* to make thinkable the decisive question of God's created speech, but in the fifth century the Caliph al-Qādir made this question unthinkable by imposing, in his famous *ʿAqīda*, the dogma of the uncreated Quran as the "orthodox" belief (cf. George Makdisi, *Ibn Aqil et la resurgence de l'Islam traditionalite au XIeme* siecle, Damascus, 1963).

As we have said, the unthinkable or the not yet thought (*l'impense*) in Islamic thought has been enlarged since intellectual modernity was elaborated in the West. All the theories developed by sociology and anthropology on religion are still unknown, or rejected as irrelevant, by most contemporary Islamic thought without any intellectual argument or scientific consideration.

It is true that traditional religions play decisive roles in our secularized, modernized societies. We even see secular religions emerging in industrialized societies, like fascism in Germany and Italy, Stalinism and Maoism in the Communist world, and many new sects in liberal democracies. If we look at the revealed religions through the parameters set by recent secular religions, we are obliged to introduce new criteria to define religion as a universal phenomenon. To the traditional view of religion a totally revealed, created, and given by God, we cannot simply substitute the sociological theory of religion generated by a socio-historical process according to the cultural values and representations available in each group, community, or society. We must rethink the whole question of the nature and the functions of religion through the traditional theory of divine origin and the modern secular explanation of religion as a social historical production.

This means, in the case of Islam, rewriting the whole history of Islam as a revealed religion and as an active factor, among others, in the historical evolution of societies where it has been or still is received as a religion. Orientalist scholars have already started this study, inquiring even into the social and cultural conditions of the *jāhilīyya* period in which Islam emerged; but I do not know any Orientalist who has raised the epistemological problems implicit in this historicist approach. No single intellectual effort is devoted to considering the consequences of historicist presentations of the origins and functions of a religion *given* and *received* as being *revealed.*[5]

We need to create an intellectual and cultural framework in which all historical, sociological, anthropological, and psychological presentations of revealed religions could be integrated into a system of thought and evolving as irrelevant to human and social studies and let it be monopolized by theological speculation. One has to ask, then, why sociology and anthropology have been interested in the question of the sacred and in ritual, but not in revelation. Why, conversely, has theology considered revelation, but not so much the sacred and the secular, until it has been influenced by anthropology and social sciences.

To move a step further in these complex interrelated difficulties and theories, let us try to work out the concept of the "Societies of the Book" (*Sociétes du Livre*).

The Societies of the Book

I introduce this concept as a historical category to deepen the analysis of the revealed religions. I emphasize first the significant fact that the three revealed religions have not yet been studied comparatively as we have suggested above. Instead, there is an ancient polemical literature. A descriptive literature, especially on Islam and Christianity, is being developed in line with the Islamic-Christian dialogue, but the theological postulates received in each tradition are still dominating the analyses of the revealed religions.

Scholarship has not yet contributed to changing the intellectual approach in this field of research and reflection. Departments of history of religions or of comparative religions devote a larger place to Judaism and Christianity than to Islam. There are many departments of religion in very famous universities, like Princeton or the Sorbonne, where no chair exists for teaching Islam, and I know that these departments do not even utilize the existing departments of Near Eastern studies or languages, because they have different scientific concerns. The books written by Orientalists on Islam are limited and often irrelevant in terms of this approach. They do not show any comparative curiosity or epistemological critique beyond the traditional theological definitions of the different schools.[6]

This is why the problem of revelation is one of the key topics, but it has been neglected by modern scholarship despite its fundamental role in the historical genesis of societies where Judaic, Christian, and Islamic expressions are found.

I call Societies of the Book those that have been shaped since the Middle Ages by the Book as a religious and a cultural phenomenon. The Book has two meanings in this perspective. The Heavenly Book preserved by God and containing the entire word of God is called *Umm al-kitāb* in the Quran. Geo Widengren has demonstrated the very ancient origin of this conception in Near East religious history (cf. his *Muhammad, The Apostle of God and the Heavenly Book*, Uppsala, 1955). The importance of this belief for our purpose is that it refers to the verticality which has constituted the religious *imaginaire* in the Near East. Truth is located in Heaven with God, who reveals it in time and through the medium He chooses: the prophets, Himself incarnated in the "Son" who lived among people, the Book transmitted by the messenger Muhammad. There are different *modalities* for the delivery of parts (not the whole) of the Heavenly Book, but the Word of God as God Himself is the same from the point of view of the anthropological structures of religious *imaginaire*.

The modalities for the delivery of parts of the Heavenly Book have been interpreted by each community, raised and guided by a prophet, as the absolute expression of God Himself. The cultural, linguistic, and social aspects of these modalities were unthinkable in the mythical framework of knowledge particular to people who receive the "revelations". When theologians came to systematize in conceptual, demonstrative ways the relations between the Word of God (*Umm al-kitāb*) and its manifested forms in Hebrew, Aramaic, and Arabic, they used either literalist exegesis of the scripture itself or rational categories and procedures influenced by Greek philosophy. Grammar and logic have been used as two different ways to reach and to deliver the meaning of the manifested revelation in relation to the grammatical and logical "reading," but they did not lead to a radical critique of the postulates used in the different exegeses developed in the Middle Ages. This issue needs to be rethought today in light of the new knowledge of language, mind, logic, and history, which means that all the ancient exegesis has to be reworked, too.

We are obliged today to consider differently the second meaning of the concept of Book in our expression "Societies of the Book". The Muʿtazila touched on this point in their theory of God's created speech. The Quran, as well as the Bible, are the manifested, *incarnated* word of God in human languages, transmitted orally by human voices, or fixed in written material. One has to answer here to a Christian objection on the specificity of Christian revelation made through Jesus as the incarnated God, not through human mediators. As I said, this is a difference in modality, not in the relation between the Heavenly Book and its terrestrial manifestations through religious *imaginaire*. Theological theorization transformed into substantial transcendental truths revealed by God what, in fact, had been historical, social, and cultural events and manifestations. The delivery of the Word of God by Jesus in a given society and period of history, using the Aramaic language, is a historical event just like the delivery of the Quran by Muhammad. That Jesus is presented as the "Son of God" and the Quran a speech worded by God Himself are theological definitions used in systems of beliefs and non-beliefs particular to Christian and Islamic dogma. These definitions do not change the linguistic and historical fact that the messages of Jesus, Muhammad, (and, of course, the prophets of Israel) are transmitted in human languages and collected in an "orthodox" closed corpus (Bible, Gospels, and Quran) in concrete historical conditions. Then, the Heavenly Book is accessible to the believers *only* through the *written* version of the books or scriptures adopted by the three communities. This second aspect of the Book is then submitted to all the constraints of arbitrary historicity. The books or scriptures are read and interpreted by the historical communities in concrete, changing, social, political, and cultural situations.

The societies where the Book - or Holy Scriptures - is used as the revelation of the divine will developed a global vision of the world, history, meaning, and human destiny by the use of hermeneutic procedures. All juridical, ethical, political, and intellectual norms had to be derived from the textual forms of the revelation. The Torah, Canon Law, and the *Sharīʿa* have been elaborated on the basis of the same vision of revealed Truth and "rational" procedures from which norms have been derived. There is a common conception of human destiny commanded by the eschatological perspective (the search for salvation by obedience to God's will) and guided in this world by the norms of the law.

The new dimension which I aim to explain by the concept of the Societies of the Book is the process of *historicization* of a divine law derived from Revelation is not subject to historicity. It cannot be changed by any human legislation and it is a totally *rationalized* law. Scientific knowledge cannot demonstrate that this belief is based on a wrong assumption, but it can explain how it is possible psychologically to maintain the affirmation of a revealed law in the form presented in the Torah, Canon Law, and the *Sharīʿa*, against the evidence of its historicity.

Traditional theological thought has not used the concept of social *imaginaire* and the related notions of myth, symbol, sign, or metaphor in the new meanings already mentioned. It refers constantly to *reason* as the faculty of true knowledge, differentiated from knowledge based on the representations of the imagination. The methodology elaborated and used by jurists-theologians shares with the Aristotelian tradition the same postulate of rationality as founding the true knowledge and excluding the constructions of the imagination. In fact, an analysis of the discourse produced by both trends of thinking - the theological and the philosophical - reveals a simultaneous use of reason and imagination. Beliefs and convictions are often used as "arguments" to "demonstrate" propositions of knowledge. In this stage of thinking, metaphor is understood and used as a rhetorical device to add an aesthetic emotion to the "real" content of the words; it was not perceived in its creative force as a semantic innovation or in its power to shift the discourse to a global metaphorical organization requiring the full participation of a coherent imagination. The philosophers, however, recognized the power that imagination as a faculty of privileged knowledge bestowed on the prophet especially. Ibn Sīnā and Ibn Tufayl used this faculty in each of their accounts of *Hayy ibn Yaqzān*, but this did not create a trend comparable to the logocentrism of the jurists, the theologians, and the *falāsifa* who favored Aristoteliansim.

This lack of attention to the imagination did not prevent the general activity of social *imaginaire* - the collective representations of the realities according to the system of beliefs and non-beliefs introduced by revelation in the Societies of the Book. The social *imaginaire* is partially elaborated and controlled by the *'ulamā'* with their *Aqa 'īd* (like the one written by Ibn Batta, French translation by H. Laoust, *La profession de foi d'Ibn Batta*, Damascus, 1958); but it is structured as well by beliefs and representations taken from the cultures preceding Islam. In all Islamic societies, there are two levels of traditions - the deepest archaic level going back to the *jāhilīyya* of each society and the more recent level represented by Islamic beliefs, norms and practices as they have been developed since the foundation of the Muslim state. The revealed Book assumed a great importance because it provided a strategy of integration for all norms, beliefs, and practices proper to each social group. This means that the social *imaginaire* is generated by the interacting layers of traditions, so that it is not correct from an anthropological point of view to describe the Societies of the Book as if they were produced exclusively by the Book used as their constitution. The revealed Book had an influence on all cultural activities and political institutions to some extent. It generated a civilization of written culture opposed to, or differentiated from, the oral civilization.

The key to the Societies of the Book is thus the intensive dialectic developed everywhere between two strongly competitive forces: On the one hand, there is the state, using the phenomenon of the Book in its two dimensions - the transcendent, divine, ontological message and the written literature and culture derived from it. This comprises the official culture produced and used under the ideological supervision of the state, that is, the orthodox religion defined and enforced by doctors of law (jurists-theologians). On the other hand, there are the non-integrated, resisting groups using oral, non-official culture and keeping alive non-orthodox beliefs (called heresies and condemned by the official *ʿulamā*ʾ). The struggle between the reformed church and the Catholic church in the sixteenth century is a typical example of this competition. In Islam, we have many examples in history from the first century to the contemporary revivalist movements. The segmentary groups perpetuating oral cultures and traditions and adhering to archaic beliefs under the name of Islam, have resisted their integration into the Muslim state. This is why the *ʿulamā*ʾ - ancient and contemporary - regularly condemned the "superstitions" and "heresies" of these groups, as long as they resisted the norms of the Societies of the Book.

This model is more than a contemplative *Weltanschauung*; it is and remains an active paradigm of historical action with which the Societies of the Book generated their structure and destiny. Religions are superior to any scientific theory because they give imaginative solutions to permanent issues in human life, and they mobilize the social *imaginaire* with beliefs, mythical explanations, and rites. (For more explanations, see my *Lectures du Coran*, *op. cit*.)

Strategies for Deconstruction

Thus far, we have presented elements and forces acting in the Societies of the Book. This is not sufficient for thinking in new ways about the opposition between Societies of the Book and secularized societies. Thinking about this opposition is thinking from a new perspective about human destiny with two major historical results. The Societies of the Book, as well as the secularized societies, have shown the intellectual limits and the empirical failures of their respective paradigms for historical action.

Thinking about our new historical situation is a positive enterprise. We are not aiming for a negative critique of the previous attempts at emancipation of human existence as much as we wish to propose relevant answers to pending and pressing questions. This is why we prefer to speak about a strategy for deconstruction. We need to deconstruct the social *imaginaire* structured over centuries by the phenomenon of the Book as well as the secularizing forces of the material civilization[7] since the seventeenth century.

We speak of one social *imaginaire* because secularization has not totally eliminated from any society all the elements, principles and postulates organizing the social *imaginaire* in the Societies of the Book.

This is, I know, a controversial point among historians. Karl Lowith, *Meaning in History: the Theological Implications of the Philosophy of History*, (Chicago: University of Chicago Press, 1949), has shown that so-called modern ideas are just the secularized reshaping and re-expressing of medieval Christian ideas. More recently, Regis Debray (*Critique de la raison politique*, Paris, Gallimard, 1981) has underlined the Christian origins of the present socialist utopia.

Hans Blumenberg tried to refute these positions in his doctoral dissertation on *The Legitimacy of the Modern Age* (Cambridge: The MIT Press, 1983). He showed how modernity is an alternative to Christian medieval conceptions. According to him, the modern idea of progress of development rather than a messianic one. Long-term scientific progress guided by pluralist method and experimentation, continuity of *problems* rather than *solutions*, and history as a positive, whole process cut from the transcendent God, are characteristics of the modern age. Should one, then, accept the definition of secularization as a long-term process through which religious ties, attitudes toward transcendence, the expectation of an afterlife, ritual performances, firmly established forms of speech, a typical structure of the individual *imaginaire*, specific articulation and use of reason and imagination, become a private concern separated from public life? One could add the triumph of *pragmatism*, which gives priority to action over contemplation, verification over truth, method over system, logic over rhetoric, future over past, and becoming over being.

Along this line of thinking, secularization is usually presented as one of the following: a decaying of the former capacity for receiving divine inspiration and guidance; a cultural and political program of emancipation from theological thinking and ecclesiastical dominance; the domination of nature to increase the powers of man; or the substitution of a public system of education for the private one. This is known in France as *laicité*, which often has been expressed as a militant attitude against the religious vision of the world, such as we saw during 1982-1983 when the socialist government wanted to "unify" the national educational system (cf. Guy Gautier, *La laicité en miroir*, Paris: Grasset, 1985).

Whatever the relevance of these observations to the long-term process of change undertaken first in Western societies and extended more and more to the rest of the world, two remarks are in order. First, references to traditional religions - especially the three revealed religions - are frequent and even dominating everywhere. Second, secular "religions", like fascism, Stalinism, and Maoism, are produced by contemporary societies and govern the social *imaginaire* with their so-called values, norms, aims, beliefs, and representations. Secularism appears, then, as a change of methods, styles, procedures, and forms of expression in human existence; but it does not affect the ultimate force structuring and generating the human condition through existential and historical process.

How can we obtain a clear vision of this force and describe it? Religions have mobilized it, shaped it, formulated it by using various cultural systems, myths, rites, beliefs, and institutions. Modern ideologies do the same by using secularized languages and collective organizations. What is the common unifying reality of all these religious and ideological constructions? To answer this question we must avoid the usual opposition between the "true" religious teaching and the "false" secularist conceptions. We will be better able to discover the reality if we deconstruct methodically all the manifested cultural constructions in the various societies. Returning to the Societies of the Book, we can show a deep, common mechanism described by Marcel Gauchet (*Le désenchantement du monde*, Paris: Gallimard, 1985), as "the debt of meaning".

All known societies are built on an *order*, a hierarchy of values and powers maintained and enforced by a political power. On what conditions is a political power accepted and obeyed by the members of the society?

How is it legitimized? There is no possible legitimization of any exercised power without an authority spontaneously internalized by each individual as an ultimate reference to the absolute truth. In traditional societies, authority is the privilege of a charismatic leader able to mediate the meaning located in an extra - or super-worldliness, meaning possessed by a god (or gods), and this leader delivers it in various ways to human beings. Thus, this process creates a recognition of *debt* in each individual consciousness and, consequently, an adherence to all the commandments of the leader.

The example of Islam gives a clear illustration of this general mechanism, one which is at thc same time psychological, social, political, and cultural. A very small group of believers followed Muhammad, a charismatic leader related to the known paradigm of prophets and messengers of God in the history of salvation common to the "People of the Book". Muhammad, supported and inspired by God, had the ability to create a new relationship to the divine through two simultaneous and interacting initiatives as all charismatic leaders do with different levels of success and innovation. He announced the absolute truth in an unusual Arabic form of expression, and he engaged the group in successive, concrete experiences of social, political, and institutional change. The Revelation translated into a sublime, symbolic, and transcendental language to the daily public life of the group whose identity and *imaginaire* were separated from the hostile, non-converted groups (called infidels, hypocrites, enemies of God, errants, and bedouins). We can follow in the Quran the growth of a new collective social-cultural *imaginaire* nourished by new systems of connotation whose semantic substance was not primarily an abstract vision of an idealistic dreaming mind but the historic crystallization of events shared at the time by all members of the group.

The "debt of meaning" incurred in such conditions is the most constraining for the individuals who are the actors of their own destiny. The relation to the source of authority is not separated from obedience to the political power exercised in the name of this authority. But already, in this first stage of setting up and internalizing the debt of meaning, we must pay special attention to a structural process not yet deconstructed by historians and anthropologists.

When we write the history of these twenty years (612-632) during which Muhammad created a new community, we mention the principal events in a narrative style. We neglect to point out the use made of these events by later generations of believers. In other words, how does the "debt of meaning" historically operate on the collective *imaginaire* to produce the concrete destiny of each group in each society? There is, in fact, a double line to follow in writing the history of societies commanded by an initial "debt of meaning" incurred in the Inaugural Age. The first is to index, describe, and articulate all the significant events and facts that occurred in each period; the second is to analyze the mental representations of these events, facts, and actions shaping the collective *imaginaire* which becomes the moving force of history. This study of psychological discussions of history is more explanatory than the positivist narration of "objective" history. It shows the powerful capacity of imagination to create symbolic figures and paradigms of meaning from very ordinary events and persons, at the first stage, then the transformation of these symbols into collective representations structuring the social *imaginaire*.

Thus, the idealized figures of Muhammad, ʿAlī, Husayn, and other imāms have been constructed to enlighten and legitimize the historical development of the community. The biographies (*sīra*) of Muhammad and ʿAlī, as they have been fixed in the Sunnī and Shīʿī traditions, are the typical production of the same social *imaginaire* influenced by a highly elaborated mythical vision provided by the Quran. The whole Quranic discourse is already a perfect sublimation of the concrete history produced by the small group of "believers" in Mecca and Medina.

The point I want to make here is that historians of Islam, so far, have not considered the question of the *imaginaire* as an important historical field. I have mentioned this concept several times because it is unavoidable when we want to relate political, social, and cultural events to their psychological origins and impacts. The narrative history suggests that all the events are understandable according to a "rational" system of knowledge. No one historian raises the question: How does one rationalize, for example, the history of Salvation as it is proposed by the Holy Scriptures - Bible, Gospels, and Quran - and as it is received, integrated, and used by the individual and the collective *imaginaire*? There is no possibility to interpret the whole literature derived from those Scriptures without taking into account the representations of Salvation perpetuated in the behaviors and the thinking activity of all believers, so that all history produced in the Societies of the Book is legitimized and assimilated by the *imaginaire* of Salvation, not by any "rational" construction. The theological and juridical systems elaborated by so-called "reason" are also related to the *imaginaire* of Salvation.

The writing and the understanding of the so-called "Islamic" history would change totally if we accept to open the field of research on social *imaginaire*, and the anthropological structures of this *imaginaire* as we can describe it, for example, through *Ihyā' ʿulūm al-dīn* of Ghazālī, the literature of Quran exegesis, the present discourse of Islamist movements (I refer to my essay, "L'Islam dans l'histoire", in *Maghreb-Mashreq* 1985, no. 102.)

Revelation and History

The strategy of deconstruction leads to the ultimate decisive confrontation in the Societies of the Book. When we discover the function of social *imaginaire* as producing the history of the group, we cannot maintain the theory of revelation as it has been elaborated previously, that ius, as images produced by the complex phenomenon of prophetic intervention

The Quran insists on the necessity of human beings to listen, to be aware, to reflect, to penetrate, to understand, and to meditate. All these verbs refer to intellectual activities leading to a kind of rationalization based on existential paradigms revealed with the history of Salvation. Medieval thought derived from this an essential, substantist, and unchangeable concept of rationality guaranteed by a divine intellect. Modern knowledge, on the contrary, is based on the concept of social-historical space continuously constructed and deconstructed by the activities of the social actors. Each group fights to impose its hegemony over the others not only through political power (control of the state) but also through a cultural system presented as the universal one. Seen from this perspective, the Quran is the expression of the historical process which led the small group of believers to power. This process is social, political, cultural, and psychological. Through it, the Quran presented as the revelation and received as such by the individual and the collective memory, is continuously reproduced, re-written, re-read, and re-expressed in a changing social-historical space.

History is the actual incarnation of the revelation as it is interpreted by the *ʿulamā*ʾ and preserved in the collective memory. Revelation maintains the possibility of giving a "transcendent" legitimization to the social order and the historical process accepted by the group. But this possibility can be maintained only as long as the cognitive system, based on social *imaginaire*, is not replaced by a new, more plausible rationality linked to a different organization of the social-historical space. This is one reason for the known opposition between *falāsifa* and *mutakallimūn*, or *fuqahā*ʾ.

The struggle between the inherited thinkable and the not yet thought has become more intense in Muslim societies since the violent introduction of intellectual modernity; but, as we have seen, the same struggle between the paradigms of knowledge and action started in Western societies in the sixteenth century. The result has been the inversion of the priorities fixed by the revelation. Economic life and thought had been submitted to ethical-religious principles until the triumph of the capitalist system of production and exchange, which replaced the symbolic exchanges practiced in traditional societies with the rule of profit.

Within this new value system, ethical thinking has less relevance than the technical regulations of the market and the efficient control of productive forces. Democracy limits the source of authority to the acquiescence expressed in different circumstances of various professional or political groups. There is no longer any reference to the transcendental origin of authority. The question of revelation is thus eliminated; it is neither solved intellectually nor maintained as a plausible truth according to the pragmatic reason prevailing in so-called modern thought. All relations are based on the respective power of nations, groups, and individuals; ethical principles, founded on metaphysical or religious visions, lose their appeal. I do not mean that we have to go back to the "revealed" truth according to *islāḥī* thinking. I am stressing a major difficulty of our time: the rupture between ethics and materialism. At the same time, social *imaginaire* is not more controlled or used in a better way by "scientific" knowledge. Rather, it is mobilized more than ever by ideologues who take advantage of the modern mass media to disseminate slogans taken from religious (in Muslim societies) or secular ideologies, or from a mixture of both (in the so-called socialist regimes).

If we sum up the foregoing analysis and observations, we can stress the following propositions:

1) The social-historical space in which religions emerged, exercised their functions, and shaped cultures and collective sensibilities is being replaced by the secular positivist space of scientific knowledge, technological activities, material civilization, individual pragmatic ethics and law.

2) Scientific knowledge is divided into separate, technical, highly specialized disciplines. Religions, on the contrary, have provided global, unified, and unifying systems of beliefs and non-beliefs, knowledge and practice, as well as pragmatic solutions to the fundamental problems of human destiny: life, death, love, justice, hope, truth, eternity, transcendence, and the absolute. The nostalgia for a unified vision explains the re-emergence of religion.

3) Positivist scientific knowledge has discredited or eliminated religious functions in society without providing an adequate alternative to religion as a symbol of human existence and a source of unifying ethical values for the group. This happened in Western societies under the name of

secularism (or *laicisme* in French), liberalism, and socialism.

4) Present thought has not yet recognized the positive aspect of secularism as a cultural and intellectual way to overcome fanatic divisions imposed by the dogmatic, superstitious use of religion. At the same time, the specific role of religion as a source for symbols in human existence also goes unrecognized.

5) Islam is not better prepared than Christianity to face the challenge of secularism, intellectual modernity, and technological civilization. The so-called religious revivalism is a powerful secular movement disguised by a religious discourse, rites, and collective behavior; but is a secularization without the intellectual support needed to maintain the metaphysical mode of thinking and to search for an ethical coherence in human behavior. Theological and ethical thinking has reappeared in contemporary Islamic thought in the form of the ideology of liberation (political and economic). There is little intellectual concern with genuine religious issues like the consciousness of culpability, the eschatological perspective, or revelation as a springboard for mythical, or symbolic thinking.

6) The concept that the Societies of the Book could help to build a new humanism which would integrate religions as cultures and not as dogmas for confessional groups (or *tawāif*, as in Lebanon or Ireland) is not taken seriously either in theology or in the social scientific study of religions. But there is hope that semiotics and linguistics can create the possibility of reading religious texts in the new way we have mentioned.

7) The study of Islam today suffers particularly from the ideological obstacles created, since the nineteenth century, by the decay of the Muslim intellectual tradition, as it had developed from the first to the fifth century *Hijra*, and by the economic pressure of the West, the general trend of positivist rationalism and material civilization, the powerful impact of demography since the late fifties and the necessity of building a modern state and unifying the nation.

8) World system economists insist on the opposition between the center and the periphery. Likewise, in intellectual evolution, we should pay attention to the increasing domination of Western patterns of thought which

have not been duly criticized, controlled, or mastered in Western societies themselves. Islam, which has a rich cultural tradition, is facing major issues in a generalized climate of semantic disorder; our thinking should be directed to the dangers resulting from this threat.

9) We should not forget that man agrees to obey, to be devoted, and to obligate his life when he feels a "debt of meaning" to a natural or a supernatural being. This may be the ultimate legitimacy of the state understood as the power accepted and obeyed by a group, community, or nation. The crisis of meaning started when each individual claimed himself as the source of all or true meaning; in this case, there is no longer any transcendent authority. Relations of power are substituted for relations of symbolic exchanges of meaning. To whom do we owe a "debt of meaning"?

It is our responsibility to answer this question after man has changed himself by his own initiatives, discoveries, performances, and errors. It seems that the answer will be conjectural and more and more bound to empirical research instead of to divine guidance taught by traditional religions. I learned through the Algerian war of liberation how all revolutionary movements need to be backed by a struggle for meaning, and I discovered how meaning is manipulated by forces devoted to the conquest of power. The conflict between meaning and power has been, is, and will be the permanent condition through which man tries to emerge as a thinking being.

In the full light of this experience, the question arises again: Should we Islamicize knowledge according to the revealed discourse, or should we consider Islam in the context of a universal quest for meaning? Many paths are open again. Let us explore them with confidence, hope, and lucidity.

Notes

1. I prefer to use the French word for this important concept because it has no exact correspondent in English. Cf. C. Castoriadis, *L'institution imaginaire de la société*, Paris: Seuil, 1977.
2. Cf. my *Ta'rīkhiyyāt al-fikr al-ʿarabī al-islāmī,* Dār al-inmā' al-ʿarabī, Beirut, 1985.
3. Miskawayh did this before in his philosophical and historiographical works. Cf. my *Humanisme arabe au IVᵉ/Xᵉ siecle*, 2nd. Edition, Paris: Vrin, 1982.
4. Cf. my essays in Pour une *Critique de la Raison Islamique*, Paris, Maissoneuve et Larose, 1984; and *L'islam, morale et politique*, Paris: Desclee De Brouwer, 1986.
5. Given and received are technical terms in linguistic and literary analyses. Islam is given as revealed in the grammatical structure of Quranic discourse, and it is received as such by the psychological consciousness generated by this discourse and the ritual performances prescribed by it. For more thorough elaboration of this approach, I refer to my essay, *The Concept of Revelation: From Ahl al-Kitab to the Societies of the Book*, The Claremont Graduate School, California, 1987.
6. The comparative approach, attempted by L. Gardet and G. Anawati in their *Introduction a la theologie musulmane*, is commanded by the postulates of Thomist theology. W.C. Smith has tried to open the field including the case of Islam. Cf. also the recent book by Hans Kung, J. Van Ess, H. Von Stietenbron, H. Becher, *Le Christianisme et les religions du monde*, *Islam, Hindouisme, Bouddhisme*, translated from German by Joseph Feisthauer, ed. Paris: Seuil, 1986. See also my article, "Islamic Studies: Methodologies", *The Oxford Encyclopedia of the Modern Islamic World*, Vol. 2, pp. 332-340.
7. I use this expression according to its historical elaboration by the French historian, Fernand Braudel.

Selected Bibliography

Abbott, Nabia. *Aisha the Beloved of Mohammad*. Chicago: University of Chicago Press, 1942.

Abbott, Nabia. *Two Queens of Baghdad*. Chicago: University of Chicago Press, 1946.

Abbott, Nabia. *Studies in Arabic Literary Papyri*. Oriental Institute Publications, vols. 75-77. 3 vols. Chicago: University of Chicago Press, 1957-72.

Abdel-Malek, Anouar. "Orientalism in Crisis". *Diogenes* 44 (1963): 103-140.

Abed, Shukri. *Israeli Arabism: The Latest Incarnation of Orientalism in the Muslim World*. Washington, D.C.: International Center for Research and Public Policy, 1988.

Adams, Charles. "The Development of Islamic Studies in Canada". *The Muslim Community in North America*. Edited by Earle Waugh, et al. Edmonton: University of Alberta Press, 1983. 185-201.

Ahmed, Akbar. *Post Modernism and Islam: Predicament and Promise*. London and New York: Routledge, 1992.

Ahmed, Akbar. *Toward Islamic Anthropology*. Ann Arbor, Mich.: New Era Publications, 1986.

Ahsan, M. Manazir. "Orientalism and the Study of Islam in the West: A Select Bibliography". *Muslim World Book Review* 1, no. 4 (1981): 51-60.

Akhtar, Shabir. *Be Careful with Muhammad*! London: Bellew, 1989.

Alverny, Marie - Therese d'. *La Conaissance de l'Islam dans l'occident medieval*. Edited by Charles Burnett. Aldershot: Variorum, 1994.

Ahmad, Leila. *Edward William Lane: A Study of His Life and Works and of British Ideas of the Middle East in the 19th Century*. London; New York: Longman, 1978.

Al-Attas, S.M.N. *Islam and Secularism*. Kuala Lumpur: Abina, 1978.

Al-Azm, Sadiq. *Naqd al-Fikr al-Dīnī*. Beirut: Dār al-Taliʿah, 1970.

Al-Azm, Sadiq. "Orientalism and Orientalism in Reverse". *Khamsin* 7 (1980): 5-26.

Al-Faruqi, Ismail. *Islamization of Knowledge: General Principles and Work Plan*. Washington, D.C.: International Institute of Islamic Thought, 1982.

Algar, Hamid. "The Problems of Orientalists". *Islamic Literature* (Lahore) 17 no. 2 (1971): 95-106.

Anderson, Benedict. *Imagined Communities*. London: Verso, 1983.

Arkoun, Mohammed. *Pour une critique de la raison islamique*. Paris: Maissonneuve and Larose, 1984.

Asad, Talal, ed. *Anthropology and the Colonial Encounter*. Atlantic Highlands, N.J.: Humanities Press, 1973.

Asad, Talal. *Genealogies of Religion: Discipline and Reasons of Power in Christianity and Islam*. Baltimore, Md.: The Johns Hopkins University Press, 1993.

"Asianists in Europe". *Preliminary Guide to Asian Studies in Europe '95*. Leiden: International Institute for Asian Studies, (1995): 5-8. [List of names of scholars, arranged by European country and area of interest.]

Azmeh, Aziz A. "Ibn Khaldun in Modern Scholarship: A Study in Orientalism". *Journal of Near Eastern Studies* 46 no. 3 (1987): 233-34.

Azmeh, Aziz A. *Islamic Studies and the European Imagination*. Exeter: 1986.

Azmeh, Aziz A. *Islams and Modernities*. London: Verso, 1993.

Badawi, Abdurrahman. *Al-Turāth al-Yunānī fi al-Hadara al-Islāmiyya: Dirāsat li-Kibāl al-Mustashriqīn*. Cairo: Maktabat al-Nahda al-Misriyya, 1946.

Badawi, Abdurrahman. *Ruh al-Hadara al-ʿArabiyya*. Beirut: Dār al- ʿIlm lil-Malayin, 1949.

Batunsky, M. "Russian Clerical Islamic Studies in the Late 19th and Early 20th Centuries". *Central Asian Survey*, 13 ii (1994): 213-35.

Becker, Carl H. *Vom Werden und Wesen der Islamischen Welt: Islam studien*. 2 vols. Leipzig: Verlag Quelle & Meyer, 1924-32.

Becker, Carl H. *Das Erbe der Antike im Orient und Okzident*. Leipzig: Verlag Quelle & Meyer, 1931.

Beckingham, C.F. *Between Islam and Christendom*. London: Variorum Reprints, 1983.

Benaboud, M'hammad. "Orientalism and the Arab Elite". *Islamic Quarterly* 26, no. 1 (1982): 3-14.

Benaboud, M'hammad. "The Prophet's Revelation and 20th Century Orientalists: The Case of W.M. Watt and M. Rodinson". *Revue d'Histoire Maghrebine* 13, no. 41-42 (1986): 143-61.

Benaboud, M'hammad. "The Methodology of Orientalism in Islamic History". *Melanges Robert Mantran.* Edited by A. Termini. Zaghouan: 1988. 51-82.

Bernal, Martin. *Black Athena. The Afro-Asian Roots of Classical Civilization.* London: Free Association Press, 1987.

Bennett, C. ed. *Victorian Images of Islam.* London: Grey Seal Books, 1992.

Bergstrasser, Gotthelf. Hunain ibn Ishaq über die syrischen und arabischen Galenuberzetzungen. Abhandlungen für die Kunde des Morgen--landes. Edited by the Deutsche Morgenländische Gesellschaft. Vol. 17, no. 2. Leipzig: F.A. Brockhaus, 1925.

Bijlefeld, Willem A. "Islamic Studies within the Perspective of the History of Religions". *The Muslim World* 62 (1972): 1-11.

Binder, Leonard. *The Study of the Middle East: Research and Scholarship in the Humanities and the Social Sciences.* New York: Wiley, 1976.

Binder, Leonard. *Islamic Liberalism.* Chicago: University of Chicago Press, 1988.

Bosworth, C. E. "Orientalism and Orientalists". *Arab-Islamic Bibliography.* Edited by Diana Grimwood-Jones, et al. Hassocks: Harvester Press, 1977. 148-56.

Bowen, John. *Muslims through Discourse.* Princeton, N.J.: Princeton University Press, 1993.

Breasted, James H. *The Oriental Institute.* University of Chicago Survey. vol. 12. Chicago: University of Chicago Press, 1933.

Breckenridge, Carol and Peter Van der Veer, eds. *Orientalism and the Post Colonial Predicament.* Philadelphia: University of Pennsylvania Press, 1993.

Bürgel, J. C. et al. *Les études moyen-orientales en Suisse: propositions et recommandations*. Berne: Conseil Suisse de la/Science, 1993 (Détection Avancée en Politique de la Recherche, 135a). [In French and German.]

Buttner, Friedemann. "Situation, Structure and Functions of Contemporary Oriental Studies in the Federal Republic of Germany: Spiritual Imperialism or Bridge of Intercultural Communication"? *Europe's Future in the Arab View*... ed. Bielenstein. 71-86.

Buttner, Friedemann. "Des contre-orients aux contre-occidents". *Etudes Orientalies* 1 (1988): 5-16.

Clifford, J. *The Predicament of Culture*. Cambridge, Mass.: Harvard University Press, 1988.

Cohen, Warren C. *Reflections on Orientalism* . East Lansing, Mich.: Asian Studies Center, 1983.

Cohen, Warren C. "Edward Said and the Orientalists". *Mélanges de l'Institut Dominicain d'Études Orientales du Caire* 15 (1982): 211-22.

Corbin, Henry. *Avicenne et le recit visionnaire*. Bibliotheque Iranienne, vol. 4. Tehran: Department d'Iranologie de l'Institute Franco-Iranie; Paris: Librarie d'Amerique et d'Orient Adrien-Maisonneuve, 1954.

Corbin, Henry. *Avicenna and the Visionary Recital*. Translated from the French by Willard R. Trask. Bollingen series, no.66. New York: Pantheon Books, 1960.

Daiber, H. And W. Raven. "Recent Islamic and Arabic Studies in the Netherlands". *Asian Research Trends*, 4 (1994): 1-24.

De Jong, Frederich. "Middle Eastern Studies in the Netherlands". *Middle East Studies Association Bulletin* 20, no. 2 (1986): 171-86.

Djait, Hichem. *L'Europe et l'Islam*. Paris: 1978. Translated as *Europe and Islam*. Translated by Peter Heinegg. Berkeley: University of California Press, 1985.

Eccel, Chris. *Egypt, Islam and Social Change: Al-Azhar in Conflict and Accommodation*. Berlin: Klaus Schwarz Verlag, 1984.

Eickelman, Dale ed. *Russia's Muslim Frontiers: New Directions in Cross-Cultural Analysis*. Bloomington: Indiana University Press, 1994.

Escovitz, Joseph H. "Orientalists and Orientalism in the Writings of Muhammad Kurd ʿAli". *International Journal of Middle East Studies* 15 (1983): 95-109.

Ess, Josef van. "From Wellhausen to Becker: The Emergence of "Kulturgeschichte" in Islamic Studies". *Islamic Studies*. Edited by Malcolm Kerr. Malibu, Calif.: Undena Books, 1980.

Evers, S. And P. van der Velde. "Charting Asian Studies in Europe I: Preliminary Guide to Asian Studies in Europe (GASE)". *Preliminary Guide to Asian Studies in Europe '95*. Leiden: International Institute for Asian Studies, (1995): 2-3.

Fahndrich, Hartmut. "Invariable Factors Underlying the Historical Perspective in Theodor Noldeke's Orientalische Skizzen". *Akten des VII. Kongresses für Arabistik Islamwissenschaft*. Edited by A. Dietrich. Gottingen: Vanden-noeck and Ruprecht, 1976. 146-54.

Fahndrich, Hartmut. "Orientalismus und Orientalismus: Überlegungen zu Edward Said, Michel Foucault und westlichen Islamstudien". *Welt des Islam* 28 (1988): 178-86.

Fahndrich, Hartmut. "Islam as a Historical Problem in European Historiography since 1800". *Historians of the Middle East*. Edited by B. Lewis and P. M. Holt. London and New York: Oxford University Press, 1962. 303-14.

Gabrieli, Francesco. "Apology for Orientalism". *Diogenes* 50 (1965): 128-36.

Gallagher, Nancy, ed. *Approaches to the History of the Middle East: Interviews with Leading Middle East Historians*. Reading, U.K.: Garnet, 1995.

Geertz, C. *Local Knowledge: Further Essays in Interpretive Anthropology*. New York: Basic Books, 1983.

Geertz, C. *After the Fact: Two Countries, Four Decades, One Anthropologist*. Cambridge, Mass.: Harvard University Press, 1995.

Gelb, Ignace J., *et al.*, eds. *The Assyrian Dictionary of the Oriental Institute of the University of Chicago*. Chicago: Oriental Institute, 1956.

Gibb, H.A.R. *Modern Trends in Islam*. Chicago: University of Chicago Press, 1947.

Gibb, H.A.R. *Mohammedanism: An Historical Survey*. Home University Library of Modern Knowledge, no. 197. London: Oxford University Press, 1953 [1949].

Gibb, H.A.R. "The Islamic Background of Ibn Khaldun's Political Theory". *Studies on the Civilization of Islam*. Edited by Stanford J. Shaw and William Polk. Boston: Beacon Press, 1962.

Gibb, H.A.R., *et al.*, eds. *The Encyclopedia of Islam*. (New Edition. Prepared by a number of leading Orientalists under the patronage of the International Union of Academies.) Leiden: E.J. Brill; London: Luzac, 1960-.

Goitein, Shlomo D. "Humanistic Aspects of Oriental Studies". *Jerusalem Studies of Arabic and Islam* 9 (1987): 1-12.

Gost, R. *Directory of Near and Middle East and North Africa Research Institutions in Western Europe (except Federal Republic of Germany): Instutitions in Research and Teaching, Libraries, Documentation Centres and Museums*. Bielefeld: Sociology of Development Research Centre, University of Bielefeld; Hamburg: German Overseas Institute, Overseas Documentation, 1993.

Graham-Brown, Sarah. *Images of Women*. New York: Columbia University Press, 1992.

Grunebaum, Gustav E. von. *Medieval Islam: A Study in Cultural Orientation*. Chicago: University of Chicago Press, 1947.

Haarmann, Ulrich. "Die islamische Moderne bei den deutschen Orientalisten". *Araber und Deutsche: Begegnungen in einem Jahrtausend*. Edited by F. Kochwasser and R. Roemer. Tübingen: 1974. 56-91.

Halbfass, Wilhelm. *India and Europe: An Essay in Understanding*. Albany: State University of New York Press, 1988.

Hanotaux, Gabriel/Abdou. *Mohammed: L'Europe et l'Islam* (avec preface de M. Tallat Harb Bey). Cairo: 1905.

Hamilton, A. *Europe and the Arab World: Five Centuries of Books by European Scholars and Travellers From the Libraries of the Arcadian Group*. Translated by R. Crevier. Oxford: Oxford University Press, for Azimuth Editions, 1994.

Harrison, P. *"Religion" and the Religions in the English Enlightenment*. Cambridge: Cambridge University Press, 1990.

Hermansen, M. K. "Trends in Islamic Studies in the United States and Canada since the 1970s". *American Journal of Islamic Social Sciences*, 10 I (1993): 96-118.

Hobsbawm, Eric and Terence Ranger, eds. *The Invention of Tradition*. Cambridge: Cambridge University Press, 1983.

Hodgson, M.G.S. *Rethinking World History: Essays on Europe, Islam and World History*. Cambridge and New York: Cambridge University Press, 1993.

Hodgson, M.G.S. *The Venture of Islam: Conscience and History in a World Civilization*. 3 vols. Chicago: University of Chicago Press, 1974.

Holt, P.M. and Bernard Lewis, eds. *Historians of the Middle East*. London and New York: Oxford University Press, 1962.

Hourani, Albert. *Europe and the Middle East*. Berkeley: University of California Press, 1980.

Hourani, Albert. *Islam in European Thought*. Cambridge: Cambridge University Press, 1991.

Huntington, Samuel. "Clash of Civilizations". *Foreign Affairs* 71, no. 3 (Summer 93): 22-8.

Husain Taha. *Fi'l Adab al-Jāhilī*. Cairo: Dār al-Kutūb, 1927.

Hussain, A., et al., eds. *Orientalism, Islam and Islamists*. Brattleboro, Vt.: Amana Books, 1984.

Hussain, Asaf. "The Ideology of Orientalism". *Orientalism, Islam and Islamists*. Brattleboro, Vt.: Amana Books, 1984. 5-21.

Ibrahim Saad Eddin and Nicholas Hopkins, eds. *Arab Society: Social Science Perspectives*. Cairo: American University in Cairo Press, 1985.

Inden, Ronald. *Imagining India*. Oxford: Blackwell, 1990.

"Institutes, Universities, and Museums in Europe". *Preliminary Guide to Asian Studies in Europe '95*. Leiden: International Institute for Asian Studies, (1995): 9-24.

Ismael, Tareq, ed. *Middle East Studies: International Perspectives on the State of the Art*. New York: Praeger Publishers, 1990.

International Islamic Colloqium Papers. Lahore, Panjab University. (Dec. 29, 1957-Jan. 8, 1958). Lahore: Punjab University Press, 1960.

Johansen, Baber. *Muhammad Husain Haikal: Europa und der Orient im Weltbild eines typischen Liberalen*. Beiruter Texte und Studien, no. 5. Wiesbaden: Otto Harrassowitz, 1967.

Johansen, Baber. "Politics and Scholarship: The Development of Islamic Studies in the Federal Republic of Germany". *Middle East Studies: International Perspectives on the State of the Art*. Edited by Tareq Ismael. New York: Praeger Publishers, 1990. 71-130.

Johansen, Baber. "Politics, Paradigms and the Progress of Oriental Studies: the German Oriental Society" (Deutsche Morgenländische Gesellschaft) 1845-1989. *Mars: Le Monde Arabe dans la Recherche Scientifique. The Arab World in Scientific Research*, (1994): 79-94.

Jones, W. *Discourses Delivered at the Asiatick Society 1785-1792*/with a new introduction by R. Harris ad a short bibliography on eighteenth-century linguistics by K. Thomson. London: Routledge/Thoemmes, 1993. [A reprint from volume III of the *Works of William Jones*, 1807.]

Kabbani, Rana. *Europe's Myths of the Orient*. Bloomington: Indiana University Press, 1986.

Kapp, Robert A., et al., Dalby, M., Kopf, D. "Review Symposium: Edward Said's Orientalism". *Journal of Asian Studies* 39 (1980): 481-506.

Kedouri, Elie. "Islam and the Orientalists: Some Recent Discussion". *British Journal of Sociology* 7, no. 3 (1956): 217-25.

Kemp, Paul E. "Orientalistes éconduits, orientalistes reconduits". *Arabica* 27 (1980): 154-79.

Kerr, Malcolm E., ed. *Islamic Studies: A Tradition and its Problems*. Malibu, Calif.: Undena Books, 1980.

Kopf, David. *British Orientalism and the Bengal Renaissance*. Berkeley: University of California Press, 1969.

Kraus, Paul. *Jabir Ibn Hayyan: Contribution a l'histoire des idees scientifiques dans l'Islam*. Memoires de l'Institute d'Egypt, 2 vols. Cairo: Institut Francais d'Archeologie Orientale, 1942-43. 44-45.

Kritzeck, James. *Peter the Venerable and Islam*. Princeton, N.J.: Princeton University Press, 1964.

Lach, Donald and Edwin Van Kley. *Asia in the Making of Europe*. Vol. 3. Chicago: University of Chicago Press, 1993.

Lambropoulous, Yassilis. *The Rise of Eurocentrism: Anatomy of Interpretation*. Princeton, N.J.: Princeton University Press, 1993.

Laroui, Abdallah. *The Crisis of the Arab Intellectual: Traditionalism or Historicism*. Translated by Diarmid Cammell. Berkeley: University of California Press, 1976.

Laroui, Abdallah. *L'Ideologie arabe contemporaier*. Preface de Maxime Rodinson Foundations. Paris: F. Maspero, 1982 [1967].

Leask, Nigel. *British Romantic Writers and the East: Anxieties of Empire*. Cambridge: Cambridge University Press, 1993.

Lewis, Bernard. *Islam and the West*. New York: Oxford University Press, 1993.

Lewis, Bernard. *History: Remembered, Recovered, Invented*. Princeton, N.J.: Princeton University Press, 1975.

Little, Donald P. "Three Arab Critiques of Orientalism". *The Muslim World* 69 (1979): 110-31.

Lyotard, Jean-François. *The Postmodern Condition: A Report on Knowledge*. Translated by Geoff Bennington and Brian Massumi. Minneapolis: University of Minnesota Press, 1984.

Mackenzie, J. M. *Orientalism: History, Theory and the Arts*. Manchester: Manchester University Press, 1995.

Mahdi, Muhsin. "Islamic Philosophy in Contemporary Islamic Thought". *God and Man in Contemporary Islamic Thought*. Edited by Charles Malik. [American University of Beirut Centennial Publications.] Beirut: American University of Beirut, 1972. 99-111.

Mahdi, Muhsin. "In Memoriam". *Middle East Studies Association* [of North America] *Bulletin*. [In honour of H.A.R. Gibb] 6 (1972): 88.
Mahdi, Muhsin. "The Book and the Master as Poles of Cultural Change in Islam". *Islam and Cultural Change in the Middle Ages*. Edited by Speros Vryonis, Jr. Giorgio Levi Della Vilda Biennial Conference Publications, no. 4. [In honour of Gustav E. von Grunebaum], Wiesbaden: Otto Harrassowitz, 1975. 3-15.
Mahdi, Muhsin. Foreword. *Journal of Near Eastern Studies*. [In honour of Nabia Abbott] 40 (1981): 163-64.
Mahdi, Muhsin. "Al-Fārābī's Imperfect State". *Journal of the American Oriental Society* 110, no. 4 (1990): 691-726.
Malti-Douglas, Fedwa. "Re-Orienting Orientalism". *The Virginia Quarterly Review* 55 (1979): 724-33.
Malti-Douglas, Fedwa. "In the Eyes of Others: The Middle Eastern Response and Reaction to Western Scholarship". *As Others See Us: Mutual Perceptions East and West*. Edited by Bernard Lewis, et al. *Comparative Civilizations Review* 13-14 (1985/86): 36-55.
Manzoor, S. Parvez. "Method against Truth: Orientalism and Quranic Studies". Muslim World Review 7, no. 4 (1987): 33-49.
Martin, Richard C., ed. *Approaches to Islam in Religious Studies*. Tucson: University of Arizona Press, 1985.
Mazrui, Ali. *The Africans: A Triple Heritage*. London: British Broadcasting Corporation, 1986.
Mernissi, Fatima. *Sexe, Ideologie, Islam*. Paris: Tiense, 1983.
Metcalf, Barbara Daly. *Islamic Revival in British India: Deoband, 1860-1900*. Princeton, N.J.: Princeton University Press, 1982.
Middle East Studies in Denmark. Ed. Erslev Andersen, L. Odense: Odense University Press, 1994.
Morgan, J. "Religion and Culture as Meaning Systems: A Dialogue between Geertz and Tillich". *Journal of Religion* 57 (1977): 363-75.
Mottahedeh, Roy. *The Mantle of the Prophet: Religion and Politics in Iran*. New York: Simon and Schuster, 1985.

Mudimbe, V. *The Invention of Africa: Gnosis, Philosophy, and the Order of Knowledge*. Bloomington: Indiana University Press, 1988.

Murphy, E., G. Nonneman and N. Quilliam. *European Expertise on the Middle East and North Africa: A Directory of Specialists and Institutions*. Exeter: EURAMES, the European Association for Middle Eastern Studies, for the Commission of the European Communities, 1993.

Nagel, Tilman. "Gedanken über die europäische Islamforschung und ihr Echo im Orient". *Zeitschrift für Missionswissenschaft und Religionswissenschaft* 62 (1978): 21-39.

Nanji, Azim, ed. *The Muslim Almanac: A Reference Book on the History, Faith, Culture and Peoples of Islam*. Detroit: Gale, 1996.

Nyang, Sulayman S. "Bernard Lewis and Islamic Studies: An Assessment". *Orientalism, Islam and Islamists*. ed. A Hussain and R. Olson. Brattleboro, Vt.: Amana Books, 1984, 259-84.

"Organisations in Europe". *Preliminary Guide to Asian Studies in Europe '95*. Leiden: International Institute for Asian Studies, (1995): 25-7. [Listed by acronym.]

Oxtoby Williard G. "Western Perceptions of Islam and the Arabs". *The American Media and the Arabs*. Edited by M.C. Hudson. Washington, D.C.: Center for Contemporary Arab Studies, 1980. 3-12.

Parry, Benita. *Connad and Imperialism: Ideological Boundaries and Visionary Frontiers*. London: Macmillan, 1984.

Partington, D. H. "Towards a History of Middle Eastern Studies at Harvard: Early Harvard and Radcliffe Ph.D. Dissertations". *Harvard Middle Eastern and Islamic Review*, 1 I (1994): 138-49.

Paths to the Middle East Scholars Look Back. Ed. T. Naff. Albany: State University of New York Press, 1993.

Pearson, James D. "History of Oriental Studies". *Oriental and Asian Bibliography*. Edited by James D. Pearson. London: Lockwood, 1966. 21-33.

Peters, Rudolph. *Abendländische Islamkunde aus morgenländischer Sicht in Wij en het midden-oosten: midden-oosten en Islamstudies in ander perspective*. Nijmegen: 1978. 61-72.

Peters, Rudolph. "The Mysteries of the Oriental Mind: Some Remarks on the Development of Western Stereotypes of the Arabs". *The Challenge of the Middle East: Middle Eastern Studies at the University of Amsterdam*. Edited by I. el-Sheikh. Amsterdam: 1982. 73-90.

Preliminary Guide to Asian Studies in Europe '95. Leiden: International Institute for Asian Studies, 1995.

Pruett, Gordon E. "Duncan Black Macdonald: Christian Islamicist". *Orientalism, Islam and Islamists*. A. Hussain; R. Olson, et al, eds. Brattleboro, Vt.: Amana Books, 1984. 125-76.

Qureshi, Jamil. "Alongsidedness - in good faith: an essay on Kenneth Cragg". *Orientalism, Islam and Islamists*. Eds. A Hussain; R Olson, et al, Brattleboro, Vt.: Amana Books, 1984. 203-58.

Qutb, Sayyid. *Milestones*. Chicago: Kazi Publications, 1981.

Rahman, Fazlur. "Islamic Studies and the Future of Islam". *Malcolm Kerr*, ed. Islamic Studies: A Tradition and its Problems. Malibu, Calif.: Undena Books, 1980. 125-133.

Reid, Donald M. *The Odyssey of Farah Antun: a Syrian Christian's Quest for Secularism*. Minneapolis: Bibliotheca Islamica, 1975.

Reid, Donald M. *Cairo University and the Making of a Modern Egypt*. Cambridge and New York: Cambridge University Press, 1990.

Reid, Donald M. "Orientalisme et ethnocentrisme". *Vortrage des 21. Deutschen Orientalistentages*. Edited by F. Steppat. Berlin, 1980; Wiesbaden 1983 (Zeitschrift der Deutshen Morgenländischen Gesellschaft, Suppl.,: 5): 77-86.

Reig, Daniel. *Homo orientaliste: La langue arabe en France depuis XIXe siècle*. Paris: Maisonneuve and Larose, 1988.

Renan, Ernest. *Averroes et l'averroisme essai historique*. 2d ed. Paris: Michel Levy Freres, 1961 [1852].

Rodinson, Maxime. *La fascination de l'Islam.* Paris: F. Maspero, 1981. Translated as *Europe and the Mystique of Islam.* Translated by Roger Veinus. Seattle: University of Washington Press, 1987.

Rodinson, Maxime. "The Western Image and Western Studies of Islam". *Legacy of Islam.* 2d ed. Edited by Joseph Schacht. Oxford: Clarendon Press, 1974. 9-62.

Roper, G. J. "Islamic Bibliography Unit, Cambridge University Library". *Cambridge Bibliographical Society Newsletter*, (Autumn 1993): 6-7.

Rosenthal, Franz. "Die Krise der Orientalistik". *Vortrage des 21. Deutschen Orientalistentages.* Edited by F. Steppat. Berlin 1980. Wiesbaden 1983 (ZDMG, Suppl., 5). 10-21.

Rudolph, Ekkehard. "Eine neue Phase im Verstandnis der Orientalistik 7 Bemerkungen zu einem Gemeinschaftwerk arabischer Wissenschaftler". *Orient* 29 (1988): 505-09.

Sadowski, Yahya. "The New Orientalism and the Democracy Debate". *Middle East Report*, 23 iv/183 (1993): 14-21; 40.

Sahlins, Marshall. *Islands of History.* Chicago: University of Chicago Press, 1985.

Said, Edward. *Orientalism.* 2d. ed. New York: Pantheon, 1995.

Said, Edward. "Orientalism: An Exchange". *New York Review of Books* 29 (August, 12, 1982): 44.

Said, Edward. "Orientalism Reconsidered". *Race and Class* 27, no. 2 (1985): 1-15.

Said, Edward. *Culture and Imperialism.* New York: Knopf, 1993.

Schaeder, Hans Heinrich. "Der Orient und das griechische Erbe". *Die Antike* [Dedicated to Werner Jaeger, editor of *Die Antike*] 4 (1928): 226-65.

Schoeberlein-Engel, J. S. *Guide to Scholars of the History and Culture of Central Asia.* Cambridge, Mass.: Harvard Central Asia Forum, Harvard University, 1995.

A Scholars' Guide to Humanities and Social Sciences in the Soviet Successor States: The Academies of Sciences of Russia, Armenia, Azerbaidzhan, Belarus, Estonia, Georgia, Kazakhstan, Kirgizstan,

Latvia, Lithuania, Moldova, Tadzhikistan, Turkmenistan, Ukraine, and Uzbekistan. 2nd ed. Ed. by V. A. Vinogradov, B. A. Ruble, M. H. Teeter, and and V. G. Osinov. Armonk: Sharpe, 1993.

Schwab, Raymond. *La renaissance orientale*. Paris: Payot, 1950. Translated into English as *Oriental Renaissance: Europe's Rediscovery of India and the East*, 1680-1880. New York: Columbia University Press, 1984.

Shaban, Fuad. *Islam and Arabs in Early American Thought: The Roots of Orientalism in America*. New York: Acorn Press, 1991.

Sharabi, Hisham. *Arab Intellectuals and the West: The Formative Years 1875-1914*. Baltimore: Johns Hopkins University Press, 1970.

Sharabi, Hisham. *Neopatriarchy: A Theory of Distorted Change in Contemporary Arab Society*. Oxford: Oxford University Press, 1988.

Sharafuddin, Mohammed. *Islam and Romantic Orientalism: Literary Encounters with the Orient*. London: Tauris, 1994.

Shawqī, Ahmad. *Majnun Layla*. Cairo: Matba ʿat Misr, 1916.

Simon, David. *Orientalism and History*. 2d ed. Bloomington: Indiana University Press, 1970.

Sivan, Emmanuel. "Orientalism, Islam and Cultural Revolution". Jerusalem Quarterly 5 (1977): 84-93.

Sivan, Emmanuel. *Interpretations of Islam: Past and Present*. Princeton, N.J.: Darwin Press, 1985.

Smith, Byron Porter. *Islam in English Literature*. Delmar, N.Y.: Caravan Books, 1977.

Smith, Charles D. "The Crisis of Orientation: The Shift of Egyptian Intellectuals to Islamic Subjects in the 1930s". *International Journal of Middle East Studies* 4 (1973): 382-410.

Southern, Richard. *Western Views of Islam in the Middle Ages*. Cambridge: Cambridge University Press, 1962.

Sprinkler, Michael, ed. *Edward Said: A Critical Reader*. Oxford: Blackwell, 1992.

Stover, Dale. "Orientalism and the Otherness of Islam". *Studies in Religion* 17 (1988): 27-40.

Sweetman, John. *The Oriental Obsession: Islamic Inspiration in British and American Art and Architecture, 1500-1920*. Cambridge and New York: Cambridge University Press, 1988.

Tanaka, Stefan. *Japan's Orient: Rendering Pasts into History*. Berkeley and Oxford: University of California Press, 1993.

Thomas, Nicholas. *Colonialism's Culture: Anthropology, Travel and Government*. Princeton, N.J.: Princeton University Press, 1994.

Tibawi, Abdel-Latif. "English-speaking Orientalists: A Critique of their Approach to Islam and Arab Nationalism". *The Muslim World* 53 (1963): 185-204; 298-313.

Tibawi, Abdel-Latif. *Second Critique of English-speaking Orientalists and Their Approach to Islam and the Arabs*. London: 1979.

Tibawi, Abdel-Latif. "On the Orientalists Again". *The Muslim World* 70 (1980): 56-60.

Tibi, Bassam. *Die Krise des modernen Islams: Eine vorindustrielle Kultur im wissenschaftlich-technischen Zeitalter*. Munich: C. H. Becksche, 1981. Translated as *The Crisis of Modern Islam: A Preindustrial Culture in the Scientific-technological Age*. Translated by Judith von Sivers. Salt Lake City: University of Utah Press, 1988.

Tolan, John Victor. *Medieval Christian Perceptions of Islam*. New York: Garland Publishers, 1996.

Toll, Christopher. "The Purpose of Islamic Studies". *Islam, State and Society*. Edited by Klaus Ferdinand and Mehdi Mozaffari. London: Curzon, 1988. 13-25.

Turner, Bryan S. *Marx and the End of Orientalism*. London: Allen and Unwin, 1978.

Turner, Bryan S. *Orientalism, Post Modernism and Globalism*. London and New York: Routledge, 1994.

Van Ess, Joseph. *Theologie und Gesellschaft im 2, und 3.* Jahrundent Hidschra: Eine Geschichte des religiösen Denkens im frühen Islam. Berlin: 1991-92.

Wagner, Peter, et al., eds. *Social Sciences and Modern States: National Experiences and Theoretical Crossroads*. Cambridge and New York: Cambridge University Press, 1991.

Watt, William Montgomery. *Muslim-Christian Encounters: Perceptions and Misperceptions*. London and New York: Routledge, 1991.

White, Hayden. *Metahistory: The Historical Imagination in Nineteenth-Century Europe*. Baltimore, Md.: The Johns Hopkins University Press, 1973.

Wolf, E. *Europe and the People Without History*. Berkeley: University of California Press, 1982.